NON SANZ DROICT.

Much adoe about Nothing.

As it hath been sundrie times publikely
acted by the right honourable, the Lord
Chamberlaine his seruants.

Written by William Shakespeare.

LONDON
Printed by V.S. for Andrew Wise, and
William Aspley.
1600.

Title page of the earliest and most authoritative edition of the play,
the Quarto of 1600

William Shakespeare

Much Ado
About Nothing

With New and Updated
Critical Essays
and a Revised Bibliography

Edited by David L. Stevenson

THE SIGNET CLASSIC SHAKESPEARE
General Editor: Sylvan Barnet

A SIGNET CLASSIC

SIGNET CLASSIC
Published by New American Library, a division of
Penguin Group (USA) Inc., 375 Hudson Street,
New York, New York 10014, U.S.A.
Penguin Books Ltd, 80 Strand,
London WC2R 0RL, England
Penguin Books Australia Ltd, 250 Camberwell Road,
Camberwell, Victoria 3124, Australia
Penguin Books Canada Ltd, 10 Alcorn Avenue,
Toronto, Ontario, Canada M4V 3B2
Penguin Books (NZ), cnr Airborne and Rosedale Roads,
Albany, Auckland 1310, New Zealand

Penguin Books Ltd, Registered Offices:
80 Strand, London WC2R 0RL, England

Published by Signet Classic, an imprint of New American Library,
a division of Penguin Group (USA) Inc. The Signet Classic edition of *Much Ado
About Nothing* was first published in 1964, and an updated edition was published
in 1989.

First Signet Classic Printing (Second Revised Edition), July 1998
20   19   18

Ⓒ REGISTERED TRADEMARK—MARCA REGISTRADA

Library of Congress Catalog Card Number: 97-62387

Printed in the United States of America

Contents

Shakespeare: An Overview

Biographical Sketch

Between the record of his baptism in Stratford on 26 April 1564 and the record of his burial in Stratford on 25 April 1616, some forty official documents name Shakespeare, and many others name his parents, his children, and his grandchildren. Further, there are at least fifty literary references to him in the works of his contemporaries. More facts are known about William Shakespeare than about any other playwright of the period except Ben Jonson. The facts should, however, be distinguished from the legends. The latter, inevitably more engaging and better known, tell us that the Stratford boy killed a calf in high style, poached deer and rabbits, and was forced to flee to London, where he held horses outside a playhouse. These traditions are only traditions; they may be true, but no evidence supports them, and it is well to stick to the facts.

Mary Arden, the dramatist's mother, was the daughter of a substantial landowner; about 1557 she married John Shakespeare, a tanner, glove-maker, and trader in wool, grain, and other farm commodities. In 1557 John Shakespeare was a member of the council (the governing body of Stratford), in 1558 a constable of the borough, in 1561 one of the two town chamberlains, in 1565 an alderman (entitling him to the appellation of "Mr."), in 1568 high bailiff—the town's highest political office, equivalent to mayor. After 1577, for an unknown reason he drops out of local politics. What *is* known is that he had to mortgage his wife's property, and that he was involved in serious litigation.

The birthday of William Shakespeare, the third child and the eldest son of this locally prominent man, is unrecorded, but the Stratford parish register records that the infant was baptized on 26 April 1564. (It is quite possible that he was born on 23 April, but this date has probably been assigned by tradition because it is the date on which, fifty-two years later, he died, and perhaps because it is the feast day of St. George, patron saint of England.) The attendance records of the Stratford grammar school of the period are not extant, but it is reasonable to assume that the son of a prominent local official attended the free school—it had been established for the purpose of educating males precisely of his class—and received substantial training in Latin. The masters of the school from Shakespeare's seventh to fifteenth years held Oxford degrees; the Elizabethan curriculum excluded mathematics and the natural sciences but taught a good deal of Latin rhetoric, logic, and literature, including plays by Plautus, Terence, and Seneca.

On 27 November 1582 a marriage license was issued for the marriage of Shakespeare and Anne Hathaway, eight years his senior. The couple had a daughter, Susanna, in May 1583. Perhaps the marriage was necessary, but perhaps the couple had earlier engaged, in the presence of witnesses, in a formal "troth plight" which would render their children legitimate even if no further ceremony were performed. In February 1585, Anne Hathaway bore Shakespeare twins, Hamnet and Judith.

That Shakespeare was born is excellent; that he married and had children is pleasant; but that we know nothing about his departure from Stratford to London or about the beginning of his theatrical career is lamentable and must be admitted. We would gladly sacrifice details about his children's baptism for details about his earliest days in the theater. Perhaps the poaching episode is true (but it is first reported almost a century after Shakespeare's death), or perhaps he left Stratford to be a schoolmaster, as another tradition holds; perhaps he was moved (like Petruchio in *The Taming of the Shrew*) by

> Such wind as scatters young men through the world,
> To seek their fortunes farther than at home
> Where small experience grows.   (1.2.49–51)

In 1592, thanks to the cantankerousness of Robert Greene, we have our first reference, a snarling one, to Shakespeare as an actor and playwright. Greene, a graduate of St. John's College, Cambridge, had become a playwright and a pamphleteer in London, and in one of his pamphlets he warns three university-educated playwrights against an actor who has presumed to turn playwright:

> There is an upstart crow, beautified with our feathers, that with his *tiger's heart wrapped in a player's hide* supposes he is as well able to bombast out a blank verse as the best of you, and being an absolute Johannes-factotum [i.e., jack-of-all-trades] is in his own conceit the only Shake-scene in a country.

The reference to the player, as well as the allusion to Aesop's crow (who strutted in borrowed plumage, as an actor struts in fine words not his own), makes it clear that by this date Shakespeare had both acted and written. That Shakespeare is meant is indicated not only by *Shake-scene* but also by the parody of a line from one of Shakespeare's plays, *3 Henry VI*: "O, tiger's heart wrapped in a woman's hide" (1.4.137). If in 1592 Shakespeare was prominent enough to be attacked by an envious dramatist, he probably had served an apprenticeship in the theater for at least a few years.

In any case, although there are no extant references to Shakespeare between the record of the baptism of his twins in 1585 and Greene's hostile comment about "Shake-scene" in 1592, it is evident that during some of these "dark years" or "lost years" Shakespeare had acted and written. There are a number of subsequent references to him as an actor. Documents indicate that in 1598 he is a "principal comedian," in 1603 a "principal tragedian," in 1608 he is one of the "men players." (We do not have, however, any solid information about which roles he may have played; later traditions say he played Adam in *As You Like It* and the ghost in *Hamlet*, but nothing supports the assertions. Probably his role as dramatist came to supersede his role as actor.) The profession of actor was not for a gentleman, and it occasionally drew the scorn of university men like Greene who resented writing speeches for persons less educated than themselves, but it was respectable enough; players, if prosperous, were in effect members of the bourgeoisie, and there is nothing to suggest that Stratford considered William Shakespeare less than a solid citizen. When, in 1596, the Shakespeares were granted a coat of arms—i.e., the right to be considered gentlemen—the grant was made to Shakespeare's father, but probably William Shakespeare had arranged the matter on his own behalf. In subsequent transactions he is occasionally styled a gentleman.

Although in 1593 and 1594 Shakespeare published two narrative poems dedicated to the Earl of Southampton, *Venus and Adonis* and *The Rape of Lucrece*, and may well have written most or all of his sonnets in the middle nineties, Shakespeare's literary activity seems to have been almost entirely devoted to the theater. (It may be significant that the two narrative poems were written in years when the plague closed the theaters for several months.) In 1594 he was a charter member of a theatrical company called the Chamberlain's Men, which in 1603 became the royal company, the King's Men, making Shakespeare the king's playwright. Until he retired to Stratford (about 1611, apparently), he was with this remarkably stable company. From 1599 the company acted primarily at the Globe theater, in which Shakespeare held a one-tenth interest. Other Elizabethan dramatists are known to have acted, but no other is known also to have been entitled to a share of the profits.

Shakespeare's first eight published plays did not have his name on them, but this is not remarkable; the most popular play of the period, Thomas Kyd's *The Spanish Tragedy*, went through many editions without naming Kyd, and Kyd's authorship is known only because a book on the profession of acting happens to quote (and attribute to Kyd) some lines on the interest of Roman emperors in the drama. What is remarkable is that after 1598 Shakespeare's name commonly appears on printed plays—some of which are not his. Presumably his name was a drawing card, and publishers used it to attract potential buyers. Another indication of his popularity comes from Francis Meres, author of *Palladis Tamia: Wit's Treasury* (1598). In this anthology of snippets accompanied by an essay on literature, many playwrights are mentioned, but Shakespeare's name occurs more often than any other, and Shakespeare is the only play-wright whose plays are listed.

From his acting, his play writing, and his share in a playhouse, Shakespeare seems to have made considerable money. He put it to work, making substantial investments in Stratford real estate. As early as 1597 he bought New Place, the second-largest house in Stratford. His family moved in soon afterward, and the house remained in the family until a granddaughter died in 1670. When Shakespeare made his will in 1616, less than a month before he died, he sought to leave his property intact to his descendants. Of small bequests to relatives and to friends (including three actors, Richard Burbage, John Heminges, and Henry Condell), that to his wife of the second-best bed has provoked the most comment. It has sometimes been taken as a sign of an unhappy marriage (other supposed signs are the apparently hasty marriage, his wife's seniority of eight years, and his residence in London without his family). Perhaps the second-best bed was the bed the couple had slept in, the best bed being reserved for visitors. In any case, had Shakespeare not excepted it, the bed would have gone (with the rest of his household possessions) to his daughter and her husband.

On 25 April 1616 Shakespeare was buried within the chancel of the church at Stratford. An unattractive monu-ment to his memory, placed on a wall near the grave, says that he died on 23 April. Over the grave itself are the lines, perhaps by Shakespeare, that (more than his literary fame) have kept his bones undisturbed in the crowded burial ground where old bones were often dislodged to make way for new:

> Good friend, for Jesus' sake forbear
> To dig the dust enclosed here.
> Blessed be the man that spares these stones
> And cursed be he that moves my bones.

A Note on the Anti-Stratfordians, Especially Baconians and Oxfordians

Not until 1769—more than a hundred and fifty years after Shakespeare's death—is there any record of anyone

expressing doubt about Shakespeare's authorship of the plays
and poems. In 1769, however, Herbert Lawrence nominated
Francis Bacon (1561–1626) in *The Life and Adventures of
Common Sense*. Since then, at least two dozen other nomi-
nees have been offered, including Christopher Marlowe, Sir
Walter Raleigh, Queen Elizabeth I, and Edward de Vere,
17th earl of Oxford. The impulse behind all anti-Stratfordian
movements is the scarcely concealed snobbish opinion that
"the man from Stratford" simply could not have written the
plays because he was a country fellow without a university
education and without access to high society. Anyone, the
argument goes, who used so many legal terms, medical
terms, nautical terms, and so forth, and who showed some
familiarity with classical writing, must have attended a university, and anyone who knew so much about courtly elegance and courtly deceit must himself have moved among
courtiers. The plays do indeed reveal an author whose inter-
ests were exceptionally broad, but specialists in any given
field—law, medicine, arms and armor, and so on—soon find
that the plays do not reveal deep knowledge in specialized
matters; indeed, the playwright often gets technical details
wrong.

The claim on behalf of Bacon, forgotten almost as soon as
it was put forth in 1769, was independently reasserted by
Joseph C. Hart in 1848. In 1856 it was reaffirmed by W. H.
Smith in a book, and also by Delia Bacon in an article; in
1857 Delia Bacon published a book, arguing that Francis
Bacon had directed a group of intellectuals who wrote the
plays.

Francis Bacon's claim has largely faded, perhaps because
it was advanced with such evident craziness by Ignatius
Donnelly, who in *The Great Cryptogram* (1888) claimed to
break a code in the plays that proved Bacon had written not
only the plays attributed to Shakespeare but also other
Renaissance works, for instance the plays of Christopher
Marlowe and the essays of Montaigne.

Consider the last two lines of the Epilogue in *The
Tempest*:

> As you from crimes would pardoned be,
> Let your indulgence set me free.

What was Shakespeare—sorry, Francis Bacon, Baron Verulam—*really* saying in these two lines? According to Baconians, the lines are an anagram reading, "Tempest of Francis Bacon, Lord Verulam; do ye ne'er divulge me, ye words." Ingenious, and it is a pity that in the quotation the letter *a* appears only twice in the cryptogram, whereas in the deciphered message it appears three times. Oh, no problem; just alter "Verulam" to "Verul'm" and it works out very nicely.

Most people understand that with sufficient ingenuity one can torture any text and find in it what one wishes. For instance: Did Shakespeare have a hand in the King James Version of the Bible? It was nearing completion in 1610, when Shakespeare was forty-six years old. If you look at the 46th Psalm and count forward for forty-six words, you will find the word *shake*. Now if you go to the end of the psalm and count backward forty-six words, you will find the word *spear*. Clear evidence, according to some, that Shakespeare slyly left his mark in the book.

Bacon's candidacy has largely been replaced in the twentieth century by the candidacy of Edward de Vere (1550–1604), 17th earl of Oxford. The basic ideas behind the Oxford theory, advanced at greatest length by Dorothy and Charlton Ogburn in *This Star of England* (1952, rev. 1955), a book of 1297 pages, and by Charlton Ogburn in *The Mysterious William Shakespeare* (1984), a book of 892 pages, are these: (1) The man from Stratford could not possibly have had the mental equipment and the experience to have written the plays—only a courtier could have written them; (2) Oxford had the requisite background (social position, education, years at Queen Elizabeth's court); (3) Oxford did not wish his authorship to be known for two basic reasons: writing for the public theater was a vulgar pursuit, and the plays show so much courtly and royal disreputable behavior that they would have compromised Oxford's position at court. Oxfordians offer countless details to support the claim. For example, Hamlet's phrase "that ever I was born to set it right" (1.5.89) barely conceals "E. Ver, I was born to set it right," an unambiguous announcement of de Vere's authorship, according to *This Star of England* (p. 654). A second example: Consider Ben

Jonson's poem entitled "To the Memory of My Beloved Master William Shakespeare," prefixed to the first collected edition of Shakespeare's plays in 1623. According to Oxfordians, when Jonson in this poem speaks of the author of the plays as the "swan of Avon," he is alluding not to William Shakespeare, who was born and died in Stratford-on-Avon and who throughout his adult life owned property there; rather, he is alluding to Oxford, who, the Ogburns say, used "William Shakespeare" as his pen name, and whose manor at Bilton was on the Avon River. Oxfordians do not offer any evidence that Oxford took a pen name, and they do not mention that Oxford had sold the manor in 1581, forty-two years before Jonson wrote his poem. Surely a reference to the Shakespeare who was born in Stratford, who had returned to Stratford, and who had died there only seven years before Jonson wrote the poem is more plausible. And exactly why Jonson, who elsewhere also spoke of Shakespeare as a playwright, and why Heminges and Condell, who had acted with Shakespeare for about twenty years, should speak of Shakespeare as the author in their dedication in the 1623 volume of collected plays is never adequately explained by Oxfordians. Either Jonson, Heminges and Condell, and numerous others were in on the conspiracy, or they were all duped—equally unlikely alternatives. Another difficulty in the Oxford theory is that Oxford died in 1604, and some of the plays are clearly indebted to works and events later than 1604. Among the Oxfordian responses are: At his death Oxford left some plays, and in later years these were touched up by hacks, who added the material that points to later dates. *The Tempest,* almost universally regarded as one of Shakespeare's greatest plays and pretty clearly dated to 1611, does indeed date from a period after the death of Oxford, but it is a crude piece of work that should not be included in the canon of works by Oxford.

The anti-Stratfordians, in addition to assuming that the author must have been a man of rank and a university man, usually assume two conspiracies: (1) a conspiracy in Elizabethan and Jacobean times, in which a surprisingly large number of persons connected with the theater knew that the actor Shakespeare did not write the plays attributed to him but for some reason or other pretended that he did; (2) a conspiracy of today's Stratfordians, the professors who teach Shakespeare in the colleges and universities, who are said to have a vested interest in preserving Shakespeare as the author of the plays they teach. In fact, (1) it is inconceivable that the secret of Shakespeare's non-authorship could have been preserved by all of the people who supposedly were in on the conspiracy, and (2) academic fame awaits any scholar today who can disprove Shakespeare's authorship.

The Stratfordian case is convincing not only because hundreds or even thousands of anti-Stratford arguments—of the sort that say "ever I was born" has the secret double meaning "E. Ver, I was born"—add up to nothing at all but also because irrefutable evidence connects the man from Stratford with the London theater and with the authorship of particular plays. The anti-Stratfordians do not seem to understand that it is not enough to dismiss the Stratford case by saying that a fellow from the provinces simply couldn't have written the plays. Nor do they understand that it is not enough to dismiss all of the evidence connecting Shakespeare with the plays by asserting that it is perjured.

The Shakespeare Canon

We return to William Shakespeare. Thirty-seven plays as well as some nondramatic poems are generally held to constitute the Shakespeare canon, the body of authentic works. The exact dates of composition of most of the works are highly uncertain, but evidence of a starting point and/or of a final limiting point often provides a framework for informed guessing. For example, *Richard II* cannot be earlier than 1595, the publication date of some material to which it is indebted; *The Merchant of Venice* cannot be later than 1598, the year Francis Meres mentioned it. Sometimes arguments for a date hang on an alleged topical allusion, such as the lines about the unseasonable weather in *A Midsummer Night's Dream*, 2.1.81–117, but such an allusion, if indeed it is an allusion to an event in the real world, can be variously interpreted, and in any case there is always the possibility that a topical allusion was inserted years later, to bring the play up to date. (The issue of alterations in a text between the time that Shakespeare drafted it and the time that it was printed—alterations due to censorship or playhouse practice or Shakespeare's own second thoughts—will be discussed in "The Play Text as a Collaboration" later in this overview.) Dates are often attributed on the basis of style, and although conjectures about style usually rest on other conjectures (such as Shakespeare's development as a playwright, or the appropriateness of lines to character), sooner or later one must rely on one's literary sense. There is no documentary proof, for example, that *Othello* is not as early as *Romeo and Juliet*, but one feels that *Othello* is a later, more mature work, and because the first record of its performance is 1604, one is glad enough to set its composition at that date and not push it back into Shakespeare's early years. (*Romeo and Juliet* was first published in 1597, but evidence suggests that it was written a little earlier.) The following chronology, then, is indebted not only to facts but also to informed guesswork and sensitivity. The dates, necessarily imprecise for some works, indicate something like a scholarly consensus concerning the time of original composition. Some plays show evidence of later revision.

Plays. The first collected edition of Shakespeare, published in 1623, included thirty-six plays. These are all accepted as Shakespeare's, though for one of them, *Henry VIII*, he is thought to have had a collaborator. A thirty-seventh play, *Pericles*, published in 1609 and attributed to Shakespeare on the title page, is also widely accepted as being partly by Shakespeare even though it is not included in the 1623 volume. Still another play not in the 1623 volume, *The Two Noble Kinsmen*, was first published in 1634, with a title page attributing it to John Fletcher and Shakespeare. Probably most students of the subject now believe that Shakespeare did indeed have a hand in it. Of the remaining plays attributed at one time or another to Shakespeare, only one, *Edward III*, anonymously published in 1596, is now regarded by some scholars as a serious candidate. The prevailing opinion, however, is that this rather simple-minded play is not Shakespeare's; at most he may have revised some passages, chiefly scenes with the Countess of

Salisbury. We include *The Two Noble Kinsmen* but do not include *Edward III* in the following list.

1588–94	*The Comedy of Errors*
1588–94	*Love's Labor's Lost*
1589–91	*2 Henry VI*
1590–91	*3 Henry VI*
1589–92	*1 Henry VI*
1592–93	*Richard III*
1589–94	*Titus Andronicus*
1593–94	*The Taming of the Shrew*
1592–94	*The Two Gentlemen of Verona*
1594–96	*Romeo and Juliet*
1595	*Richard II*
1595–96	*A Midsummer Night's Dream*
1596–97	*King John*
1594–96	*The Merchant of Venice*
1596–97	*1 Henry IV*
1597	*The Merry Wives of Windsor*
1597–98	*2 Henry IV*
1598–99	*Much Ado About Nothing*
1598–99	*Henry V*
1599	*Julius Caesar*
1599–1600	*As You Like It*
1599–1600	*Twelfth Night*
1600–1601	*Hamlet*
1601–1602	*Troilus and Cressida*
1602–1604	*All's Well That Ends Well*
1603–1604	*Othello*
1604	*Measure for Measure*
1605–1606	*King Lear*
1605–1606	*Macbeth*
1606–1607	*Antony and Cleopatra*
1605–1608	*Timon of Athens*
1607–1608	*Coriolanus*
1607–1608	*Pericles*
1609–10	*Cymbeline*
1610–11	*The Winter's Tale*
1611	*The Tempest*

| 1612–13 | *Henry VIII* |
| 1613 | *The Two Noble Kinsmen* |

Poems. In 1989 Donald W. Foster published a book in which he argued that "A Funeral Elegy for Master William Peter," published in 1612, ascribed only to the initials W.S., *may* be by Shakespeare. Foster later published an article in a scholarly journal, *PMLA* 111 (1996), in which he asserted the claim more positively. The evidence begins with the initials, and includes the fact that the publisher and the printer of the elegy had published Shakespeare's *Sonnets* in 1609. But such facts add up to rather little, especially because no one has found any connection between Shakespeare and William Peter (an Oxford graduate about whom little is known, who was murdered at the age of twenty-nine). The argument is based chiefly on statistical examinations of word patterns, which are said to correlate with Shakespeare's known work. Despite such correlations, however, many readers feel that the poem does not sound like Shakespeare. True, Shakespeare has a great range of styles, but one quality that unites his work is that it is imaginative and interesting. Many readers find neither of these qualities in "A Funeral Elegy."

1592–93	*Venus and Adonis*
1593–94	*The Rape of Lucrece*
1593–1600	*Sonnets*
1600–1601	*The Phoenix and the Turtle*

Shakespeare's English

1. Spelling and Pronunciation. From the philologist's point of view, Shakespeare's English is modern English. It requires footnotes, but the inexperienced reader can comprehend substantial passages with very little help, whereas for the same reader Chaucer's Middle English is a foreign language. By the beginning of the fifteenth century the chief grammatical changes in English had taken place, and the final unaccented *-e* of Middle English had been lost (though it survives even today in spelling, as in *name*); during the fifteenth century the dialect of London, the commercial and political center, gradually displaced the provincial dialects, at least in writing; by the end of the century, printing had helped to regularize and stabilize the language, especially spelling. Elizabethan spelling may seem erratic to us (there were dozens of spellings of *Shakespeare*, and a simple word like *been* was also spelled *beene* and *bin*), but it had much in common with our spelling. Elizabethan spelling was conservative in that for the most part it reflected an older pronunciation (Middle English) rather than the sound of the language as it was then spoken, just as our spelling continues to reflect medieval pronunciation—most obviously in the now silent but formerly pronounced letters in a word such as *knight*. Elizabethan pronunciation, though not identical with ours, was much closer to ours than to that of the Middle Ages. Incidentally, though no one can be certain about what Elizabethan English sounded like, specialists tend to believe it was rather like the speech of a modern stage Irishman (*time* apparently was pronounced *toime*, *old* pronounced *awld*, *day* pronounced *die*, and *join* pronounced *jine*) and not at all like the Oxford speech that most of us think it was.

An awareness of the difference between our pronunciation and Shakespeare's is crucial in three areas—in accent, or number of syllables (many metrically regular lines may look irregular to us); in rhymes (which may not look like rhymes); and in puns (which may not look like puns). Examples will be useful. Some words that were at least on occasion stressed differently from today are *aspèct*, *còmplete*, *fòrlorn*, *revènue*, and *sepùlcher*. Words that sometimes had an additional syllable are *emp[e]ress*, *Hen[e]ry*, *mon[e]th*, and *villain* (three syllables, *vil-lay-in*). An additional syllable is often found in possessives, like *moon*'s (pronounced *moones*) and in words ending in *-tion* or *-sion*. Words that had one less syllable than they now have are *needle* (pronounced *neel*) and *violet* (pronounced *vilet*). Among rhymes now lost are *one* with *loan*, *love* with *prove*, *beast* with *jest*, *eat* with *great*. (In reading, trust your sense of metrics and your ear, more than your eye.) An example of a pun that has become obliterated by a change in pronunciation is Falstaff's reply to Prince Hal's "Come, tell us your

reason" in *1 Henry IV*: "Give you a reason on compulsion?
If reasons were as plentiful as blackberries, I would give no
man a reason upon compulsion, I" (2.4.237–40). The *ea* in
reason was pronounced rather like a long *a*, like the *ai* in
raisin, hence the comparison with blackberries.

Puns are not merely attempts to be funny; like metaphors
they often involve bringing into a meaningful relationship
areas of experience normally seen as remote. In *2 Henry IV*,
when Feeble is conscripted, he stoically says, "I care not. A
man can die but once. We owe God a death" (3.2.242–43),
punning on *debt*, which was the way *death* was pronounced.
Here an enormously significant fact of life is put into simple
commercial imagery, suggesting its commonplace quality.
Shakespeare used the same pun earlier in *1 Henry IV,* when
Prince Hal says to Falstaff, "Why, thou owest God a death,"
and Falstaff replies, " 'Tis not due yet: I would be loath
to pay him before his day. What need I be so forward with
him that calls not on me?" (5.1.126–29).

Sometimes the puns reveal a delightful playfulness;
sometimes they reveal aggressiveness, as when, replying to
Claudius's "But now, my cousin Hamlet, and my son,"
Hamlet says, "A little more than kin, and less than kind!"
(1.2.64–65). These are Hamlet's first words in the play, and
we already hear him warring verbally against Claudius.
Hamlet's "less than kind" probably means (1) Hamlet is not
of Claudius's family or nature, *kind* having the sense it still
has in our word *mankind*; (2) Hamlet is not kindly (affec-
tionately) disposed toward Claudius; (3) Claudius is not
naturally (but rather unnaturally, in a legal sense incestu-
ously) Hamlet's father. The puns evidently were not put in
as sops to the groundlings; they are an important way of
communicating a complex meaning.

2. *Vocabulary.* A conspicuous difficulty in reading Shakespeare is rooted in the fact that some of his words are no
longer in common use—for example, words concerned with
armor, astrology, clothing, coinage, hawking, horsemanship, law, medicine, sailing, and war. Shakespeare had a
large vocabulary—something near thirty thousand words—
but it was not so much a vocabulary of big words as a
vocabulary drawn from a wide range of life, and it is partly

his ability to call upon a great body of concrete language that gives his plays the sense of being in close contact with life. When the right word did not already exist, he made it up. Among words thought to be his coinages are *accommodation, all-knowing, amazement, bare-faced, countless, dexterously, dislocate, dwindle, fancy-free, frugal, indistinguishable, lackluster, laughable, overawe, premeditated, sea change, star-crossed.* Among those that have not survived are the verb *convive,* meaning to feast together, and *smilet,* a little smile.

Less overtly troublesome than the technical words but more treacherous are the words that seem readily intelligible to us but whose Elizabethan meanings differ from their modern ones. When Horatio describes the Ghost as an "erring spirit," he is saying not that the ghost has sinned or made an error but that it is wandering. Here is a short list of some of the most common words in Shakespeare's plays that often (but not always) have a meaning other than their most usual modern meaning:

'a	he
abuse	deceive
accident	occurrence
advertise	inform
an, and	if
annoy	harm
appeal	accuse
artificial	skillful
brave	fine, splendid
censure	opinion
cheer	(1) face (2) frame of mind
chorus	a single person who comments on the events
closet	small private room
competitor	partner
conceit	idea, imagination
cousin	kinsman
cunning	skillful
disaster	evil astrological influence
doom	judgment
entertain	receive into service

envy	malice
event	outcome
excrement	outgrowth (of hair)
fact	evil deed
fancy	(1) love (2) imagination
fell	cruel
fellow	(1) companion (2) low person (often an insulting term if addressed to someone of approximately equal rank)
fond	foolish
free	(1) innocent (2) generous
glass	mirror
hap, haply	chance, by chance
head	army
humor	(1) mood (2) bodily fluid thought to control one's psychology
imp	child
intelligence	news
kind	natural, acting according to nature
let	hinder
lewd	base
mere(ly)	utter(ly)
modern	commonplace
natural	a fool, an idiot
naughty	(1) wicked (2) worthless
next	nearest
nice	(1) trivial (2) fussy
noise	music
policy	(1) prudence (2) stratagem
presently	immediately
prevent	anticipate
proper	handsome
prove	test
quick	alive
sad	serious
saw	proverb
secure	without care, incautious
silly	innocent

sensible	capable of being perceived by the senses
shrewd	sharp
so	provided that
starve	die
still	always
success	that which follows
tall	brave
tell	count
tonight	last night
wanton	playful, careless
watch	keep awake
will	lust
wink	close both eyes
wit	mind, intelligence

All glosses, of course, are mere approximations; sometimes one of Shakespeare's words may hover between an older meaning and a modern one, and as we have seen, his words often have multiple meanings.

3. Grammar. A few matters of grammar may be surveyed, though it should be noted at the outset that Shakespeare sometimes made up his own grammar. As E.A. Abbott says in *A Shakespearian Grammar,* "Almost any part of speech can be used as any other part of speech": a noun as a verb ("he childed as I fathered"); a verb as a noun ("She hath made compare"); or an adverb as an adjective ("a seldom pleasure"). There are hundreds, perhaps thousands, of such instances in the plays, many of which at first glance would not seem at all irregular and would trouble only a pedant. Here are a few broad matters.

Nouns: The Elizabethans thought the *-s* genitive ending for nouns (as in *man's*) derived from *his;* thus the line " 'gainst the count his galleys I did some service," for "the count's galleys."

Adjectives: By Shakespeare's time adjectives had lost the endings that once indicated gender, number, and case. About the only difference between Shakespeare's adjectives and ours is the use of the now redundant *more* or *most* with the comparative ("some more fitter place") or superlative

("This was the most unkindest cut of all"). Like double comparatives and double superlatives, double negatives were acceptable; Mercutio "will not budge for no man's pleasure."

Pronouns: The greatest change was in pronouns. In Middle English *thou, thy,* and *thee* were used among familiars and in speaking to children and inferiors; *ye, your,* and *you* were used in speaking to superiors (servants to masters, nobles to the king) or to equals with whom the speaker was not familiar. Increasingly the "polite" forms were used in all direct address, regardless of rank, and the accusative *you* displaced the nominative *ye.* Shakespeare sometimes uses *ye* instead of *you,* but even in Shakespeare's day *ye* was archaic, and it occurs mostly in rhetorical appeals.

Thou, thy, and *thee* were not completely displaced, however, and Shakespeare occasionally makes significant use of them, sometimes to connote familiarity or intimacy and sometimes to connote contempt. In *Twelfth Night* Sir Toby advises Sir Andrew to insult Cesario by addressing him as *thou:* "If thou thou'st him some thrice, it shall not be amiss" (3.2.46–47). In *Othello* when Brabantio is addressing an unidentified voice in the dark he says, "What are you?" (1.1.91), but when the voice identifies itself as the foolish suitor Roderigo, Brabantio uses the contemptuous form, saying, "I have charged thee not to haunt about my doors" (93). He uses this form for a while, but later in the scene, when he comes to regard Roderigo as an ally, he shifts back to the polite *you,* beginning in line 163, "What said she to you?" and on to the end of the scene. For reasons not yet satisfactorily explained, Elizabethans used *thou* in addresses to God—"O God, thy arm was here," the king says in *Henry V* (4.8.108)—and to supernatural characters such as ghosts and witches. A subtle variation occurs in *Hamlet.* When Hamlet first talks with the Ghost in 1.5, he uses *thou,* but when he sees the Ghost in his mother's room, in 3.4, he uses *you,* presumably because he is now convinced that the Ghost is not a counterfeit but is his father.

Perhaps the most unusual use of pronouns, from our point of view, is the neuter singular. In place of our *its, his* was often used, as in "How far that little candle throws *his* beams." But the use of a masculine pronoun for a neuter noun came to seem unnatural, and so *it* was used for the possessive as well as the nominative: "The hedge-sparrow fed the cuckoo so long / That it had it head bit off by it young." In the late sixteenth century the possessive form *its* developed, apparently by analogy with the *-s* ending used to indicate a genitive noun, as in *book*'s, but *its* was not yet common usage in Shakespeare's day. He seems to have used *its* only ten times, mostly in his later plays. Other usages, such as "you have seen Cassio and she together" or the substitution of *who* for *whom*, cause little problem even when noticed.

Verbs, Adverbs, and Prepositions: Verbs cause almost no difficulty: The third person singular present form commonly ends in *-s*, as in modern English (e.g., "He blesses"), but sometimes in *-eth* (Portia explains to Shylock that mercy "blesseth him that gives and him that takes"). Broadly speaking, the *-eth* ending was old-fashioned or dignified or "literary" rather than colloquial, except for the words *doth*, *hath*, and *saith*. The *-eth* ending (regularly used in the King James Bible, 1611) is very rare in Shakespeare's dramatic prose, though not surprisingly it occurs twice in the rather formal prose summary of the narrative poem *Lucrece*. Sometimes a plural subject, especially if it has collective force, takes a verb ending in *-s*, as in "My old bones aches." Some of our strong or irregular preterites (such as *broke*) have a different form in Shakespeare (*brake*); some verbs that now have a weak or regular preterite (such as *helped*) in Shakespeare have a strong or irregular preterite (*holp*). Some adverbs that today end in *-ly* were not inflected: "grievous sick," "wondrous strange." Finally, prepositions often are not the ones we expect: "We are such stuff as dreams are made on," "I have a king here to my flatterer."

Again, none of the differences (except meanings that have substantially changed or been lost) will cause much difficulty. But it must be confessed that for some elliptical passages there is no widespread agreement on meaning. Wise editors resist saying more than they know, and when they are uncertain they add a question mark to their gloss.

Shakespeare's Theater

In Shakespeare's infancy, Elizabethan actors performed wherever they could—in great halls, at court, in the courtyards of inns. These venues implied not only different audiences but also different playing conditions. The innyards must have made rather unsatisfactory theaters: on some days they were unavailable because carters bringing goods to London used them as depots; when available, they had to be rented from the innkeeper. In 1567, presumably to avoid such difficulties, and also to avoid regulation by the Common Council of London, which was not well disposed toward theatricals, one John Brayne, brother-in-law of the carpenter turned actor James Burbage, built the Red Lion in an eastern suburb of London. We know nothing about its shape or its capacity; we can say only that it may have been the first building in Europe constructed for the purpose of giving plays since the end of antiquity, a thousand years earlier. Even after the building of the Red Lion theatrical activity continued in London in makeshift circumstances, in marketplaces and inns, and always uneasily. In 1574 the Common Council required that plays and playing places in London be licensed because

> sundry great disorders and inconveniences have been found to ensue to this city by the inordinate haunting of great multitudes of people, specially youth, to plays, interludes, and shows, namely occasion of frays and quarrels, evil practices of incontinency in great inns having chambers and secret places adjoining to their open stages and galleries.

The Common Council ordered that innkeepers who wished licenses to hold performance put up a bond and make contributions to the poor.

The requirement that plays and innyard theaters be licensed, along with the other drawbacks of playing at inns and presumably along with the success of the Red Lion, led James Burbage to rent a plot of land northeast of the city walls, on property outside the jurisdiction of the city. Here he built England's second playhouse, called simply the Theatre. About all that is known of its construction is that it was wood. It soon had imitators, the most famous being the Globe (1599), essentially an amphitheater built across the Thames (again outside the city's jurisdiction), constructed with timbers of the Theatre, which had been dismantled when Burbage's lease ran out.

Admission to the theater was one penny, which allowed spectators to stand at the sides and front of the stage that jutted into the yard. An additional penny bought a seat in a covered part of the theater, and a third penny bought a more comfortable seat and a better location. It is notoriously difficult to translate prices into today's money, since some things that are inexpensive today would have been expensive in the past and vice versa—a pipeful of tobacco (imported, of course) cost a lot of money, about three pennies, and an orange (also imported) cost two or three times what a chicken cost—but perhaps we can get some idea of the low cost of the penny admission when we realize that a penny could also buy a pot of ale. An unskilled laborer made about five or sixpence a day, an artisan about twelve pence a day, and the hired actors (as opposed to the sharers in the company, such as Shakespeare) made about ten pence a performance. A printed play cost five or sixpence. Of course a visit to the theater (like a visit to a baseball game today) usually cost more than the admission since the spectator probably would also buy food and drink. Still, the low entrance fee meant that the theater was available to all except the very poorest people, rather as movies and most athletic events are today. Evidence indicates that the audience ranged from apprentices who somehow managed to scrape together the minimum entrance fee and to escape from their masters for a few hours, to prosperous members of the middle class and aristocrats who paid the additional fee for admission to the galleries. The exact proportion of men to women cannot be determined, but women of all classes certainly were present. Theaters were open every afternoon but Sundays for much of the year, except in times of plague, when they were closed because of fear of infection. By the way, no evidence suggests the presence of toilet facilities. Presumably the patrons relieved themselves by making a quick trip to the fields surrounding the playhouses.

There are four important sources of information about the

structure of Elizabethan public playhouses—drawings, a contract, recent excavations, and stage directions in the plays. Of drawings, only the so-called de Witt drawing (c. 1596) of the Swan—really his friend Aernout van Buchell's copy of Johannes de Witt's drawing—is of much significance. The drawing, the only extant representation of the interior of an Elizabethan theater, shows an amphitheater of three tiers, with a stage jutting from a wall into the yard or

Johannes de Witt, a Continental visitor to London, made a drawing of the Swan theater in about the year 1596. The original drawing is lost; this is Aernout van Buchell's copy of it.

center of the building. The tiers are roofed, and part of the stage is covered by a roof that projects from the rear and is supported at its front on two posts, but the groundlings, who paid a penny to stand in front of the stage or at its sides, were exposed to the sky. (Performances in such a playhouse were held only in the daytime; artificial illumination was not used.) At the rear of the stage are two massive doors; above the stage is a gallery.

The second major source of information, the contract for the Fortune (built in 1600), specifies that although the Globe (built in 1599) is to be the model, the Fortune is to be square, eighty feet outside and fifty-five inside. The stage is to be forty-three feet broad, and is to extend into the middle of the yard, i.e., it is twenty-seven and a half feet deep.

The third source of information, the 1989 excavations of the Rose (built in 1587), indicate that the Rose was fourteen-sided, about seventy-two feet in diameter with an inner yard almost fifty feet in diameter. The stage at the Rose was about sixteen feet deep, thirty-seven feet wide at the rear, and twenty-seven feet wide downstage. The relatively small dimensions and the tapering stage, in contrast to the rectangular stage in the Swan drawing, surprised theater historians and have made them more cautious in generalizing about the Elizabethan theater. Excavations at the Globe have not yielded much information, though some historians believe that the fragmentary evidence suggests a larger theater, perhaps one hundred feet in diameter.

From the fourth chief source, stage directions in the plays, one learns that entrance to the stage was by the doors at the rear (*"Enter one citizen at one door, and another at the other"*). A curtain hanging across the doorway—or a curtain hanging between the two doorways—could provide a place where a character could conceal himself, as Polonius does, when he wishes to overhear the conversation between Hamlet and Gertrude. Similarly, withdrawing a curtain from the doorway could "discover" (reveal) a character or two. Such discovery scenes are very rare in Elizabethan drama, but a good example occurs in *The Tempest* (5.1.171), where a stage direction tells us, *"Here Prospero discovers Ferdinand and Miranda playing at chess."* There was also some sort of playing space "aloft" or "above" to represent, for instance, the top of a city's walls or a room above the street. Doubtless each theater had its own peculiarities, but perhaps we can talk about a "typical" Elizabethan theater if we realize that no theater need exactly fit the description, just as no mother is the average mother with 2.7 children.

This hypothetical theater is wooden, round, or polygonal (in *Henry V* Shakespeare calls it a "wooden *O*") capable of holding some eight hundred spectators who stood in the yard around the projecting elevated stage—these spectators were the "groundlings"—and some fifteen hundred additional spectators who sat in the three roofed galleries. The stage, protected by a "shadow" or "heavens" or roof, is entered from two doors; behind the doors is the "tiring house" (attiring house, i.e., dressing room), and above the stage is some sort of gallery that may sometimes hold spectators but can be used (for example) as the bedroom from which Romeo—according to a stage direction in one text—"goeth down." Some evidence suggests that a throne can be lowered onto the platform stage, perhaps from the "shadow"; certainly characters can descend from the stage through a trap or traps into the cellar or "hell." Sometimes this space beneath the stage accommodates a sound-effects man or musician (in *Antony and Cleopatra* "*music of the hautboys* [oboes] *is under the stage*") or an actor (in *Hamlet* the "*Ghost cries under the stage*"). Most characters simply walk on and off through the doors, but because there is no curtain in front of the platform, corpses will have to be carried off (Hamlet obligingly clears the stage of Polonius's corpse, when he says, "I'll lug the guts into the neighbor room"). Other characters may have fallen at the rear, where a curtain on a doorway could be drawn to conceal them.

Such may have been the "public theater," so called because its inexpensive admission made it available to a wide range of the populace. Another kind of theater has been called the "private theater" because its much greater admission charge (sixpence versus the penny for general admission at the public theater) limited its audience to the wealthy or the prodigal. The private theater was basically a large room, entirely roofed and therefore artificially illuminated, with a stage at one end. The theaters thus were distinct in two ways: One was essentially an amphitheater that catered to the general public; the other was a hall that catered to the wealthy. In 1576 a hall theater was established in Blackfriars, a Dominican priory in London that had been suppressed in 1538 and confiscated by the Crown and thus was not under the city's jurisdiction. All the actors in this Blackfriars theater were boys about eight to thirteen years old (in the public theaters similar boys played female parts; a boy Lady Macbeth played to a man Macbeth). Near the end of this section on Shakespeare's theater we will talk at some length about possible implications in this convention of using boys to play female roles, but for the moment we should say that it doubtless accounts for the relative lack of female roles in Elizabethan drama. Thus, in *A Midsummer Night's Dream*, out of twenty-one named roles, only four are female; in *Hamlet*, out of twenty-four, only two (Gertrude and Ophelia) are female. Many of Shakespeare's characters have fathers but no mothers—for instance, King Lear's daughters. We need not bring in Freud to explain the disparity; a dramatic company had only a few boys in it.

To return to the private theaters, in some of which all of the performers were children—the "eyrie of . . . little eyases" (nest of unfledged hawks—2.2.347–48) which Rosencrantz mentions when he and Guildenstern talk with Hamlet. The theater in Blackfriars had a precarious existence, and ceased operations in 1584. In 1596 James Burbage, who had already made theatrical history by building the Theatre, began to construct a second Blackfriars theater. He died in 1597, and for several years this second Blackfriars theater was used by a troupe of boys, but in 1608 two of Burbage's sons and five other actors (including Shakespeare) became joint operators of the theater, using it in the winter when the open-air Globe was unsuitable. Perhaps such a smaller theater, roofed, artificially illuminated, and with a tradition of a wealthy audience, exerted an influence in Shakespeare's late plays.

Performances in the private theaters may well have had intermissions during which music was played, but in the public theaters the action was probably uninterrupted, flowing from scene to scene almost without a break. Actors would enter, speak, exit, and others would immediately enter and establish (if necessary) the new locale by a few properties and by words and gestures. To indicate that the scene took place at night, a player or two would carry a torch. Here are some samples of Shakespeare establishing the scene:

This is Illyria, lady.   (*Twelfth Night*, 1.2.2)

Well, this is the Forest of Arden.   (*As You Like It*, 2.4.14)

This castle has a pleasant seat; the air
Nimbly and sweetly recommends itself
Unto our gentle senses.   (*Macbeth*, 1.6.1–3)

The west yet glimmers with some streaks of day.
                                            (*Macbeth*, 3.3.5)

Sometimes a speech will go far beyond evoking the minimal setting of place and time, and will, so to speak, evoke the social world in which the characters move. For instance, early in the first scene of *The Merchant of Venice* Salerio suggests an explanation for Antonio's melancholy. (In the following passage, *pageants* are decorated wagons, floats, and *cursy* is the verb "to curtsy," or "to bow.")

Your mind is tossing on the ocean,
There where your argosies with portly sail—
Like signiors and rich burghers on the flood,
Or as it were the pageants of the sea—
Do overpeer the petty traffickers
That cursy to them, do them reverence,
As they fly by them with their woven wings.   (1.1.8–14)

Late in the nineteenth century, when Henry Irving produced the play with elaborate illusionistic sets, the first scene showed a ship moored in the harbor, with fruit vendors and dock laborers, in an effort to evoke the bustling and exotic life of Venice. But Shakespeare's words give us this exotic, rich world of commerce in his highly descriptive language when Salerio speaks of "argosies with portly sail" that fly with "woven wings"; equally important, through Salerio Shakespeare conveys a sense of the orderly, hierarchical society in which the lesser ships, "the petty traffickers," curtsy and thereby "do . . . reverence" to their superiors, the merchant prince's ships, which are "Like signiors and rich burghers."

On the other hand, it is a mistake to think that except for verbal pictures the Elizabethan stage was bare. Although Shakespeare's Chorus in *Henry V* calls the stage an "unworthy scaffold" (Prologue 1.10) and urges the spectators to "eke out our performance with your mind" (Prologue 3.35), there was considerable spectacle. The last act of *Macbeth,* for instance, has five stage directions calling for *"drum and colors,"* and another sort of appeal to the eye is indicated by the stage direction *"Enter Macduff, with Macbeth's head."* Some scenery and properties may have been substantial; doubtless a throne was used, but the pillars supporting the roof would have served for the trees on which Orlando pins his poems in *As You Like It.*

Having talked about the public theater—"this wooden *O*"—at some length, we should mention again that Shakespeare's plays were performed also in other locales. Alvin Kernan, in *Shakespeare, the King's Playwright: Theater in the Stuart Court 1603–1613* (1995) points out that "several of [Shakespeare's] plays contain brief theatrical performances, set always in a court or some noble house. When Shakespeare portrayed a theater, he did not, except for the choruses in *Henry V,* imagine a public theater" (p. 195). (Examples include episodes in *The Taming of the Shrew, A Midsummer Night's Dream, Hamlet,* and *The Tempest.*)

A Note on the Use of Boy Actors in Female Roles

Until fairly recently, scholars were content to mention that the convention existed; they sometimes also mentioned that it continued the medieval practice of using males in female roles, and that other theaters, notably in ancient Greece and in China and Japan, also used males in female roles. (In classical Noh drama in Japan, males still play the female roles.) Prudery may have been at the root of the academic failure to talk much about the use of boy actors, or maybe there really is not much more to say than that it was a convention of a male-centered culture (Stephen Greenblatt's view, in *Shakespearean Negotiations* [1988]). Further, the very nature of a convention is that it is not thought about: Hamlet is a Dane and Julius Caesar is a Roman, but in Shakespeare's plays they speak English, and we in the audience never give this odd fact a thought. Similarly, a character may speak in the presence of others and we understand, again without thinking about it, that he or she is not heard by the figures on the stage (the aside); a character alone on the stage may speak (the soliloquy), and we do not take the character to be unhinged; in a realistic (box) set, the fourth wall, which allows us to see what is going on, is miraculously missing. The no-nonsense view, then, is that the boy actor was an accepted convention, accepted unthinkingly—just as today we know that Kenneth Branagh is not Hamlet, Al Pacino is not Richard II, and Denzel Washington is not the Prince of Aragon. In this view, the audience takes the performer for the role, and that is that; such is the argument we now make for race-free casting, in which African-Americans and Asians can play roles of persons who lived in medieval Denmark and ancient Rome. But gender perhaps is different, at least today. It is a matter of abundant academic study: The Elizabethan theater is now sometimes called a transvestite theater, and we hear much about cross-dressing.

Shakespeare himself in a very few passages calls attention to the use of boys in female roles. At the end of *As You Like It* the boy who played Rosalind addresses the audience, and says, "O men, . . . if I were a woman, I would kiss as many of you as had beards that pleased me." But this is in the Epilogue; the plot is over, and the actor is stepping out of the play and into the audience's everyday world. A second reference to the practice of boys playing female roles occurs in *Antony and Cleopatra*, when Cleopatra imagines that she and Antony will be the subject of crude plays, her role being performed by a boy:

> The quick comedians
> Extemporally will stage us, and present
> Our Alexandrian revels: Antony
> Shall be brought drunken forth, and I shall see
> Some squeaking Cleopatra boy my greatness.   (5.2.216–20)

In a few other passages, Shakespeare is more indirect. For
instance, in *Twelfth Night* Viola, played of course by a boy,
disguises herself as a young man and seeks service in the
house of a lord. She enlists the help of a Captain, and (by
way of explaining away her voice and her beardlessness)
says,

> I'll serve this duke
> Thou shalt present me as an eunuch to him.   (1.2.55–56)

In *Hamlet*, when the players arrive in 2.2, Hamlet jokes with
the boy who plays a female role. The boy has grown since
Hamlet last saw him: "By'r Lady, your ladyship is nearer to
heaven than when I saw you last by the altitude of a chopine"
(a lady's thick-soled shoe). He goes on: "Pray God your
voice . . . be not cracked" (434–38).

Exactly how sexual, how erotic, this material was and is,
is now much disputed. Again, the use of boys may have been
unnoticed, or rather not thought about—an unexamined
convention—by most or all spectators most of the time, perhaps *all* of the time, except when Shakespeare calls the convention to the attention of the audience, as in the passages
just quoted. Still, an occasional bit seems to invite erotic
thoughts. The clearest example is the name that Rosalind
takes in *As You Like It*, Ganymede—the beautiful youth
whom Zeus abducted. Did boys dressed to play female roles
carry homoerotic appeal for straight men (Lisa Jardine's
view, in *Still Harping on Daughters* [1983]), or for gay men,
or for some or all women in the audience? Further, when the
boy actor played a woman who (for the purposes of the plot)
disguised herself as a male, as Rosalind, Viola, and Portia
do—so we get a boy playing a woman playing a man—what
sort of appeal was generated, and for what sort of spectator?

Some scholars have argued that the convention empow-
ered women by letting female characters display a freedom
unavailable in Renaissance patriarchal society; the convention, it is said, undermined rigid gender distinctions. In this
view, the convention (along with plots in which female characters for a while disguised themselves as young men)
allowed Shakespeare to say what some modern gender

critics say: Gender is a constructed role rather than a bio-logical given, something we make, rather than a fixed binary opposition of male and female (see Juliet Dusinberre, in *Shakespeare and the Nature of Women* [1975]). On the other hand, some scholars have maintained that the male disguise assumed by some female characters serves only to reaffirm traditional social distinctions since female characters who don male garb (notably Portia in *The Merchant of Venice* and Rosalind in *As You Like It*) return to their female garb and at least implicitly (these critics say) reaffirm the status quo. (For this last view, see Clara Claiborne Park, in an essay in *The Woman's Part*, ed. Carolyn Ruth Swift Lenz et al. [1980].) Perhaps no one answer is right for all plays; in *As You Like It* cross-dressing empowers Rosalind, but in *Twelfth Night* cross-dressing comically traps Viola.

Shakespeare's Dramatic Language: Costumes, Gestures and Silences; Prose and Poetry

Because Shakespeare was a dramatist, not merely a poet, he worked not only with language but also with costume, sound effects, gestures, and even silences. We have already discussed some kinds of spectacle in the preceding section, and now we will begin with other aspects of visual language; a theater, after all, is literally a "place for seeing." Consider the opening stage direction in *The Tempest*, the first play in the first published collection of Shakespeare's plays: *"A tempestuous noise of thunder and Lightning heard: Enter a Ship-master, and a Boteswain."*

Costumes: What did that shipmaster and that boatswain wear? Doubtless they wore something that identified them as men of the sea. Not much is known about the costumes that Elizabethan actors wore, but at least three points are clear: (1) many of the costumes were splendid versions of contemporary Elizabethan dress; (2) some attempts were made to approximate the dress of certain occupations and of antique or exotic characters such as Romans, Turks, and Jews; (3) some costumes indicated that the wearer was supernatural. Evidence for elaborate Elizabethan clothing can be found in the plays themselves and in contemporary comments about the "sumptuous" players who wore the discarded clothing of noblemen, as well as in account books that itemize such things as "a scarlet cloak with two broad gold laces, with gold buttons down the sides."

The attempts at approximation of the dress of certain occupations and nationalities also can be documented from the plays themselves, and it derives additional confirmation from a drawing of the first scene of Shakespeare's *Titus Andronicus*—the only extant Elizabethan picture of an identifiable episode in a play. (See pp. xxxviii–xxxix.) The drawing, probably done in 1594 or 1595, shows Queen Tamora pleading for mercy. She wears a somewhat medieval-looking robe and a crown; Titus wears a toga and a wreath, but two soldiers behind him wear costumes fairly close to Elizabethan dress. We do not know, however, if the drawing represents an actual stage production in the public theater, or perhaps a private production, or maybe only a reader's visualization of an episode. Further, there is some conflicting evidence: In *Julius Caesar* a reference is made to Caesar's doublet (a close-fitting jacket), which, if taken literally, suggests that even the protagonist did not wear Roman clothing; and certainly the lesser characters, who are said to wear hats, did not wear Roman garb.

It should be mentioned, too, that even ordinary clothing can be symbolic: Hamlet's "inky cloak," for example, sets him apart from the brightly dressed members of Claudius's court and symbolizes his mourning; the fresh clothes that are put on King Lear partly symbolize his return to sanity. Consider, too, the removal of disguises near the end of some plays. For instance, Rosalind in *As You Like It* and Portia and Nerissa in *The Merchant of Venice* remove their male attire, thus again becoming fully themselves.

Gestures and Silences: Gestures are an important part of a dramatist's language. King Lear kneels before his daughter Cordelia for a benediction (4.7.57–59), an act of humility that contrasts with his earlier speeches banishing her and that contrasts also with a comparable gesture, his ironic

kneeling before Regan (2.4.153–55). Northumberland's failure to kneel before King Richard II (3.3.71–72) speaks volumes. As for silences, consider a moment in *Coriolanus*: Before the protagonist yields to his mother's entreaties (5.3.182), there is this stage direction: *"Holds her by the hand, silent."* Another example of "speech in dumbness" occurs in *Macbeth*, when Macduff learns that his wife and children have been murdered. He is silent at first, as Malcolm's speech indicates: "What, man! Ne'er pull your hat upon your brows. Give sorrow words" (4.3.208–09). (For a discussion of such moments, see Philip C. McGuire's *Speechless Dialect: Shakespeare's Open Silences* [1985].)

Of course when we think of Shakespeare's work, we think primarily of his language, both the poetry and the prose.

Prose: Although two of his plays (*Richard II* and *King John*) have no prose at all, about half the others have at least one quarter of the dialogue in prose, and some have notably more: *1 Henry IV* and *2 Henry IV*, about half; *As You Like It*

and *Twelfth Night,* a little more than half; *Much Ado About Nothing,* more than three quarters; and *The Merry Wives of Windsor,* a little more than five sixths. We should remember that despite Molière's joke about M. Jourdain, who was amazed to learn that he spoke prose, most of us do not speak prose. Rather, we normally utter repetitive, shapeless, and often ungrammatical torrents; prose is something very different—a sort of literary imitation of speech at its most coherent.

Today we may think of prose as "natural" for drama; or even if we think that poetry is appropriate for high tragedy we may still think that prose is the right medium for comedy. Greek, Roman, and early English comedies, however, were written in verse. In fact, prose was not generally considered a literary medium in England until the late fifteenth century; Chaucer tells even his bawdy stories in verse. By the end of the 1580s, however, prose had established itself on the English comic stage. In tragedy, Marlowe made some use of prose, not simply in the speeches of clownish servants but even in the speech of a tragic hero, Doctor Faustus. Still, before Shakespeare, prose normally was used in the theater only for special circumstances: (1) letters and proclamations, to set them off from the poetic dialogue; (2) mad characters, to indicate that normal thinking has become disordered; and (3) low comedy, or speeches uttered by clowns even when they are not being comic. Shakespeare made use of these conventions, but he also went far beyond them. Sometimes he begins a scene in prose and then shifts into verse as the emotion is heightened; or conversely, he may shift from verse to prose when a speaker is lowering the emotional level, as when Brutus speaks in the Forum.

Shakespeare's prose usually is not prosaic. Hamlet's prose includes not only small talk with Rosencrantz and Guildenstern but also princely reflections on "What a piece of work is a man" (2.2.312). In conversation with Ophelia, he shifts from light talk in verse to a passionate prose denunciation of women (3.1.103), though the shift to prose here is perhaps also intended to suggest the possibility of madness. (Consult Brian Vickers, *The Artistry of Shakespeare's Prose* [1968].)

Poetry: Drama in rhyme in England goes back to the Middle Ages, but by Shakespeare's day rhyme no longer dominated poetic drama; a finer medium, blank verse (strictly speaking, unrhymed lines of ten syllables, with the stress on every second syllable) had been adopted. But before looking at unrhymed poetry, a few things should be said about the chief uses of rhyme in Shakespeare's plays. (1) A couplet (a pair of rhyming lines) is sometimes used to convey emotional heightening at the end of a blank verse speech; (2) characters sometimes speak a couplet as they leave the stage, suggesting closure; (3) except in the latest plays, scenes fairly often conclude with a couplet, and sometimes, as in *Richard II*, 2.1.145–46, the entrance of a new character within a scene is preceded by a couplet, which wraps up the earlier portion of that scene; (4) speeches of two characters occasionally are linked by rhyme, most notably in *Romeo and Juliet*, 1.5.95–108, where the lovers speak a sonnet between them; elsewhere a taunting reply occasionally rhymes with the

previous speaker's last line; (5) speeches with sententious
or gnomic remarks are sometimes in rhyme, as in the
duke's speech in *Othello* (1.3.199–206); (6) speeches of
sardonic mockery are sometimes in rhyme—for example,
Iago's speech on women in *Othello* (2.1.146–58)—and
they sometimes conclude with an emphatic couplet, as in
Bolingbroke's speech on comforting words in *Richard II*
(1.3.301–2); (7) some characters are associated with rhyme,
such as the fairies in *A Midsummer Night's Dream*; (8) in
the early plays, especially *The Comedy of Errors* and *The
Taming of the Shrew*, comic scenes that in later plays would
be in prose are in jingling rhymes; (9) prologues, choruses,
plays-within-the-play, inscriptions, vows, epilogues, and so
on are often in rhyme, and the songs in the plays are rhymed.

Neither prose nor rhyme immediately comes to mind
when we first think of Shakespeare's medium: It is blank
verse, unrhymed iambic pentameter. (In a mechanically
exact line there are five iambic feet. An iambic foot consists
of two syllables, the second accented, as in *away*; five feet
make a pentameter line. Thus, a strict line of iambic pentameter contains ten syllables, the even syllables being
stressed more heavily than the odd syllables. Fortunately,
Shakespeare usually varies the line somewhat.) The first
speech in *A Midsummer Night's Dream*, spoken by Duke
Theseus to his betrothed, is an example of blank verse:

> Now, fair Hippolyta, our nuptial hour
> Draws on apace. Four happy days bring in
> Another moon; but, O, methinks, how slow
> This old moon wanes! She lingers my desires,
> Like to a stepdame, or a dowager,
> Long withering out a young man's revenue.   (1.1.1–6)

As this passage shows, Shakespeare's blank verse is not
mechanically unvarying. Though the predominant foot is
the iamb (as in *apace* or *desires*), there are numerous varia-
tions. In the first line the stress can be placed on "fair," as the
regular metrical pattern suggests, but it is likely that "Now"
gets almost as much emphasis; probably in the second line
"Draws" is more heavily emphasized than "on," giving us a

trochee (a stressed syllable followed by an unstressed one); and in the fourth line each word in the phrase "This old moon wanes" is probably stressed fairly heavily, conveying by two spondees (two feet, each of two stresses) the oppressive tedium that Theseus feels.

In Shakespeare's early plays much of the blank verse is end-stopped (that is, it has a heavy pause at the end of each line), but he later developed the ability to write iambic pentameter verse paragraphs (rather than lines) that give the illusion of speech. His chief techniques are (1) enjambing, i.e., running the thought beyond the single line, as in the first three lines of the speech just quoted; (2) occasionally replacing an iamb with another foot; (3) varying the position of the chief pause (the caesura) within a line; (4) adding an occasional unstressed syllable at the end of a line, traditionally called a feminine ending; (5) and beginning or ending a speech with a half line.

Shakespeare's mature blank verse has much of the rhythmic flexibility of his prose; both the language, though richly figurative and sometimes dense, and the syntax seem natural. It is also often highly appropriate to a particular character. Consider, for instance, this speech from *Hamlet*, in which Claudius, King of Denmark ("the Dane"), speaks to Laertes:

> And now, Laertes, what's the news with you?
> You told us of some suit. What is't, Laertes?
> You cannot speak of reason to the Dane
> And lose your voice. What wouldst thou beg, Laertes,
> That shall not be my offer, not thy asking?   (1.2.42–46)

Notice the short sentences and the repetition of the name "Laertes," to whom the speech is addressed. Notice, too, the shift from the royal "us" in the second line to the more intimate "my" in the last line, and from "you" in the first three lines to the more intimate "thou" and "thy" in the last two lines. Claudius knows how to ingratiate himself with Laertes.

For a second example of the flexibility of Shakespeare's blank verse, consider a passage from *Macbeth*. Distressed by the doctor's inability to cure Lady Macbeth and by the imminent battle, Macbeth addresses some of his remarks to the doctor and others to the servant who is arming him. The entire speech, with its pauses, interruptions, and irresolution (in "Pull't off, I say," Macbeth orders the servant to remove the armor that the servant has been putting on him), catches Macbeth's disintegration. (In the first line, *physic* means "medicine," and in the fourth and fifth lines, *cast the water* means "analyze the urine.")

> Throw physic to the dogs, I'll none of it.
> Come, put mine armor on. Give me my staff.
> Seyton, send out.—Doctor, the thanes fly from me.—
> Come, sir, dispatch. If thou couldst, doctor, cast
> The water of my land, find her disease
> And purge it to a sound and pristine health,
> I would applaud thee to the very echo,
> That should applaud again.—Pull't off, I say.—
> What rhubarb, senna, or what purgative drug,
> Would scour these English hence? Hear'st thou of them?
>
> (5.3.47–56)

Blank verse, then, can be much more than unrhymed iambic pentameter, and even within a single play Shakespeare's blank verse often consists of several styles, depending on the speaker and on the speaker's emotion at the moment.

The Play Text as a Collaboration

Shakespeare's fellow dramatist Ben Jonson reported that the actors said of Shakespeare, "In his writing, whatsoever he penned, he never blotted out line," i.e., never crossed out material and revised his work while composing. None of Shakespeare's plays survives in manuscript (with the possible exception of a scene in *Sir Thomas More*), so we cannot fully evaluate the comment, but in a few instances the published work clearly shows that he revised his manuscript. Consider the following passage (shown here in facsimile) from the best early text of *Romeo and Juliet*, the Second Quarto (1599):

Ro. Would I were sleepe and peace so sweet to rest
The grey eyde morne smiles on the frowning night,
Checkring the Easterne Clouds with streaks of light,
And darknesse fleckted like a drunkard reeles,
From forth daies pathway,made by *Tytans* wheeles.
Hence will I to my ghostly Friers close cell,
His helpe to craue,and my deare hap to tell.

Exit.

Enter Frier alone with a basket.   (night,
Fri. The grey-eyed morne smiles on the frowning
Checking the Easterne clowdes with streaks of light:
And fleckeld darknesse like a drunkard reeles,
From forth daies path,and *Titans* burning wheeles:
Now ere the sun aduance his burning eie,

Romeo rather elaborately tells us that the sun at dawn is
dispelling the night (morning is smiling, the eastern clouds
are checked with light, and the sun's chariot—Titan's
wheels—advances), and he will seek out his spiritual father,
the Friar. He exits and, oddly, the Friar enters and says pretty
much the same thing about the sun. Both speakers say that
"the gray-eyed morn smiles on the frowning night," but there
are small differences, perhaps having more to do with the
business of printing the book than with the author's
composition: For Romeo's "checkring," "fleckted," and
"pathway," we get the Friar's "checking," "fleckeld," and
"path." (Notice, by the way, the inconsistency in Elizabethan
spelling: Romeo's "clouds" become the Friar's "clowdes.")
    Both versions must have been in the printer's copy, and it
seems safe to assume that both were in Shakespeare's manuscript. He must have written one version—let's say he first
wrote Romeo's closing lines for this scene—and then he
decided, no, it's better to give this lyrical passage to the
Friar, as the opening of a new scene, but neglected to delete
the first version. Editors must make a choice, and they may
feel that the reasonable thing to do is to print the text as
Shakespeare intended it. But how can we know what he
intended? Almost all modern editors delete the lines from

Romeo's speech, and retain the Friar's lines. They don't do this because they know Shakespeare's intention, however. They give the lines to the Friar because the first published version (1597) of *Romeo and Juliet* gives only the Friar's version, and this text (though in many ways inferior to the 1599 text) is thought to derive from the memory of some actors, that is, it is thought to represent a performance, not just a script. Maybe during the course of rehearsals Shakespeare—an actor as well as an author—unilaterally decided that the Friar should speak the lines; if so (remember that we don't know this to be a fact) his final intention was to give the speech to the Friar. Maybe, however, the actors talked it over and settled on the Friar, with or without Shakespeare's approval. On the other hand, despite the 1597 version, one might argue (if only weakly) on behalf of giving the lines to Romeo rather than to the Friar, thus: (1) Romeo's comment on the coming of the daylight emphasizes his separation from Juliet, and (2) the figurative language seems more appropriate to Romeo than to the Friar. Having said this, in the Signet edition we have decided in this instance to draw on the evidence provided by earlier text and to give the lines to the Friar, on the grounds that since Q1 reflects a production, in the theater (at least on one occasion) the lines were spoken by the Friar.

A playwright sold a script to a theatrical company. The script thus belonged to the company, not the author, and author and company alike must have regarded this script not as a literary work but as the basis for a play that the actors would create on the stage. We speak of Shakespeare as the author of the plays, but readers should bear in mind that the texts they read, even when derived from a single text, such as the First Folio (1623), are inevitably the collaborative work not simply of Shakespeare with his company—doubtless during rehearsals the actors would suggest alterations—but also with other forces of the age. One force was governmental censorship. In 1606 parliament passed "an Act to restrain abuses of players," prohibiting the utterance of oaths and the name of God. So where the earliest text of *Othello* gives us "By heaven" (3.3.106), the first Folio gives "Alas," presumably reflecting the compliance of stage practice with the law. Similarly, the 1623 version of *King Lear* omits the oath "Fut" (probably from "By God's foot") at 1.2.142, again presumably reflecting the line as it was spoken on the stage. Editors who seek to give the reader the play that Shakespeare initially conceived—the "authentic" play conceived by the solitary Shakespeare—probably will restore the missing oaths and references to God. Other editors, who see the play as a collaborative work, a construction made not only by Shakespeare but also by actors and compositors and even government censors, may claim that what counts is the play as it was actually performed. Such editors regard the censored text as legitimate, since it is the play that was (presumably) finally put on. A performed text, they argue, has more historical reality than a text produced by an editor who has sought to get at what Shakespeare initially wrote. In this view, the text of a play is rather like the script of a film; the script is not the film, and the play text is not the performed play. Even if we want to talk about the play that Shakespeare "intended," we will find ourselves talking about a script that he handed over to a company with the intention that it be implemented by actors. The "intended" play is the one that the actors—we might almost say "society"—would help to construct.

Further, it is now widely held that a play is also the work of readers and spectators, who do not simply receive meaning, but who create it when they respond to the play. This idea is fully in accord with contemporary post-structuralist critical thinking, notably Roland Barthes's "The Death of the Author," in *Image-Music-Text* (1977) and Michel Foucault's "What Is an Author?," in *The Foucault Reader* (1984). The gist of the idea is that an author is not an isolated genius; rather, authors are subject to the politics and other social structures of their age. A dramatist especially is a worker in a collaborative project, working most obviously with actors—parts may be written for particular actors—but working also with the audience. Consider the words of Samuel Johnson, written to be spoken by the actor David Garrick at the opening of a theater in 1747:

> The stage but echoes back the public voice;
> The drama's laws, the drama's patrons give,
> For we that live to please, must please to live.

The audience—the public taste as understood by the play-wright—helps to determine what the play is. Moreover, even members of the public who are not part of the playwright's immediate audience may exert an influence through censorship. We have already glanced at governmental censorship, but there are also other kinds. Take one of Shakespeare's most beloved characters, Falstaff, who appears in three of Shakespeare's plays, the two parts of *Henry IV* and *The Merry Wives of Windsor*. He appears with this name in the earliest printed version of the first of these plays, *1 Henry IV*, but we know that Shakespeare originally called him (after an historical figure) Sir John Oldcastle. Oldcastle appears in Shakespeare's source (partly reprinted in the Signet edition of *1 Henry IV*), and a trace of the name survives in Shakespeare's play, 1.2.43–44, where Prince Hal punningly addresses Falstaff as "my old lad of the castle." But for some reason—perhaps because the family of the historical Oldcastle complained—Shakespeare had to change the name. In short, the play as we have it was (at least in this detail) subject to some sort of censorship. If we think that a text should present what we take to be the author's intention, we probably will want to replace *Falstaff* with *Oldcastle*. But if we recognize that a play is a collaboration, we may welcome the change, even if it was forced on Shakespeare. Somehow *Falstaff*, with its hint of *false-staff*, i.e., inadequate prop, seems just right for this fat knight who, to our delight, entertains the young prince with untruths. We can go as far as saying that, at least so far as a play is concerned, an insistence on the author's original intention (even if we could know it) can sometimes impoverish the text.

The tiny example of Falstaff's name illustrates the point that the text we read is inevitably only a version—something in effect produced by the collaboration of the playwright with his actors, audiences, compositors, and editors—of a fluid text that Shakespeare once wrote, just as the *Hamlet* that we see on the screen starring Kenneth Branagh is not the *Hamlet* that Shakespeare saw in an open-air playhouse starring Richard Burbage. *Hamlet* itself, as we shall note in a moment, also exists in several versions. It is not surprising that there is now much talk about the *instability* of Shakespeare's texts.

Because he was not only a playwright but was also an actor and a shareholder in a theatrical company, Shakespeare probably was much involved with the translation of the play from a manuscript to a stage production. He may or may not have done some rewriting during rehearsals, and he may or may not have been happy with cuts that were made. Some plays, notably *Hamlet* and *King Lear*, are so long that it is most unlikely that the texts we read were acted in their entirety. Further, for both of these plays we have more than one early text that demands consideration. In *Hamlet*, the Second Quarto (1604) includes some two hundred lines not found in the Folio (1623). Among the passages missing from the Folio are two of Hamlet's reflective speeches, the "dram of evil" speech (1.4.13–38) and "How all occasions do inform against me" (4.4.32–66). Since the Folio has more numerous and often fuller stage directions, it certainly looks as though in the Folio we get a theatrical version of the play, a text whose cuts were probably made—this is only a hunch, of course—not because Shakespeare was changing his conception of Hamlet but because the playhouse demanded a modified play. (The problem is complicated, since the Folio not only cuts some of the Quarto but adds some material. Various explanations have been offered.)

Or take an example from *King Lear*. In the First and Second Quarto (1608, 1619), the final speech of the play is given to Albany, Lear's surviving son-in-law, but in the First Folio version (1623), the speech is given to Edgar. The Quarto version is in accord with tradition—usually the highest-ranking character in a tragedy speaks the final words. Why does the Folio give the speech to Edgar? One possible answer is this: The Folio version omits some of Albany's speeches in earlier scenes, so perhaps it was decided (by Shakespeare? by the players?) not to give the final lines to so pale a character. In fact, the discrepancies are so many between the two texts, that some scholars argue we do not simply have texts showing different theatrical productions. Rather, these scholars say, Shakespeare substantially revised the play, and we really have two versions of *King Lear* (and of *Othello* also, say some)—two different plays—not simply two texts, each of which is in some ways imperfect.

In this view, the 1608 version of *Lear* may derive from Shakespeare's manuscript, and the 1623 version may derive from his later revision. The Quartos have almost three hundred lines not in the Folio, and the Folio has about a hundred lines not in the Quartos. It used to be held that all the texts were imperfect in various ways and from various causes— some passages in the Quartos were thought to have been set from a manuscript that was not entirely legible, other passages were thought to have been set by a compositor who was new to setting plays, and still other passages were thought to have been provided by an actor who misremembered some of the lines. This traditional view held that an editor must draw on the Quartos and the Folio in order to get Shakespeare's "real" play. The new argument holds (although not without considerable strain) that we have two authentic plays, Shakespeare's early version (in the Quarto) and Shakespeare's—or his theatrical company's—revised version (in the Folio). Not only theatrical demands but also Shakespeare's own artistic sense, it is argued, called for extensive revisions. Even the titles vary: Q1 is called *True Chronicle Historie of the life and death of King Lear and his three Daughters*, whereas the Folio text is called *The Tragedie of King Lear*. To combine the two texts in order to produce what the editor thinks is the play that Shakespeare intended to write is, according to this view, to produce a text that is false to the history of the play. If the new view is correct, and we do have texts of two distinct versions of *Lear* rather than two imperfect versions of one play, it supports in a textual way the poststructuralist view that we cannot possibly have an unmediated vision of (in this case) a play by Shakespeare; we can only recognize a plurality of visions.

Editing Texts

Though eighteen of his plays were published during his lifetime, Shakespeare seems never to have supervised their publication. There is nothing unusual here; when a playwright sold a play to a theatrical company he surrendered his ownership to it. Normally a company would not publish the play, because to publish it meant to allow competitors to acquire the piece. Some plays did get published: Apparently hard-up actors sometimes pieced together a play for a publisher; sometimes a company in need of money sold a play; and sometimes a company allowed publication of a play that no longer drew audiences. That Shakespeare did not concern himself with publication is not remarkable; of his contemporaries, only Ben Jonson carefully supervised the publication of his own plays.

In 1623, seven years after Shakespeare's death, John Heminges and Henry Condell (two senior members of Shakespeare's company, who had worked with him for about twenty years) collected his plays—published and unpublished—into a large volume, of a kind called a folio. (A folio is a volume consisting of large sheets that have been folded once, each sheet thus making two leaves, or four pages. The size of the page of course depends on the size of the sheet—a folio can range in height from twelve to sixteen inches, and in width from eight to eleven; the pages in the 1623 edition of Shakespeare, commonly called the First Folio, are approximately thirteen inches tall and eight inches wide.) The eighteen plays published during Shakespeare's lifetime had been issued one play per volume in small formats called quartos. (Each sheet in a quarto has been folded twice, making four leaves, or eight pages, each page being about nine inches tall and seven inches wide, roughly the size of a large paperback.)

Heminges and Condell suggest in an address "To the great variety of readers" that the republished plays are presented in better form than in the quartos:

> Before you were abused with diverse stolen and surreptitious copies, maimed and deformed by the frauds and stealths of injurious impostors that exposed them; even those, are now offered to your view cured and perfect of their limbs, and all the rest absolute in their numbers, as he [i.e., Shakespeare] conceived them.

There is a good deal of truth to this statement, but some of the quarto versions are better than others; some are in fact preferable to the Folio text.

Whoever was assigned to prepare the texts for publication

in the first Folio seems to have taken the job seriously and yet not to have performed it with uniform care. The sources of the texts seem to have been, in general, good unpublished copies or the best published copies. The first play in the collection, *The Tempest*, is divided into acts and scenes, has unusually full stage directions and descriptions of spectacle, and concludes with a list of the characters, but the editor was not able (or willing) to present all of the succeeding texts so fully dressed. Later texts occasionally show signs of carelessness: in one scene of *Much Ado About Nothing* the names of actors, instead of characters, appear as speech prefixes, as they had in the Quarto, which the Folio reprints; proofreading throughout the Folio is spotty and apparently was done without reference to the printer's copy; the pagination of *Hamlet* jumps from 156 to 257. Further, the proofreading was done while the presses continued to print, so that each play in each volume contains a mix of corrected and uncorrected pages.

Modern editors of Shakespeare must first select their copy; no problem if the play exists only in the Folio, but a considerable problem if the relationship between a Quarto and the Folio—or an early Quarto and a later one—is unclear. In the case of *Romeo and Juliet*, the First Quarto (Q1), published in 1597, is vastly inferior to the Second (Q2), published in 1599. The basis of Q1 apparently is a version put together from memory by some actors. Not surprisingly, it garbles many passages and is much shorter than Q2. On the other hand, occasionally Q1 makes better sense than Q2. For instance, near the end of the play, when the parents have assembled and learned of the deaths of Romeo and Juliet, in Q2 the Prince says (5.3.208–9),

> Come, *Montague;* for thou art early vp
> To see thy sonne and heire, now earling downe.

The last three words of this speech surely do not make sense, and many editors turn to Q1, which instead of "now earling downe" has "more early downe." Some modern editors take only "early" from Q1, and print "now early down"; others take "more early," and print "more early down." Further, Q1 (though, again, quite clearly a garbled and abbreviated text) includes some stage directions that are not found in Q2, and today many editors who base their text on Q2 are glad to add these stage directions, because the directions help to give us a sense of what the play looked like on Shakespeare's stage. Thus, in 4.3.58, after Juliet drinks the potion, Q1 gives us this stage direction, not in Q2: *"She falls upon her bed within the curtains."*

In short, an editor's decisions do not end with the choice of a single copy text. First of all, editors must reckon with Elizabethan spelling. If they are not producing a facsimile, they probably modernize the spelling, but ought they to preserve the old forms of words that apparently were pronounced quite unlike their modern forms—*lanthorn, alablaster*? If they preserve these forms are they really preserving Shakespeare's forms or perhaps those of a compositor in the printing house? What is one to do when one finds *lanthorn* and *lantern* in adjacent lines? (The editors of this series in general, but not invariably, assume that words should be spelled in their modern form, unless, for instance, a rhyme is involved.) Elizabethan punctuation, too, presents problems. For example, in the First Folio, the only text for the play, Macbeth rejects his wife's idea that he can wash the blood from his hand (2.2.60–62):

> 　　No: this my Hand will rather
> The multitudinous Seas incarnardine,
> Making the Greene one, Red.

Obviously an editor will remove the superfluous capitals, and will probably alter the spelling to "incarnadine," but what about the comma before "Red"? If we retain the comma, Macbeth is calling the sea "the green one." If we drop the comma, Macbeth is saying that his bloody hand will make the sea ("the Green") *uniformly* red.

An editor will sometimes have to change more than spelling and punctuation. Macbeth says to his wife (1.7.46–47):

> I darc do all that may become a man,
> Who darcs no more, is none.

For two centuries editors have agreed that the second line is unsatisfactory, and have emended "no" to "do": "Who dares do more is none." But when in the same play (4.2.21–22) Ross says that fearful persons

> Floate vpon a wilde and violent Sea
> Each way, and mouc,

need we emend the passage? On the assumption that the compositor misread the manuscript, some editors emend "each way, and move" to "and move each way"; others emend "move" to "none" (i.e., "Each way and none"). Other editors, however, let the passage stand as in the original. The editors of the Signet Classic Shakespeare have restrained themselves from making abundant emendations. In their minds they hear Samuel Johnson on the dangers of emendation: "I have adopted the Roman sentiment, that it is more honorable to save a citizen than to kill an enemy." Some departures (in addition to spelling, punctuation, and lineation) from the copy text have of course been made, but the original readings are listed in a note following the play, so that readers can evaluate the changes for themselves.

Following tradition, the editors of the Signet Classic Shakespeare have prefaced each play with a list of characters, and throughout the play have regularized the names of the speakers. Thus, in our text of *Romeo and Juliet*, all speeches by Juliet's mother are prefixed "Lady Capulet," although the 1599 Quarto of the play, which provides our copy text, uses at various points seven speech tags for this one character: *Capu. Wi.* (i.e., Capulet's wife), *Ca. Wi., Wi., Wife, Old La.* (i.e., Old Lady), *La.*, and *Mo.* (i.e., Mother). Similarly, in *All's Well That Ends Well*, the character whom we regularly call "Countess" is in the Folio (the copy text) variously identified as *Mother, Countess, Old Countess, Lady,* and *Old Lady*. Admittedly there is some loss in regularizing, since the various prefixes may give us a hint of the way Shakespeare (or a scribe who copied Shakespeare's manuscript) was thinking of the character in a particular scene—for instance, as a mother, or as an old lady. But too much can be made of these differing prefixes, since the social relationships implied are *not* always relevant to the given scene.

We have also added line numbers and in many cases act and scene divisions as well as indications of locale at the beginning of scenes. The Folio divided most of the plays into acts and some into scenes. Early eighteenth-century editors increased the divisions. These divisions, which provide a convenient way of referring to passages in the plays, have been retained, but when not in the text chosen as the basis for the Signet Classic text they are enclosed within square brackets, [ ], to indicate that they are editorial additions. Similarly, though no play of Shakespeare's was equipped with indications of the locale at the heads of scene divisions, locales have here been added in square brackets for the convenience of readers, who lack the information that costumes, properties, gestures, and scenery afford to spectators. Spectators can tell at a glance they are in the throne room, but without an editorial indication the reader may be puzzled for a while. It should be mentioned, incidentally, that there are a few authentic stage directions—perhaps Shakespeare's, perhaps a prompter's—that suggest locales, such as *"Enter Brutus in his orchard,"* and *"They go up into the Senate house."* It is hoped that the bracketed additions in the Signet text will provide readers with the sort of help provided by these two authentic directions, but it is equally hoped that the reader will remember that the stage was not loaded with scenery.

Shakespeare on the Stage

Each volume in the Signet Classic Shakespeare includes a brief stage (and sometimes film) history of the play. When we read about earlier productions, we are likely to find them eccentric, obviously wrongheaded—for instance, Nahum Tate's version of *King Lear*, with a happy ending, which held the stage for about a century and a half, from the late seventeenth century until the end of the first quarter of the nineteenth. We see engravings of David Garrick, the greatest actor of the eighteenth century, in eighteenth-century garb

as King Lear, and we smile, thinking how absurd the production must have been. If we are more thoughtful, we say,
with the English novelist L. P. Hartley, "The past is a foreign
country: they do things differently there." But if the eighteenth-century staging is a foreign country, what of the plays
of the late sixteenth and seventeenth centuries? A foreign
language, a foreign theater, a foreign audience.

Probably all viewers of Shakespeare's plays, beginning
with Shakespeare himself, at times have been unhappy with
the plays on the stage. Consider three comments about production that we find in the plays themselves, which suggest
Shakespeare's concerns. The Chorus in *Henry V* complains
that the heroic story cannot possibly be adequately staged:

> But pardon, gentles all,
> The flat unraisèd spirits that hath dared
> On this unworthy scaffold to bring forth
> So great an object. Can this cockpit hold
> The vasty fields of France? Or may we cram
> Within this wooden *O* the very casques
> That did affright the air at Agincourt?
>
> . . . .
>
> Piece out our imperfections with your thoughts.
>
> (Prologue 1.8–14,23)

Second, here are a few sentences (which may or may not
represent Shakespeare's own views) from Hamlet's longish
lecture to the players:

> Speak the speech, I pray you, as I pronounced it to you, trippingly
> on the tongue. But if you mouth it, as many of our players do, I had
> as lief the town crier spoke my lines. . . . O, it offends me to the
> soul to hear a robustious periwig-pated fellow tear a passion to tat-
> ters, to very rags, to split the ears of the groundlings. . . . And let
> those that play your clowns speak no more than is set down for
> them, for there be of them that will themselves laugh, to set on
> some quantity of barren spectators to laugh too, though in the
> meantime some necessary question of the play be then to be con-
> sidered. That's villainous and shows a most pitiful ambition in the
> fool that uses it. (3.2.1–47)

Finally, we can quote again from the passage cited earlier in this introduction, concerning the boy actors who played the female roles. Cleopatra imagines with horror a theatrical version of her activities with Antony:

> The quick comedians
> Extemporally will stage us, and present
> Our Alexandrian revels: Antony
> Shall be brought drunken forth, and I shall see
> Some squeaking Cleopatra boy my greatness
> I' th' posture of a whore.   (5.2.216–21)

It is impossible to know how much weight to put on such passages—perhaps Shakespeare was just being modest about his theater's abilities—but it is easy enough to think that he was unhappy with some aspects of Elizabethan production. Probably no production can fully satisfy a playwright, and for that matter, few productions can fully satisfy *us;* we regret this or that cut, this or that way of costuming the play, this or that bit of business.

One's first thought may be this: Why don't they just do "authentic" Shakespeare, "straight" Shakespeare, the play as Shakespeare wrote it? But as we read the plays—words written to be performed—it sometimes becomes clear that we do not know *how* to perform them. For instance, in *Antony and Cleopatra* Antony, the Roman general who has succumbed to Cleopatra and to Egyptian ways, says, "The nobleness of life / Is to do thus" (1.1.36–37). But what is "thus"? Does Antony at this point embrace Cleopatra? Does he embrace and kiss her? (There are, by the way, very few scenes of kissing on Shakespeare's stage, possibly because boys played the female roles.) Or does he make a sweeping gesture, indicating the Egyptian way of life?

This is not an isolated example; the plays are filled with lines that call for gestures, but we are not sure what the gestures should be. *Interpretation* is inevitable. Consider a passage in *Hamlet*. In 3.1, Polonius persuades his daughter, Ophelia, to talk to Hamlet while Polonius and Claudius eavesdrop. The two men conceal themselves, and Hamlet encounters Ophelia. At 3.1.131 Hamlet suddenly says to her, "Where's your father?" Why does Hamlet, apparently out of nowhere—they have not been talking about Polonius—ask this question? Is this an example of the "antic disposition" (fantastic behavior) that Hamlet earlier (1.5.172) had told Horatio and others—including us—he would display? That is, is the question about the whereabouts of her father a seemingly irrational one, like his earlier question (3.1.103) to Ophelia, "Ha, ha! Are you honest?" Or, on the other hand, has Hamlet (as in many productions) suddenly glimpsed Polonius's foot protruding from beneath a drapery at the rear? That is, does Hamlet ask the question because he has suddenly seen something suspicious and now is testing Ophelia? (By the way, in productions that do give Hamlet a physical cue, it is almost always Polonius rather than Claudius who provides the clue. This itself is an act of inter- pretation on the part of the director.) Or (a third possibility) does Hamlet get a clue from Ophelia, who inadvertently betrays the spies by nervously glancing at their place of hiding? This is the interpretation used in the BBC television version, where Ophelia glances in fear toward the hiding place just after Hamlet says "Why wouldst thou be a breeder of sinners?" (121–22). Hamlet, realizing that he is being ob- served, glances here and there *before* he asks "Where's your father?" The question thus is a climax to what he has been doing while speaking the preceding lines. Or (a fourth inter- pretation) does Hamlet suddenly, without the aid of any clue whatsoever, intuitively (insightfully, mysteriously, wonder- fully) sense that someone is spying? Directors must decide, of course—and so must readers.

Recall, too, the preceding discussion of the texts of the plays, which argued that the texts—though they seem to be before us in permanent black on white—are unstable. The Signet text of *Hamlet*, which draws on the Second Quarto (1604) and the First Folio (1623) is considerably longer than any version staged in Shakespeare's time. Our version, even if spoken very briskly and played without any intermission, would take close to four hours, far beyond "the two hours' traffic of our stage" mentioned in the Prologue to *Romeo and Juliet*. (There are a few contemporary references to the dura- tion of a play, but none mentions more than three hours.) Of Shakespeare's plays, only *The Comedy of Errors*, *Macbeth*, and *The Tempest* can be done in less than three hours without cutting. And even if we take a play that exists only in a short text, *Macbeth*, we cannot claim that we are experiencing the very play that Shakespeare conceived, partly because some of the Witches' songs almost surely are non-Shakespearean additions, and partly because we are not willing to watch the play performed without an intermission and with boys in the female roles.

Further, as the earlier discussion of costumes mentioned, the plays apparently were given chiefly in contemporary, that is, in Elizabethan dress. If today we give them in the costumes that Shakespeare probably saw, the plays seem not contemporary but curiously dated. Yet if we use our own dress, we find lines of dialogue that are at odds with what we see; we may feel that the language, so clearly not our own, is inappropriate coming out of people in today's dress. A common solution, incidentally, has been to set the plays in the nineteenth century, on the grounds that this attractively distances the plays (gives them a degree of foreignness, allowing for interesting costumes) and yet doesn't put them into a museum world of Elizabethan England.

Inevitably our productions are adaptations, *our* adaptations, and inevitably they will look dated, not in a century but in twenty years, or perhaps even in a decade. Still, we cannot escape from our own conceptions. As the director Peter Brook has said, in *The Empty Space* (1968):

> It is not only the hair-styles, costumes and make-ups that look dated. All the different elements of staging—the shorthands of behavior that stand for emotions; gestures, gesticulations and tones of voice—are all fluctuating on an invisible stock exchange all the time. . . . A living theatre that thinks it can stand aloof from anything as trivial as fashion will wilt. (p. 16)

As Brook indicates, it is through today's hairstyles, costumes, makeup, gestures, gesticulations, tones of voice—this includes our *conception* of earlier hairstyles, costumes, and so forth if we stage the play in a period other than our own—that we inevitably stage the plays.

It is a truism that every age invents its own Shakespeare, just as, for instance, every age has invented its own classical world. Our view of ancient Greece, a slave-holding society in which even free Athenian women were severely circumscribed, does not much resemble the Victorians' view of ancient Greece as a glorious democracy, just as, perhaps, our view of Victorianism itself does not much resemble theirs. We cannot claim that the Shakespeare on our stage is the true Shakespeare, but in our stage productions we find a Shakespeare that speaks to us, a Shakespeare that our ancestors doubtless did not know but one that seems to us to be the true Shakespeare—at least for a while.

Our age is remarkable for the wide variety of kinds of staging that it uses for Shakespeare, but one development deserves special mention. This is the now common practice of race-blind or color-blind or nontraditional casting, which allows persons who are not white to play in Shakespeare. Previously blacks performing in Shakespeare were limited to a mere three roles, Othello, Aaron (in *Titus Andronicus*), and the Prince of Morocco (in *The Merchant of Venice*), and there were no roles at all for Asians. Indeed, African-Americans rarely could play even one of these three roles, since they were not welcome in white companies. Ira Aldridge (c.1806–1867), a black actor of undoubted talent, was forced to make his living by performing Shakespeare in England and in Europe, where he could play not only Othello but also—in whiteface—other tragic roles such as King Lear. Paul Robeson (1898–1976) made theatrical history when he played Othello in London in 1930, and there was some talk about bringing the production to the United States, but there was more talk about whether American audiences would tolerate the sight of a black man—a real black man, not a white man in blackface—kissing and then killing a white woman. The idea was tried out in summer stock in 1942, the reviews were enthusiastic, and in the following year Robeson opened on Broadway in a production that ran an astounding 296 performances. An occasional all-black company sometimes performed Shakespeare's plays, but otherwise blacks (and other minority members) were in effect shut out from performing Shakespeare. Only since about 1970 has it been common for nonwhites to play major roles along with whites. Thus, in a 1996–97 production of *Antony and Cleopatra*, a white Cleopatra, Vanessa Redgrave, played opposite a black Antony, David Harewood.

Multiracial casting is now especially common at the New York Shakespeare Festival, founded in 1954 by Joseph Papp, and in England, where even siblings such as Claudio and Isabella in *Measure for Measure* or Lear's three daughters may be of different races. Probably most viewers today soon stop worrying about the lack of realism, and move beyond the color of the performers' skin to the quality of the performance.

Nontraditional casting is not only a matter of color or race; it includes sex. In the past, occasionally a distinguished woman of the theater has taken on a male role—Sarah Bernhardt (1844–1923) as Hamlet is perhaps the most famous example—but such performances were widely regarded as eccentric. Although today there have been some performances involving cross-dressing (a drag *As You Like It* staged by the National Theatre in England in 1966 and in the United States in 1974 has achieved considerable fame in the annals of stage history), what is more interesting is the casting of women in roles that traditionally are male but that need not be. Thus, a 1993–94 English production of *Henry V* used a woman—*not* cross-dressed—in the role of the governor of Harfleur. According to Peter Holland, who reviewed the production in *Shakespeare Survey* 48 (1995), "having a female Governor of Harfleur feminized the city and provided a direct response to the horrendous threat of rape and murder that Henry had offered, his language and her body in direct connection and opposition" (p. 210). Ten years from now the device may not play so effectively, but today it speaks to us. Shakespeare, born in the Elizabethan Age, has been dead nearly four hundred years, yet he is, as Ben Jonson said, "not of an age but for all time." We must understand, however, that he is "for all time" precisely because each age finds in his abundance something for itself and something of itself.

And here we come back to two issues discussed earlier in this introduction—the instability of the text and, curiously, the Bacon/Oxford heresy concerning the authorship of the plays. *Of course* Shakespeare wrote the plays, and we should daily fall on our knees to thank him for them—and yet there is something to the idea that he is not their only author. Every editor, every director and actor, and every reader to some degree shapes them, too, for when we edit, direct, act, or read, we inevitably become Shakespeare's collaborator and re-create the plays. The plays, one might say, are so cunningly contrived that they guide our responses, tell us how we ought to feel, and make a mark on us, but (for better or for worse) we also make a mark on them.

—SYLVAN BARNET
Tufts University

Introduction

Much Ado About Nothing presents an editor with no significant problems as to when it was written, the correctness of the text, the kind of source material that it reanimates and makes into a play. It was published in quarto in 1600, when Shakespeare was thirty-six, with his name on the title page, and was further identified as having been "publicly acted" by the acting company for which he wrote and of which he was a member. The evidence is quite clear that it had been written within a year or a year and a half of its publication (i.e., at about mid point in Shakespeare's career as a dramatist). The text itself is an excellent one, the basis of the posthumous Folio text of 1623, with only a few minor difficulties as to the assignment of lines and as to the intent, here and there, of the original punctuation. The Hero-Claudio-Don John plot, with its lady's maid, caught with her lover, being mistaken for the lady herself, has been traced back to a Greek source of about the year 400. The sixteenth-century Italian collector of tales, Bandello, used the plot in Story XXII of his *Novelle* (1554), as did Ariosto somewhat earlier in Book V of his *Orlando Furioso*,[1] and as did Spenser in Book II, Canto 4, of the *Faerie Queene* (1590). Beatrice and Benedick, if one wishes to abstract them from the play to view them in historical context, are part of a battle of the sexes with deep roots in the culture and in the literature of the Western world (as I have tried to demonstrate in *The Love-Game Comedy,* 1946). Dogberry and Verges have self-evident origins in that which they parody.

Much Ado, moreover, has never provoked elaborate critical appraisal, perhaps because it has always seemed serenely

---

[1] The famous Elizabethan translation (1591) was by the favorite of the Queen, Sir John Harington.

self-contained, a comedy that does its work so well when seen on a stage, or when read, that it does not particularly invite extended comment. Its brilliance as a comedy, then (to justify the admirable quietness of its critics), can be briefly verbalized in two interrelated ways. We can describe the dramatic strategies employed in the play, which create its idiosyncratic "tone" as a comedy. We can also try to define the unique identity of *Much Ado* by an exploration of its substance, the special aspect of existence blocked out for dramatization in the play.

The primary identifying fact about *Much Ado*, I think, is that it is the most realistic of Shakespeare's love comedies written during the reign of Elizabeth. And it is realistic despite the basic improbability (or conventionality) of Claudio's deception by Don John. It abandons completely the romantic landscape, the romantic disguisings, the romantic dialogue of Portia's and Bassanio's Belmont, of Rosalind's and Orlando's Forest of Arden, of Viola's and Duke Orsino's Illyria. In *Much Ado* we enter a dramatic world created in very close imitation of the habitable one we know outside the theater.

From its very beginning, the play forces this real world upon us. Its characters are a small group of aristocrats who have all known each other a long time and who are introduced to us, in 1.1, talking about each other on the basis of old familiarity. Hero, for example, recognizes at once Beatrice's oblique reference to Benedick as "Signior Mountanto." Beatrice, we are to understand, has taunted Benedick's valor sometime before the immediate moments of the play and remembers that she has promised "to eat all of his killing" in the wars that have just concluded. She has also previously ridiculed his pretensions as a lover. She recalls: "He set up his bills here in Messina and challenged Cupid at the flight." Leonato refers easily to the long-standing "merry war betwixt Signior Benedick" and Beatrice. Claudio confesses to earlier amorous thoughts about Hero before he went off to the "rougher task" of the wars. Even Don John (1.3) has already been sufficiently irritated by the "exquisite" Claudio to abhor the elegance of this "very forward March-chick," this "start-up," and to be "sick in displeasure to him" (2.2).

Our sense of the close approximation of *Much Ado* to an actual social world is further enhanced by a certain casualness and easiness in the confrontations of one character with another. In this respect, and scene by scene, *Much Ado* is more like *Hamlet*, for example, than it is like *As You Like It* or *Twelfth Night*. The first and the last scene in the play are perhaps the most brilliant illustrations of this casualness, this incredible ease with which characters react to each other. But it is an ease that is completely sustained as "tone" or manner throughout the play. One finds it in Don Pedro's and in Benedick's teasing of Balthasar, for example, for his reluctance to sing in front of them (2.3). It is the element which gives credibility to Borachio's rambling discourse to Conrade on fashion (3.3). It is what makes Benedick's sudden playing the role of schoolteacher and grammarian ("How now? Interjections?") in the church scene (4.1) so believable and so desperately ironic. It is what makes so devastating the unexpected and embarrassed encounter that Don Pedro and Claudio have with Leonato and Antonio after the disgracing of Hero (5.1).

Another aspect of the sustained, mimetic realism of *Much Ado* has to do with the kind of language that makes up the complex, closely interwoven dialogue of the play. The language used to carry the interchanges between Rosalind and Orlando, or between Viola and Duke Orsino, is romantically stylized and tempts us to immerse ourselves in some ideal, golden world of love. The language used for the interchanges between characters in *Much Ado* constantly reminds us of the flow of clever discourse in the best moments of the actual world we all inhabit. And the potency of this language of *Much Ado* is such that it seems capable of generating the natural, this-worldly atmosphere of the play just in itself. It is not the formalized repartee, the carefully contrived and balanced give and take of wit in Restoration comedy. Rather, its special quality is its air of the spontaneous. In *Much Ado* it is as if the characters themselves were inventing in front of us their quick ironic retorts and their exultant gaiety at the accomplishment.

The characters in this play take their dramatic world to be so much alive that they are constantly remembering what they have said to each other earlier in the action. The most

striking example of this sort of realism is the acid repetition
to Benedick by Don Pedro and by Claudio (5.1 and 5.4) of
Benedick's extravagant description (1.1) of what may be
done to him if he ever falls in love. But Beatrice, who turns
the word "stuffed" inside out in her ridicule of Benedick
(1.1), later tempts Margaret to use it against her (3.4): "A
maid, and stuffed!" Don Pedro, with Claudio by (5.1),
catches his anger at Leonato's importunate language in the
deftly sardonic phrase, "we will not wake your patience."
Claudio, moments later in the same scene (after he learns
that he has been grossly fooled), expresses his genuine con-
trition to Leonato by slightly varying the same phrase: "I
know not how to pray your patience." Even the two members of the watch, who are worried about "one Deformed"
in 3.4, find Dogberry carefully remembering in 5.1 to have
Borachio examined "upon that point."

The sustained, conversational quality of the dialogue
of *Much Ado,* which accompanies and gives body to the
nonchalant casualness of the character confrontations in
the play, is perhaps the ultimate essence of the play's mimetic richness. The characters may individualize what they
say, but they all speak essentially the same sophisticated-
realistic language of their group. In its imagery it is much
concerned with the act of sex and with the expected cuckoldry of their society ("he that is less than a man, I am not
for him"; "Tush, fear not, man! We'll tip thy horns with
gold"). It is also full of the kind of literary reference that
would be known to a person of such a society. Hercules,
Ate, Europa and Jove, Baucis and Philemon are tossed into
the stream of discourse; Kyd's *Spanish Tragedy* and *A
Handful of Pleasant Delights* are quoted; Beatrice makes
use of current attitudes already exploited in Davies's poem
Orchestra in her description of marriage as a dance. But beyond all this sort of identifying conversational style is an
"aliveness" in what the characters say to one another. It is
this extravagant "aliveness," in combination with the play's
other dramatic devices, that gives to *Much Ado* its separate
identity of discourse. In no other of Shakespeare's comedies
could one of its characters call another, with such eloquent
understatement, "my Lady Tongue."

The substance of *Much Ado* is that of the romantic comedies, sex, love, and marriage. But this play's differentiated way of regarding this substance, its sophisticated realism, is certainly intentionally suggested by its title. Within the play itself there are two views of this substance. One view is that assumed by Claudio, Don Pedro, Leonato, and Hero. Claudio is the central, dominating voice of this group as he acts out its social assumptions. He is presented as a conventional young man, one who regards love and marriage as the making of a sensible match with a virtuous and attractive young girl who brings a good dowry and the approval of her father and of his friends. Although a young man today, a member of a similar social group, might put his feelings in somewhat more romantic terms, if he were of a "good" family in any city of the Western world, he might essentially agree with Claudio's view.

Claudio is certainly no passionate Romeo, and there is no indication in the play that he has done more than regard Hero as an attractive member of the aristocratic society to which they both belong. He is (perhaps somewhat in the position of Paris, in *Romeo and Juliet*) a young man capable of an easy romanticizing of sexual attraction, as his comment on Hero to Don Pedro fully reveals:

> . . . now I am returned and that war-thoughts
> Have left their places vacant, in their rooms
> Come thronging soft and delicate desires,
> All prompting me how fair young Hero is,
> Saying I liked her ere I went to wars.   (1.1.291–95)

Claudio, again like Paris, is the young man bent on doing "the right thing" in his society. He is attractive as a man, as his worst enemy, Don John, lets us know by his envy. But Claudio is also, as people aware only of the right thing to do tend to be, terrifyingly naïve (and terrifyingly obtuse). As Benedick puts it, Claudio reacts like a hurt bird when he thinks Don Pedro has taken Hero from him ("Alas, poor hurt fowl! Now will he creep into sedges" 2.1.200–1). And Benedick places Claudio's romantic inclinations toward Hero at the level of the feelings of a small child by comparing Claudio to a "schoolboy who, being overjoyed with finding a bird's nest, shows it his companion, and he [Don

Pedro] steals it" (220–22). Claudio's politeness, his sense of the socially appropriate, even leads him to suggest that he abandon his bride immediately after his marriage and accompany his sponsor, Don Pedro, from Messina to Aragon. Don Pedro again identifies for us the childlike quality of Claudio's feelings for Hero when he replies: "that would be as great a soil in the new gloss of your marriage as to show a child his new coat and forbid him to wear it" (3.2.5–7).

In the church scene, Claudio's turning on Hero for her supposed assignation on the eve of her marriage is wholly in keeping with the nature of his feelings for her and with the codes of his group. He moves toward his denunciation in the sententiously arrogant, teasing manner of the overly conventional person who has been fooled about something rather important and who will now take great pleasure in a measured retaliation. Claudio, the exquisite, reacts appropriately like a child cheated over a toy promised to him. And the absolute "rightness" of his attitude in the play is made quite clear by the fact that Hero's father and Don Pedro instantly agree with it. Leonato, who was as concerned as Claudio and Don Pedro with a "good" marriage, reacts, indeed, much as Capulet (also a socially conventional man) had reacted when Juliet had refused to marry Paris:

> Why had I one?
> Why ever wast thou lovely in my eyes?
> . . . mine that I was proud on, mine so much
> That I myself was to myself not mine,
> Valuing of her—why she, O, she is fall'n
> Into a pit of ink.   (4.1.128–39)

Beatrice and Benedick, wholly unchildlike, present another view of the essential stuff of this play, a view that cuts across the conventional one, and insinuates doubts lurking in sophisticated minds as to its necessary validity. They are everywhere presented as completely aware of the fact that they are playing roles with and for each other—Beatrice as shrew, Benedick as misogynist—and enjoying the playing. The subject matter of their game is a distaste for institutionalized romantic love leading to marriage, the precise kind of "love" that Claudio and Hero accept easily and without thought. The only obstacle to Claudio's pursuit would be the sort of thing he thinks had happened, a lack of sexual virtue on the part of the girl who has caught his fancy. The subtle obstacle to the union of Benedick and Beatrice is that neither is ever sure of what he or she would be like if they agreed to quit playing their respective roles. Indeed, part of the dramatic (and psychological) excitement at the play's end is that neither one of this pair is yet certain of what emotions really lie below the level of the role-playing.

The love game of Beatrice and Benedick is an intricate one in *Much Ado*, because both of them are teasing something more complicated than just conventional romantic love. They are dramatized as testing the antiromantic roles they are actually playing against their sense of what it would be like to be a Hero or a Claudio, to fall into the words and phrases and stances of institutionalized romance. Moreover, in their dueling in the self-accepted roles of the man and the woman too knowing to wear the yoke of marriage and to "sigh away Sundays," it is always made dramatically obvious that both characters are aware that with any slipping either or both could easily *become* a Hero or a Claudio and turn husband and wife. Benedick's first direct comment on Beatrice, early in the play (1.1.184–86), is, it seems to me, self-evident acknowledgment of this fact: "and she were not possessed with a fury, [Beatrice] exceeds [Hero] as much in beauty as the first of May doth the last of December."

It is this ambivalent element in their love game, I think, that made Beatrice and Benedick so fascinating to their own age, and now also to us. And the basis of the fascination is that in their own probing of their reactions to ritualized romantic love, they invite us to probe the usually inaccessible areas of our own knowing, our own awareness in such matters. More important, if we think, at the play's end, that Beatrice and Benedick merely exist for five acts to be tricked into admitting that they are fundamentally as conventionally involved in sex, love, and marriage as Hero and Claudio, we have missed the essential purport of the play.

Beatrice is the more open of the two in her acknowledgment of the ambiguity of her role-playing. Her acid remarks in the first scene of Act 1 concerning Benedick's challenge to Cupid, and her uncle's fool's response (i.e., Beatrice herself?), carry the suggestion, never made overt in the play, either that Beatrice had never been sure of her role as Lady Tongue or that she had once tried out a romantic role with Benedick himself. She is presented as openly uneasy (2.1) over the fact that Hero has got herself a husband ("I may sit in a corner and cry 'Heigh-ho for a husband!' "). And she once darkly hints an earlier involvement with Benedick when she tells Don Pedro that Benedick lent his heart to her for a while, "and I gave him use for it, a double heart for his single one. Marry, once before he won it of me with false dice" (275–78).

The ambiguousness in Benedick's role as misogynic bachelor is perhaps best suggested by the extravagant language he always uses to defend his role:

Prove that ever I lose more blood with love than I will get again with drinking, pick out mine eyes with a ballad maker's pen and hang me up at the door of a brothel house for the sign of blind Cupid.   (1.1.241–45)

His taunt to Claudio concerning Hero ("Would you buy her, that you inquire after her?" 173–74), and his headlong flight from Beatrice (2.1) with the bitter comment that "while she is here" he could live as quietly in hell, are but further illustrations of this extravagance. Dramatically, to be sure, such soaring flights of words prepare us for the irony of his surrender to love of a sort. Psychologically, they tempt us to wonder that a man could hate so vehemently what he professes to have no interest in.

The marriage of Hero and Claudio turns on the simple problem as to whether Hero is a virgin or not, i.e., as to whether she is socially and therefore personally acceptable to Claudio in his aristocratic world of arranged marriages. The marriage of Beatrice and Benedick turns on the ability of their peers to trick them out of their self-conscious role-playing. It is of interest to note that the latter pair's willingness to surrender to love and marriage takes place while Hero's virtue is still under a cloud as far as Claudio is concerned, and therefore at a moment when their previous bantering would be inappropriate. It is equally important to note that both Beatrice and Benedick, if somewhat subdued, actually bring alive again, at the play's end, something of the ambiguity toward love that they had had from the beginning of the play.

Beatrice's final words are not those of a Rosalind or a Viola:

> I yield upon great persuasion, and partly to save your life, for I was told you were in a consumption.
>
> (5.4.95–96)

Benedick's penultimate comments are addressed not to Beatrice, but rather to Don Pedro. And Benedick insists upon being as ambiguous about his feelings, now that he had agreed to conform to marriage, as he had been earlier, when he could only exclaim against it. He insists to Don Pedro that "since I do purpose to marry, I will think nothing to any purpose that the world can say against it" (104–6). He concludes that Don Pedro himself had better marry in order that he too may join the gay company of cuckolds-to-be:

> get thee a wife, get thee a wife! There is no staff more reverend than one tipped with horn.
>
> (122–24)

In *Romeo and Juliet*, written about four years before *Much Ado*, Shakespeare had dramatized the lyric, fragile love of very young people not yet wise enough to yield to the social realities—and therefore broken by them. He had presented their love as a highly perishable commodity, one as subject to accident as to time. It is not only Romeo and Juliet, but we, as audience, who acquiesce in their deaths because we are fully aware that in "reality" there can only be either slow dilution or abrupt extinction of such flower-like love. In *Twelfth Night*, written probably a year or so later than *Much Ado*, we are kept within the elegant, golden confines of courtly, aristocratic romance—a place full of music and of bodily forms (to borrow from Yeats) "of hammered gold and gold enameling," set singing to keep some "drowsy Emperor awake."

The kind of love encompassed by the dialogue of *Much Ado*, and by its two sets of lovers, is love in the social world. This comedy, indeed, is a highly novel one for Shakespeare to have written. The play ends with its characters and the audience accepting the two marriages that have been in the making from its beginning. But the power of the comedy lies not in our accepting the fragility of youthful passion or in our surrender to idyllic romance. Rather, *Much Ado*, by all its strategies of language and characterization, moves so close to reality that it cannot reach a denouement in which the simply understood mood or attitude of *Romeo and Juliet* or of *Twelfth Night* reaches final focus.

The essential uniqueness of *Much Ado* as a comedy, and its fascination, lies in the fact that it invokes our awareness of the complicated relationship between the indeterminate nature of private feeling and the simplicities of the decorous behavior which is supposed to embody such feeling. That is to say, *Much Ado* dramatizes sex, love, and marriage in close imitation of their complexity in actuality. This play, of course, is far too stylized to be "real," and it keeps us comically insulated from too deep involvement with its characters and its substance. The play's final moment of balance, of standing still, then, is necessarily somewhat different from that of the Shakespearean romances where a long ritual of wooing comes to a ritualized conclusion. In *Much Ado* we are given, in its last scene, the dramatic illusion that the pair of marriages has been created by the volition of the characters themselves. They seem to be marrying out of their own desire to find, if only momentarily, a way of being at peace with themselves and with each other.

—DAVID L. STEVENSON
Hunter College

Much adoe about *Nothing.*

*Enter Leonato gouernour of Meſſina, Innogen his wife, Hero
his daughter, and Beatrice his neece, with a
meſſenger.*

Leonato.

Learne in this letter , that don Peter of Arragon
comes this night to Meſſina.

Meſſ. ·He is very neare by this, he was not three
leagues off when I left him.

Leona. How many gentlemen haue you loſt in this action?

Meſſ. But few of any ſort, and none of name.

Leona. A victory is twice it ſelfe, when the atchiuer brings
home ful numbers: I find here, that don Peter hath beſtowed
much honour on a yong Florentine called Claudio.

Meſſ. Much deſeru'd on his part, and equally remembred
by don Pedro, he hath borne himſelfe beyond the promiſe of
his age, doing in the figure of a lamb, the feats of a lion, he hath
indeed better bettred expectation then you muſt expect of me
to tell you how.

Leo. He hath an vnckle here in Meſſina will be very much
glad of it.

Meſſ. I haue already deliuered him letters, and there ap-
peares much ioy in him, euen ſo much, that ioy could not ſhew
it ſelfe modeſt enough, without a badge of bitterneſſe.

Leo. Did he breake out into teares?

Meſſ. In great meaſure.

A 2 *Leo.*

First page of text from the Quarto of 1600. Notice that in the first stage
direction, the Governor of Messina is said to be accompanied by "Innogen his wife." Apparently when Shakespeare began writing the scene, he
thought he would include this character, but in fact she appears nowhere
in the play.

Much Ado About Nothing

Much Ado About Nothing

[ACT 1

Scene 1. *Before Leonato's house.*]

*Enter Leonato, Governor of Messina, Hero his
daughter, and Beatrice his niece, with a Messenger.*

Leonato. I learn in this letter that Don Pedro of Aragon comes this night to Messina.

Messenger. He is very near by this. He was not three
leagues off when I left him.

Leonato. How many gentlemen°[1] have you lost in this   5
action?

Messenger. But few of any sort,° and none of name.°

Leonato. A victory is twice itself when the achiever
brings home full numbers. I find here that Don
Pedro hath bestowed much honor on a young Flor-   10
entine called Claudio.

---

[1] The degree sign (°) indicates a footnote, which is keyed to the text by
line number. Text references are printed in **boldface** type; the annotation
follows in roman type.
1.1.5 **gentlemen** men of upper class   7 **sort** rank   7 **name** distinguished
family

Messenger. Much deserved on his part, and equally rememb'red by Don Pedro. He hath borne himself
beyond the promise of his age, doing, in the figure
15   of a lamb, the feats of a lion. He hath indeed better
bett'red expectation° than you must expect of me to
tell you how.

Leonato. He hath an uncle° here in Messina will be very
much glad of it.

20 *Messenger.* I have already delivered him letters, and
there appears much joy in him; even so much that
joy could not show itself modest enough without a
badge° of bitterness.

Leonato. Did he break out into tears?

25 *Messenger.* In great measure.

Leonato. A kind overflow of kindness.° There are no
faces truer than those that are so washed. How much
better is it to weep at joy than to joy at weeping!

Beatrice. I pray you, is Signior Mountanto° returned
30   from the wars or no?

Messenger. I know none of that name, lady. There was
none such in the army of any sort.

Leonato. What is he that you ask for, niece?

Hero. My cousin means Signior Benedick of Padua.

35 *Messenger.* O, he's returned, and as pleasant° as ever
he was.

Beatrice. He set up his bills° here in Messina and challenged Cupid at the flight;° and my uncle's fool,
reading the challenge, subscribed° for Cupid and
40   challenged him at the burbolt.° I pray you, how
many hath he killed and eaten in these wars? But

15–16 **better bett'red expectation** greatly exceeded anticipated valor
18 **uncle** (does not appear in the play)   23 **badge** emblem   26 **kind
overflow of kindness** natural overflow of tenderness   29 **Mountanto**
a fencing thrust   35 **pleasant** lively   37 **bills** advertising placards
38 **flight** shooting contest (i.e., he thought himself a lady-killer)   39 **sub-
scribed** signed up   40 **burbolt** blunt arrow

how many hath he killed? For indeed, I promised
to eat all of his killing.

Leonato. Faith, niece, you tax° Signior Benedick too
much; but he'll be meet° with you, I doubt it not.   45

Messenger. He hath done good service, lady, in these
wars.

Beatrice. You had musty victual, and he hath holp to
eat it. He is a very valiant trencherman;° he hath
an excellent stomach.   50

Messenger. And a good soldier too, lady.

Beatrice. And a good soldier to° a lady. But what is he
to a lord?

Messenger. A lord to a lord, a man to a man; stuffed
with all honorable virtues.   55

Beatrice. It is so, indeed; he is no less than a stuffed
man.° But for the stuffing—well, we are all mortal.

Leonato. You must not, sir, mistake my niece. There
is a kind of merry war betwixt Signior Benedick and
her. They never meet but there's a skirmish of wit   60
between them.

Beatrice. Alas, he gets nothing by that! In our last conflict four of his five wits° went halting° off, and now
is the whole man governed with one; so that if he
have wit enough to keep himself warm, let him bear   65
it for a difference between himself and his horse. For
it is all the wealth that he hath left to be known a
reasonable creature. Who is his companion now?
He hath every month a new sworn brother.

Messenger. Is't possible?   70

Beatrice. Very easily possible. He wears his faith but
as the fashion of his hat; it ever changes with the
next block.°

---

44 **tax** i.e., tease too hard   45 **meet** even   49 **trencherman** eater   52 **to**
in comparison with   56–57 **stuffed man** dummy   63 **five wits** common
sense, imagination, fancy, estimation, memory   63 **halting** limping
73 **next block** most recent shape

Messenger. I see, lady, the gentleman is not in your
75   books.°

Beatrice. No. And° he were, I would burn my study.
But I pray you, who is his companion? Is there no
young squarer° now that will make a voyage with
him to the devil?

80 *Messenger.* He is most in the company of the right
noble Claudio.

Beatrice. O Lord, he will hang upon him like a disease.
He is sooner caught than the pestilence, and the
taker runs presently° mad. God help the noble
85   Claudio if he have caught the Benedict;° it will cost
him a thousand pound ere 'a° be cured.

Messenger. I will hold friends with you, lady.

Beatrice. Do, good friend.

Leonato. You will never run mad,° niece.

90 *Beatrice.* No, not till a hot January.

Messenger. Don Pedro is approached.

*Enter Don Pedro, Claudio, Benedick, Balthasar, and
John the Bastard.*

Don Pedro. Good Signior Leonato, are you come to
meet your trouble? The fashion of the world is to
avoid cost, and you encounter it.

95 *Leonato.* Never came trouble to my house in the like-
ness of your Grace; for trouble being gone, comfort
should remain. But when you depart from me, sorrow abides, and happiness takes his leave.

Don Pedro. You embrace your charge° too willingly.
100   I think this is your daughter.

Leonato. Her mother hath many times told me so.

---

75 **books** favor   76 **And** if   78 **squarer** brawler   84 **presently** immediately (the usual sense in Shakespeare)   85 **Benedict** (the change in
spelling suggests a disease based on Benedick's name)   86 **'a** he
89 **run mad** catch the Benedict   99 **charge** burden (of my visit)

Benedick. Were you in doubt, sir, that you asked her?

Leonato. Signior Benedick, no; for then were you a
child.

Don Pedro. You have it full, Benedick. We may guess   *105*
by this what you are, being a man. Truly the lady
fathers herself.° Be happy, lady, for you are like an
honorable father.

Benedick. If Signior Leonato be her father, she would
not have his head° on her shoulders for all Messina,   *110*
as like him as she is.

Beatrice. I wonder that you will still° be talking,
Signior Benedick; nobody marks you.

Benedick. What, my dear Lady Disdain! Are you yet
living?   *115*

Beatrice. Is it possible Disdain should die while she
hath such meet food to feed it as Signior Benedick?
Courtesy itself must convert to Disdain if you come
in her presence.

Benedick. Then is courtesy a turncoat. But it is certain   *120*
I am loved of all ladies,° only you excepted; and I
would I could find in my heart that I had not a hard
heart; for truly I love none.

Beatrice. A dear happiness to women! They would else
have been troubled with a pernicious suitor. I thank   *125*
God and my cold blood, I am of your humor for
that.° I had rather hear my dog bark at a crow than
a man swear he loves me.

Benedick. God keep your ladyship still in that mind,
so some gentleman or other shall scape a predesti-   *130*
nate scratched face.

Beatrice. Scratching could not make it worse and
'twere such a face as yours were.

---

107 **fathers herself** shows who her father is by resembling him   110 **his
head** white-haired and bearded (?)   112 **still** always (the usual sense in
Shakespeare)   121 **loved of all ladies** (he had "challenged Cupid")
126–27 **of your humor for that** in agreement on that

Benedick. Well, you are a rare parrot-teacher.°

135 *Beatrice.* A bird of my tongue is better than a beast of yours.

Benedick. I would my horse had the speed of your tongue, and so good a continuer.° But keep your way, a God's name! I have done.

140 *Beatrice.* You always end with a jade's trick.° I know you of old.

Don Pedro. That is the sum of all,° Leonato. Signior Claudio and Signior Benedick, my dear friend Leonato hath invited you all. I tell him we shall stay
145 here, at the least a month, and he heartily prays some occasion may detain us longer. I dare swear he is no hypocrite, but prays from his heart.

Leonato. If you swear, my lord, you shall not be forsworn. [*To Don John*] Let me bid you welcome, my
150 lord; being reconciled to the Prince your brother, I owe you all duty.

Don John. I thank you. I am not of many words, but I thank you.

Leonato. Please it your Grace lead on?

155 *Don Pedro.* Your hand, Leonato. We will go together.
                    Exeunt. Manent° Benedick and Claudio.

Claudio. Benedick, didst thou note the daughter of Signior Leonato?

Benedick. I noted° her not, but I looked on her.

Claudio. Is she not a modest young lady?

160 *Benedick.* Do you question me as an honest man should do, for my simple true judgment? Or would

---

134 **parrot-teacher** i.e., monotonous speaker of nonsense   138 **continuer** staying power   140 **jade's trick** trick of a vicious horse (i.e., a sudden stop?)   142 **the sum of all** the end of the sparring match 155 s.d. **Manent** remain (Latin)   158 **noted** (1) scrutinized (2) set to music (3) stigmatized

you have me speak after my custom, as being a professed tyrant to their sex?

Claudio. No, I pray thee speak in sober judgment.

Benedick. Why, i' faith, methinks she's too low for a   165
high praise, too brown for a fair praise, and too little
for a great praise. Only this commendation I can
afford her, that were she other than she is, she were
unhandsome, and being no other but as she is, I
do not like her.   170

Claudio. Thou thinkest I am in sport. I pray thee tell
me truly how thou lik'st her.

Benedick. Would you buy her, that you inquire after
her?

Claudio. Can the world buy such a jewel?   175

Benedick. Yea, and a case to put it into. But speak you
this with a sad brow?° Or do you play the flouting
Jack, to tell us Cupid is a good hare-finder and
Vulcan a rare carpenter?° Come, in what key shall
a man take you to go in the song?   180

Claudio. In mine eye she is the sweetest lady that ever
I looked on.

Benedick. I can see yet without spectacles, and I see no
such matter. There's her cousin, and she were not
possessed with a fury, exceeds her as much in beauty   185
as the first of May doth the last of December. But I
hope you have no intent to turn husband, have you?

Claudio. I would scarce trust myself, though I had
sworn the contrary, if Hero would be my wife.

Benedick. Is't come to this? In faith, hath not the world 190
one man but he will wear his cap with suspicion?°

---

177 **with a sad brow** seriously   178–79 **to tell us . . . carpenter** i.e., to
mock us with nonsense (Cupid was blind, Vulcan was a blacksmith)
191 **but he . . . suspicion** who (because he is unmarried) will not fear that
he has a cuckold's horns

Shall I never see a bachelor of threescore again? Go
to, i' faith! And thou wilt needs thrust thy neck into
a yoke, wear the print of it and sigh away Sundays.°
195 Look! Don Pedro is returned to seek you.

Enter Don Pedro.

Don Pedro. What secret hath held you here, that you
followed not to Leonato's?

Benedick. I would your Grace would constrain me to
tell.

200 *Don Pedro.* I charge thee on thy allegiance.°

Benedick. You hear, Count Claudio; I can be secret as a
dumb man. I would have you think so. But, on my
allegiance—mark you this—on my allegiance! He is
in love. With who? Now that is your Grace's part.
205 Mark how short his answer is—with Hero, Leonato's short daughter.

Claudio. If this were so, so were it utt'red.

Benedick. Like the old tale, my lord: "It is not so, nor
'twas not so, but indeed, God forbid it should be so!"

210 *Claudio.* If my passion change not shortly, God forbid
it should be otherwise.

Don Pedro. Amen, if you love her, for the lady is very
well worthy.

Claudio. You speak this to fetch me in, my lord.

215 *Don Pedro.* By my troth, I speak my thought.

Claudio. And, in faith, my lord, I spoke mine.

Benedick. And, by my two faiths and troths, my lord,
I spoke mine.

Claudio. That I love her, I feel.

220 *Don Pedro.* That she is worthy, I know.

193–94 **thrust thy neck . . . Sundays** i.e., enjoy the tiresome bondage of
marriage   200 **allegiance** solemn obligation to a prince

Benedick. That I neither feel how she should be loved, nor know how she should be worthy, is the opinion that fire cannot melt out of me. I will die in it at the stake.

Don Pedro. Thou wast ever an obstinate heretic in the   225
despite of° beauty.

Claudio. And never could maintain his part but in the force of his will.°

Benedick. That a woman conceived me, I thank her; that she brought me up, I likewise give her most   230
humble thanks. But that I will have a rechate° winded in my forehead, or hang my bugle in an invisible baldrick,° all women shall pardon me. Because I will not do them the wrong to mistrust any, I will do myself the right to trust none; and the fine°   235
is (for the which I may go the finer), I will live a bachelor.

Don Pedro. I shall see thee, ere I die, look pale with love.

Benedick. With anger, with sickness, or with hunger,   240
my lord, not with love. Prove that ever I lose more blood with love than I will get again with drinking, pick out mine eyes with a ballad maker's pen and hang me up at the door of a brothel house for the sign of blind Cupid.   245

Don Pedro. Well, if ever thou dost fall from this faith, thou wilt prove a notable argument.°

Benedick. If I do, hang me in a bottle° like a cat and shoot at me; and he that hits me, let him be clapped on the shoulder and called Adam.°   250

Don Pedro. Well, as time shall try:

225–26 **in the despite of** in contempt of   228 **will** sexual appetite
231 **rechate** recheate, notes on a hunting horn   233 **baldrick** belt,
sling (the reference here, and in *rechate,* is to the horns of a cuckold)
235 **fine** finis, result   247 **notable argument** famous example   248 **bottle** basket   250 **Adam** i.e., Adam Bell, one of the three superlative
archers in the ballad "Adam Bell"

"In time the savage bull doth bear the yoke."

Benedick. The savage bull may, but if ever the sensible
     Benedick bear it, pluck off the bull's horns and set
255   them in my forehead, and let me be vilely painted,
     and in such great letters as they write "Here is good
     horse to hire," let them signify under my sign "Here
     you may see Benedick the married man."

Claudio. If this should ever happen, thou wouldst be
260   horn-mad.°

Don Pedro. Nay, if Cupid have not spent all his quiver
     in Venice,° thou wilt quake for this shortly.

Benedick. I look for an earthquake too then.

Don Pedro. Well, you will temporize with the hours.°
265   In the meantime, good Signior Benedick, repair to
     Leonato's. Commend me to him and tell him I will
     not fail him at supper; for indeed he hath made
     great preparation.

Benedick. I have almost matter° enough in me for
270   such an embassage, and so I commit you—

Claudio. To the tuition° of God. From my house, if
     I had it—

Don Pedro. The sixth of July. Your loving friend,
     Benedick.

275 *Benedick.* Nay, mock not, mock not. The body of your
     discourse is sometime guarded° with fragments,
     and the guards are but slightly basted on neither.
     Ere you flout old ends° any further, examine your
     conscience. And so I leave you.   *Exit.*

Claudio. My liege, your Highness now may do me
280   good.

---

260 **horn-mad** mad with jealousy (perhaps also "sexually insatiable")
262 **Venice** (famous for sexual license)   264 **temporize with the hours**
change temper or attitude with time   269 **matter** sense   271 **tuition** cus-
tody   276 **guarded** trimmed (used of clothing)   278 **flout old ends** i.e.,
indulge in derision at my expense

Don Pedro. My love is thine to teach. Teach it but
    how,
And thou shalt see how apt it is to learn
Any hard lesson that may do thee good.

Claudio. Hath Leonato any son, my lord?

Don Pedro. No child but Hero; she's his only heir.   *285*
    Dost thou affect° her, Claudio?

Claudio.   O my lord,
When you went onward on this ended action,°
I looked upon her with a soldier's eye,
That liked, but had a rougher task in hand
Than to drive liking to the name of love.   *290*
But now I am returned and that° war-thoughts
Have left their places vacant, in their rooms
Come thronging soft and delicate desires,
All prompting me how fair young Hero is,
Saying I liked her ere I went to wars.   *295*

Don Pedro. Thou wilt be like a lover presently
And tire the hearer with a book of words.
If thou dost love fair Hero, cherish it,
And I will break° with her and with her father,
And thou shalt have her. Was't not to this end   *300*
That thou began'st to twist so fine a story?

Claudio. How sweetly you do minister to love,
That know love's grief by his complexion!°
But lest my liking might too sudden seem,
I would have salved it with a longer treatise.   *305*

Don Pedro. What need the bridge much broader than
    the flood?
The fairest grant is the necessity.°
Look, what will serve is fit. 'Tis once,° thou lovest,
And I will fit thee with the remedy.
I know we shall have reveling tonight.   *310*

---

286 **affect** love   287 **ended action** war just concluded   291 **that** because   299 **break** open negotiations   303 **complexion** appearance
307 **The fairest grant is the necessity** the most attractive giving is when
the receiver really needs something   308 **'Tis once** in short

I will assume thy part in some disguise
And tell fair Hero I am Claudio,
And in her bosom I'll unclasp my heart
And take her hearing prisoner with the force
315   And strong encounter of my amorous tale;
Then after to her father will I break,
And the conclusion is, she shall be thine.
In practice let us put it presently.   *Exeunt.*

[Scene 2. *Leonato's house.*]

*Enter Leonato and an old man [Antonio], brother
to Leonato.*

Leonato. How now, brother? Where is my cousin°
your son? Hath he provided this music?

Antonio. He is very busy about it. But, brother, I can tell
you strange news that you yet dreamt not of.

5   *Leonato.* Are they° good?

Antonio. As the events stamps° them. But they have
a good cover, they show well outward. The Prince
and Count Claudio, walking in a thick-pleached
alley in mine orchard,° were thus much overheard
10   by a man of mine. The Prince discovered° to Claudio that he loved my niece your daughter and meant
to acknowledge it this night in a dance, and if he
found her accordant,° he meant to take the present
time by the top° and instantly break with you of it.

15   *Leonato.* Hath the fellow any wit that told you this?

1.2.1 **cousin** kinsman   5 **they** i.e., the news (plural in the sixteenth century)   6 **As the events stamps them** as the outcome proves them to be (a plural noun, especially when felt to be singular, often has a verb ending in *-s*)   8–9 **thick-pleached alley in mine orchard** walk or arbor fenced by interwoven branches in my garden   10 **discovered** disclosed   13 **accordant** agreeing   14 **top** forelock

Antonio. A good sharp fellow. I will send for him, and question him yourself.

Leonato. No, no. We will hold it as a dream till it appear itself. But I will acquaint my daughter withal, that she may be the better prepared for an answer, if peradventure this be true. Go you and tell her of it. 20

[*Enter Attendants.*]

Cousin, you know what you have to do. O, I cry you mercy,° friend. Go you with me, and I will use your skill. Good cousin, have a care this busy time. 25
Exeunt.

[Scene 3. *Leonato's house.*]

Enter Sir John the Bastard and Conrade, his companion.

Conrade. What the goodyear,° my lord! Why are you thus out of measure sad?°

Don John. There is no measure in the occasion that breeds; therefore the sadness is without limit.

Conrade. You should hear reason. 5

Don John. And when I have heard it, what blessing brings it?

Conrade. If not a present remedy, at least a patient sufferance.

Don John. I wonder that thou, being (as thou say'st thou art) born under Saturn,° goest about to apply 10

23–24 **cry you mercy** beg your pardon   1.3.1 **What the goodyear** (an expletive)   2 **out of measure sad** unduly morose   11 **under Saturn** i.e., naturally sullen

a moral medicine to a mortifying mischief.° I cannot hide what I am. I must be sad when I have
cause, and smile at no man's jests; eat when I have
15   stomach, and wait for no man's leisure; sleep when
I am drowsy, and tend on no man's business; laugh
when I am merry, and claw no man in his humor.°

Conrade. Yea, but you must not make the full show
of this till you may do it without controlment. You
20   have of late stood out against your brother, and he
hath ta'en you newly into his grace, where it is impossible you should take true root but by the fair
weather that you make yourself. It is needful that
you frame° the season for your own harvest.

25   *Don John.* I had rather be a canker° in a hedge than
a rose in his grace, and it better fits my blood to be
disdained of all than to fashion a carriage° to rob
love from any. In this, though I cannot be said to
be a flattering honest man, it must not be denied
30   but I am a plain-dealing villain. I am trusted with
a muzzle and enfranchised with a clog; therefore I
have decreed not to sing in my cage. If I had my
mouth, I would bite; if I had my liberty, I would
do my liking. In the meantime let me be that I am,
35   and seek not to alter me.

Conrade. Can you make no use of your discontent?

Don John. I make all use of it, for I use it only. Who
comes here?

Enter Borachio.

What news, Borachio?

40   *Borachio.* I came yonder from a great supper. The
Prince your brother is royally entertained by Leonato, and I can give you intelligence° of an intended
marriage.

---

12 **mortifying mischief** killing calamity   17 **claw no man in his
humor** i.e., flatter no man (**claw**=pat or scratch on the back; **humor** =
whim)   24 **frame** bring about   25 **canker** wild rose   27 **fashion a
carriage** contrive a behavior   42 **intelligence** information

Don John. Will it serve for any model to build mischief on? What is he for a fool that betroths him-   45
self to unquietness?

Borachio. Marry,° it is your brother's right hand.

Don John. Who? The most exquisite Claudio?

Borachio. Even he.

Don John. A proper squire!° And who? And who?   50
Which way looks he?

Borachio. Marry, one Hero, the daughter and heir of
Leonato.

Don John. A very forward March-chick!° How came
you to this?   55

Borachio. Being entertained for° a perfumer, as I was
smoking° a musty room, comes me the Prince and
Claudio, hand in hand in sad° conference. I whipped
me behind the arras and there heard it agreed upon
that the Prince should woo Hero for himself, and   60
having obtained her, give her to Count Claudio.

Don John. Come, come, let us thither. This may prove
food to my displeasure. That young start-up hath
all the glory of my overthrow. If I can cross him
any way, I bless myself every way. You are both   65
sure,° and will assist me?

Conrade. To the death, my lord.

Don John. Let us to the great supper. Their cheer is
the greater that I am subdued. Would the cook
were o' my mind! Shall we go prove° what's to be   70
done?

Borachio. We'll wait upon your lordship.
                                    Exit [with others].

---

47 **Marry** (an expletive, from "by the Virgin Mary")   50 **proper squire**
fine young fellow   54 **forward March-chick** precocious fellow (i.e.,
born in early spring)   56 **entertained for** employed as   57 **smoking**
fumigating (or possibly merely perfuming)   58 **sad** serious   66 **sure** re-
liable   70 **prove** try

[ACT 2

Scene 1. *Leonato's house.*]

*Enter Leonato, his brother [Antonio], Hero his
daughter, and Beatrice his niece, [also Margaret
and Ursula].*

Leonato. Was not Count John here at supper?

Antonio. I saw him not.

Beatrice. How tartly that gentleman looks! I never
can see him but I am heartburned an hour after.

5 *Hero.* He is of a very melancholy° disposition.

Beatrice. He were an excellent man that were made
just in the midway between him and Benedick. The
one is too like an image and says nothing, and the
other too like my lady's eldest son,° evermore
10 tattling.

Leonato. Then half Signior Benedick's tongue in
Count John's mouth, and half Count John's melancholy in Signior Benedick's face—

Beatrice. With a good leg and a good foot,° uncle, and
15 money enough in his purse, such a man would win
any woman in the world, if 'a could get her good
will.

2.1.5 **melancholy** ill-tempered   9 **eldest son** i.e., overly confident (as
heir presumptive)   14 **foot** (perhaps with a pun on French **foutre**, to
copulate—i.e., a good lover)

Leonato. By my troth, niece, thou wilt never get thee a husband if thou be so shrewd° of thy tongue.

Antonio. In faith, she's too curst.°   *20*

Beatrice. Too curst is more than curst. I shall lessen God's sending that way, for it is said, "God sends a curst cow short horns"; but to a cow too curst he sends none.

Leonato. So, by being too curst, God will send you no   *25*
horns.°

Beatrice. Just,° if he send me no husband; for the which blessing I am at him upon my knees every morning and evening. Lord, I could not endure a husband with a beard on his face. I had rather lie   *30*
in the woolen!°

Leonato. You may light on a husband that hath no beard.

Beatrice. What should I do with him? Dress him in my apparel and make him my waiting gentle-   *35*
woman? He that hath a beard is more than a youth, and he that hath no beard is less than a man; and he that is more than a youth is not for me; and he that is less than a man, I am not for him. Therefore I will even take sixpence in earnest° of the berrord°   *40*
and lead his apes into hell.°

Leonato. Well then, go you into hell?

Beatrice. No; but to the gate, and there will the devil meet me like an old cuckold with horns on his head, and say, "Get you to heaven, Beatrice, get you to   *45*
heaven. Here's no place for you maids." So deliver I up my apes, and away to Saint Peter. For the

---

19 **shrewd** sharp   20 **curst** shrewish   25–26 **no horns** (i.e., horn used as phallic symbol, as Beatrice's next remark makes plain)   27 **just** exactly   31 **in the woolen** between scratchy blankets   40 **in earnest** (1) advance payment (2) in all seriousness   40 **berrord** bearward, animal keeper   41 **lead his apes into hell** traditional punishment for dying unwed

heavens, he shows me where the bachelors° sit,
and there live we as merry as the day is long.

50 *Antonio.* [*To Hero*] Well, niece, I trust you will be
ruled by your father.

Beatrice. Yes, faith. It is my cousin's duty to make
cursy° and say, "Father, as it please you." But yet
for all that, cousin, let him be a handsome fellow,
55 or else make another cursy, and say, "Father, as
it please me."

Leonato. [*To Beatrice*] Well, niece, I hope to see you
one day fitted° with a husband.

Beatrice. Not till God make men of some other metal°
60 than earth. Would it not grieve a woman to be
overmastered with a piece of valiant dust? To make
an account of her life to a clod of wayward marl?°
No, uncle, I'll none. Adam's sons are my brethren,
and truly I hold it a sin to match in my kindred.

65 *Leonato.* Daughter, remember what I told you. If the
Prince do solicit you in that kind, you know your
answer.

Beatrice. The fault will be in the music, cousin, if you
be not wooed in good time. If the Prince be too
70 important,° tell him there is measure° in everything, and so dance out the answer. For, hear me,
Hero: wooing, wedding, and repenting is as a
Scotch jig, a measure, and a cinquepace.° The first
suit is hot and hasty like a Scotch jig (and full as
75 fantastical); the wedding, mannerly modest, as a
measure, full of state and ancientry; and then comes
Repentance and with his bad legs falls into the

---

48 **bachelors** unwed persons (female as well as male)   53 **cursy** curtsy
58 **fitted** (continues playful sexual innuendo of the scene)   59 **metal** substance   62 **marl** earth   70 **important** importunate   70 **measure** (1) dis-
cernible time sequence (2) moderation (the entire speech is a light parody
of Sir John Davies' *Orchestra, A Poem of Dancing* [1596]; cf. stanza 23:
"Time the measure of all moving is/And dancing is a moving all in measure")   73 **cinquepace** lively dance

cinquepace faster and faster, till he sink into his grave.

Leonato. Cousin, you apprehend passing shrewdly.   *80*

Beatrice. I have a good eye, uncle; I can see a church by daylight.

Leonato. The revelers are ent'ring, brother. Make good room.

                  [*All put on their masks.*]

    Enter Prince [Don] Pedro, Claudio, and Bene-
    dick, and Balthasar [masked; and without masks
          Borachio and] Don John.

Don Pedro. Lady, will you walk about with your   *85*
friend?°

Hero. So you walk softly and look sweetly and say nothing, I am yours for the walk; and especially when I walk away.

Don Pedro. With me in your company?   *90*

Hero. I may say so when I please.

Don Pedro. And when please you to say so?

Hero. When I like your favor,° for God defend° the lute should be like the case!°

Don Pedro. My visor° is Philemon's° roof; within the   *95*
house is Jove.

Hero. Why then, your visor should be thatched.

Don Pedro. Speak low if you speak love.
                    [*Draws her aside.*]

Benedick.° Well, I would you did like me.

---

86 **friend** lover   93 **favor** face   93 **defend** forbid   93–94 **the lute . . . case** i.e., your face be as ugly as your mask   95 **visor** mask   95 **Philemon** peasant who entertained Jove in his house   99 **Benedick** (many editors emend the Quarto, and give this and Benedick's two subsequent speeches to Balthasar; but in 5.2 Benedick and Margaret spar, and they may well do so here)

100 *Margaret.* So would not I for your own sake, for I have many ill qualities.

Benedick. Which is one?

Margaret. I say my prayers aloud.

Benedick. I love you the better. The hearers may cry
105 amen.

Margaret. God match me with a good dancer!

Balthasar. [*Interposing*] Amen.

Margaret. And God keep him out of my sight when the dance is done! Answer, clerk.

110 *Balthasar.* No more words. The clerk is answered.

Ursula. I know you well enough. You are Signior Antonio.

Antonio. At a word, I am not.

Ursula. I know you by the waggling° of your head.

115 *Antonio.* To tell you true, I counterfeit him.

Ursula. You could never do him so ill-well unless you were the very man. Here's his dry° hand up and down. You are he, you are he!

Antonio. At a word I am not.

120 *Ursula.* Come, come, do you think I do not know you by your excellent wit? Can virtue hide itself? Go to, mum, you are he. Graces will appear, and there's an end.

Beatrice. Will you not tell me who told you so?

125 *Benedick.* No, you shall pardon me.

Beatrice. Nor will you not tell me who you are?

Benedick. Not now.

Beatrice. That I was disdainful, and that I had my

---

114 **waggling** i.e., palsy   117 **dry** dried-up (with age)

good wit out of the "Hundred Merry Tales."° Well,
this was Signior Benedick that said so.   130

Benedick. What's he?

Beatrice. I am sure you know him well enough.

Benedick. Not I, believe me.

Beatrice. Did he never make you laugh?

Benedick. I pray you, what is he?   135

Beatrice. Why, he is the Prince's jester, a very dull
fool. Only his° gift is in devising impossible slanders. None but libertines delight in him, and the
commendation is not in his wit, but in his villainy;
for he both pleases men and angers them, and then   140
they laugh at him and beat him. I am sure he is in
the fleet;° I would he had boarded me.

Benedick. When I know the gentleman, I'll tell him
what you say.

Beatrice. Do, do. He'll but break a comparison or two   145
on me; which peradventure (not marked or not
laughed at), strikes him into melancholy, and then
there's a partridge wing saved, for the fool will eat
no supper that night. [*Music.*] We must follow the
leaders.   150

Benedick. In every good thing.

Beatrice. Nay, if they lead to any ill, I will leave them
at the next turning.

> *Dance. Exeunt* [*all except Don John,*
> *Borachio and Claudio*].

Don John. Sure my brother is amorous on Hero and
hath withdrawn her father to break with him about   155
it. The ladies follow her and but one visor remains.

---

129 **Hundred Merry Tales** a popular collection of amusing, coarse anec-
dotes   137 **Only his** his only   142 **fleet** group (the related meaning,
group of ships, leads to **boarded me**, but perhaps too there is an allusion
to Fleet Prison)

Borachio. And that is Claudio. I know him by his bearing.

Don John. Are not you Signior Benedick?

160 *Claudio.* You know me well. I am he.

Don John. Signior, you are very near my brother in his
love. He is enamored on Hero. I pray you dissuade
him from her; she is no equal for his birth. You may
do the part of an honest man in it.

165 *Claudio.* How know you he loves her?

Don John. I heard him swear his affection.

Borachio. So did I too, and he swore he would marry
her tonight.

Don John. Come, let us to the banquet.°

                         Exeunt. Manet Claudio.

170 *Claudio.* Thus answer I in name of Benedick
But hear these ill news with the ears of Claudio.
'Tis certain so. The Prince woos for himself.
Friendship is constant in all other things
Save in the office° and affairs of love.
175 Therefore all hearts in love use their own tongues;
Let every eye negotiate for itself
And trust no agent; for beauty is a witch
Against whose charms faith melteth into blood.°
This is an accident of hourly proof,°
180 Which I mistrusted not. Farewell therefore Hero!

                 Enter Benedick.

Benedick. Count Claudio?

Claudio. Yea, the same.

Benedick. Come, will you go with me?

---

169 **banquet** light meal, or course, of fruit, wine, and dessert   174 **office**
business   178 **blood** passion, desire   179 **accident of hourly proof**
common happening

Claudio. Whither?

Benedick. Even to the next° willow,° about your own 185
business, County.° What fashion will you wear the
garland of? About your neck, like an usurer's chain?
Or under your arm, like a lieutenant's scarf? You
must wear it one way, for the Prince hath got your
Hero. 190

Claudio. I wish him joy of her.

Benedick. Why, that's spoken like an honest drovier.°
So they sell bullocks. But did you think the Prince
would have served you thus?

Claudio. I pray you leave me. 195

Benedick. Ho! Now you strike like the blind man!
'Twas the boy that stole your meat, and you'll beat
the post.°

Claudio. If it will not be, I'll leave you.   *Exit.*

Benedick. Alas, poor hurt fowl! Now will he creep 200
into sedges. But, that my Lady Beatrice should
know me, and not know me! The Prince's fool! Ha!
It may be I go under that title because I am merry.
Yea, but so I am apt to do myself wrong. I am not
so reputed. It is the base (though bitter) disposi- 205
tion of Beatrice that puts the world into her person
and so gives me out.° Well, I'll be revenged as I
may.

Enter the Prince [Don Pedro], Hero, Leonato.

Don Pedro. Now, signior, where's the Count? Did you 210
see him?

Benedick. Troth, my lord, I have played the part of
Lady Fame.° I found him here as melancholy as a

---

185 **next** nearest   185 **willow** symbol of unrequited love   186 **County**
Count   192 **drovier** cattle dealer   197–98 **beat the post** i.e., strike out
blindly   205–07 **It is . . . gives me out** it is the low and harsh disposition
of Beatrice to assume her opinion of me is the world's opinion of
me   212 **Lady Fame** goddess of rumor

lodge in a warren.° I told him, and I think I told
him true, that your Grace had got the good will of
215 this young lady, and I off'red him my company to
a willow tree, either to make him a garland, as being
forsaken, or to bind him up a rod, as being worthy
to be whipped.

Don Pedro. To be whipped? What's his fault?

220 *Benedick.* The flat transgression of a schoolboy who,
being overjoyed with finding a bird's nest, shows it
his companion, and he steals it.

Don Pedro. Wilt thou make a trust a transgression?
The transgression is in the stealer.

225 *Benedick.* Yet it had not been amiss the rod had been
made, and the garland too; for the garland he might
have worn himself, and the rod he might have bestowed on you, who (as I take it) have stol'n his
bird's nest.

230 *Don Pedro.* I will but teach them to sing and restore
them to the owner.

Benedick. If their singing answer your saying, by my
faith you say honestly.

Don Pedro. The Lady Beatrice hath a quarrel to you.
235 The gentleman that danced with her told her she
is much wronged by you.

Benedick. O, she misused me past the endurance of a
block! An oak but with one green leaf on it would
have answered her; my very visor began to assume
240 life and scold with her. She told me, not thinking I
had been myself, that I was the Prince's jester, that
I was duller than a great thaw; huddling jest upon
jest with such impossible conveyance° upon me
that I stood like a man at a mark,° with a whole
245 army shooting at me. She speaks poniards, and
every word stabs. If her breath were as terrible as

---

213 **in a warren** i.e., in a lonely place   243 **impossible conveyance**
incredible dexterity   244 **mark** target

her terminations,° there were no living near her;
she would infect to the North Star. I would not
marry her though she were endowed with all that
Adam had left him before he transgressed. She   250
would have made Hercules have turned spit, yea,
and have cleft his club to make the fire too. Come,
talk not of her. You shall find her the infernal Ate°
in good apparel. I would to God some scholar
would conjure her,° for certainly, while she is here,   255
a man may live as quiet in hell as in a sanctuary;
and people sin upon purpose, because they would
go thither; so indeed all disquiet, horror, and per-
turbation follows her.

Enter Claudio and Beatrice.

Don Pedro. Look, here she comes.   260

Benedick. Will your Grace command me any service to
the world's end? I will go on the slightest errand
now to the Antipodes that you can devise to send
me on; I will fetch you a toothpicker now from the
furthest inch of Asia; bring you the length of Prester   265
John's° foot; fetch you a hair off the great Cham's°
beard; do you any embassage to the Pygmies—
rather than hold three words' conference with this
harpy. You have no employment for me?

Don Pedro. None, but to desire your good company.   270

Benedick. O God, sir, here's a dish I love not! I cannot
endure my Lady Tongue.   *Exit.*

Don Pedro. Come, lady, come; you have lost the heart
of Signior Benedick.

Beatrice. Indeed, my lord, he lent it me awhile, and I   275
gave him use° for it, a double heart for his single
one. Marry, once before he won it of me with false

---

247 **terminations** words   253 **Ate** goddess of discord   255 **conjure
her** i.e., exorcise the devil out of her   265–66 **Prester John** legendary
Christian king in remote Asia   266 **Cham** Khan   276 **use** interest

dice; therefore your Grace may well say I have
lost it.

280 *Don Pedro.* You have put him down, lady; you have
put him down.

Beatrice. So I would not he should do me, my lord,
lest I should prove the mother of fools.° I have
brought Count Claudio, whom you sent me to seek.

285 *Don Pedro.* Why, how now, Count? Wherefore are
you sad?

Claudio. Not sad, my lord.

Don Pedro. How then? Sick?

Claudio. Neither, my lord.

290 *Beatrice.* The Count is neither sad, nor sick, nor
merry, nor well; but civil Count, civil° as an orange,
and something of that jealous complexion.°

Don Pedro. I' faith, lady, I think your blazon° to be
true; though I'll be sworn, if he be so, his conceit°
295 is false. Here, Claudio, I have wooed in thy name,
and fair Hero is won. I have broke with her father,
and his good will obtained. Name the day of marriage, and God give thee joy!

Leonato. Count, take of me my daughter, and with
300 her my fortunes. His Grace hath made the match,
and all grace say amen to it!

Beatrice. Speak, Count, 'tis your cue.

Claudio. Silence is the perfectest herald of joy. I were
but little happy if I could say how much. Lady, as
305 you are mine, I am yours. I give away myself for
you and dote upon the exchange.

Beatrice. Speak, cousin; or (if you cannot) stop his
mouth with a kiss and let not him speak neither.

---

283 **fools** babies   291 **civil** polite (with a pun on orange of Seville)
292 **complexion** (1) disposition (2) color (i.e., yellowish for jealousy)
293 **blazon** description   294 **conceit** idea, concept

Don Pedro. In faith, lady, you have a merry heart.

Beatrice. Yea, my lord; I thank it, poor fool, it keeps *310*
on the windy° side of care. My cousin tells him in
his ear that he is in her heart.

Claudio. And so she doth, cousin.

Beatrice. Good Lord, for alliance! Thus goes every
one to the world but I, and I am sunburnt.° I may *315*
sit in a corner and cry "Heigh-ho for a husband!"

Don Pedro. Lady Beatrice, I will get you one.

Beatrice. I would rather have one of your father's
getting.° Hath your Grace ne'er a brother like you?
Your father got excellent husbands, if a maid could *320*
come by them.

Don Pedro. Will you have me, lady?

Beatrice. No, my lord, unless I might have another for
working days; your Grace is too costly to wear
every day. But I beseech your Grace pardon me. *325*
I was born to speak all mirth and no matter.

Don Pedro. Your silence most offends me, and to be
merry best becomes you, for out o' question you
were born in a merry hour.

Beatrice. No, sure, my lord, my mother cried; but *330*
then there was a star danced, and under that was
I born. Cousins, God give you joy!

Leonato. Niece, will you look to those things I told
you of?

Beatrice. I cry you mercy,° uncle. By your Grace's *335*
pardon.

Exit Beatrice.

Don Pedro. By my troth, a pleasant-spirited lady.

---

311 **windy** windward, safe   314–15 **Good Lord . . . sunburnt** i.e., everyone gets a husband but me, and I am ugly (**sunburnt**=tanned, and therefore ugly in the sixteenth century)   319 **getting** begetting   335 **cry you
mercy** beg your pardon

Leonato. There's little of the melancholy element in
her, my lord. She is never sad but when she sleeps,
340   and not ever° sad then; for I have heard my daughter say she hath often dreamt of unhappiness and
waked herself with laughing.

Don Pedro. She cannot endure to hear tell of a husband.

345 *Leonato.* O, by no means! She mocks all her wooers
out of suit.

Don Pedro. She were an excellent wife for Benedick.

Leonato. O Lord, my lord! If they were but a week
married, they would talk themselves mad.

350 *Don Pedro.* County Claudio, when mean you to go to
church?

Claudio. Tomorrow, my lord. Time goes on crutches
till Love have all his rites.

Leonato. Not till Monday, my dear son, which is hence
355   a just sevennight; and a time too brief too, to have
all things answer my mind.

Don Pedro. Come, you shake the head at so long a
breathing; but I warrant thee, Claudio, the time
shall not go dully by us. I will in the interim un-
360   dertake one of Hercules' labors, which is, to bring
Signior Benedick and the Lady Beatrice into a
mountain of affection th' one with th' other. I would
fain have it a match, and I doubt not but to fashion
it if you three will but minister such assistance as
365   I shall give you direction.

Leonato. My lord, I am for you, though it cost me ten
nights' watchings.°

Claudio. And I, my lord.

Don Pedro. And you too, gentle Hero?

340 **ever** always   366–67 **ten nights' watchings** ten nights awake

Hero. I will do any modest office, my lord, to help my   *370*
cousin to a good husband.

Don Pedro. And Benedick is not the unhopefullest
husband that I know. Thus far can I praise him: he
is of a noble strain, of approved° valor and confirmed honesty. I will teach you how to humor your   *375*
cousin, that she shall fall in love with Benedick;
and I [*to Leonato and Claudio*], with your two
helps, will so practice on° Benedick that, in despite
of his quick wit and his queasy stomach, he shall
fall in love with Beatrice. If we can do this, Cupid   *380*
is no longer an archer; his glory shall be ours, for
we are the only love-gods. Go in with me, and I
will tell you my drift.

Exit [*with the others*].

[Scene 2. *Leonato's house.*]

Enter [*Don*] *John and Borachio.*

Don John. It is so. The Count Claudio shall marry the
daughter of Leonato.

Borachio. Yea, my lord; but I can cross it.

Don John. Any bar, any cross, any impediment will
be medicinable to me. I am sick in displeasure to   *5*
him, and whatsoever comes athwart his affection
ranges evenly° with mine. How canst thou cross
this marriage?

Borachio. Not honestly, my lord; but so covertly that
no dishonesty shall appear in me.   *10*

Don John. Show me briefly how.

---

374 **approved** tested   378 **practice on** deceive   2.2.7 **ranges evenly**
goes in a straight line (i.e., suits me exactly)

Borachio. I think I told your lordship, a year since,
how much I am in the favor of Margaret, the waiting gentlewoman to Hero.

15 *Don John.* I remember.

Borachio. I can, at any unseasonable instant of the
night, appoint her to look out at her lady's chamber
window.

Don John. What life is in that to be the death of this
20   marriage?

Borachio. The poison of that lies in you to temper. Go
you to the Prince your brother; spare not to tell
him that he hath wronged his honor in marrying
the renowned Claudio (whose estimation do you
25   mightily hold up) to a contaminated stale,° such
a one as Hero.

Don John. What proof shall I make of that?

Borachio. Proof enough to misuse the Prince, to vex
Claudio, to undo Hero, and kill Leonato. Look you
30   for any other issue?

Don John. Only to despite them I will endeavor anything.

Borachio. Go then; find me a meet hour° to draw Don
Pedro and the Count Claudio alone; tell them that
35   you know that Hero loves me; intend° a kind of
zeal both to the Prince and Claudio (as in love of
your brother's honor, who hath made this match,
and his friend's reputation, who is thus like to be
cozened° with the semblance of a maid) that you
40   have discovered thus. They will scarcely believe
this without trial. Offer them instances;° which
shall bear no less likelihood than to see me at her
chamber window, hear me call Margaret Hero, hear
Margaret term me Claudio; and bring them to see
45   this the very night before the intended wedding.

---

25 **stale** prostitute   33 **meet hour** suitable time   35 **intend** pretend
39 **cozened** cheated   41 **instances** proofs

For in the meantime I will so fashion the matter
that Hero shall be absent; and there shall appear
such seeming truth of Hero's disloyalty that jeal-
ousy° shall be called assurance and all the prep-
aration overthrown.   50

Don John. Grow this to what adverse issue it can, I
will put it in practice. Be cunning in the working
this, and thy fee is a thousand ducats.

Borachio. Be you constant in the accusation, and my
cunning shall not shame me.   55

Don John. I will presently go learn their day of marriage.

                                        Exit [with Borachio].

[Scene 3. *Leonato's garden.*]

                Enter Benedick alone.

Benedick. Boy!
                    [*Enter Boy.*]

Boy. Signior?

Benedick. In my chamber window lies a book. Bring it
hither to me in the orchard.°

Boy. I am here already, sir.   5

Benedick. I know that, but I would have thee hence
and here again. (*Exit [Boy].*) I do much wonder
that one man, seeing how much another man is a
fool when he dedicates his behaviors to love, will,
after he hath laughed at such shallow follies in   10
others, become the argument° of his own scorn by

48–49 **jealousy** mistrust   2.3.4 **orchard** garden   11 **argument** subject
matter

falling in love; and such a man is Claudio. I have
known when there was no music with him but the
drum and the fife; and now had he rather hear the
15 tabor and the pipe.° I have known when he would
have walked ten mile afoot to see a good armor; and
now will he lie ten nights awake carving the fashion°
of a new doublet. He was wont to speak plain and
to the purpose, like an honest man and a soldier;
20 and now is he turned orthography;° his words are
a very fantastical banquet—just so many strange
dishes. May I be so converted and see with these
eyes? I cannot tell; I think not. I will not be sworn
but love may transform me to an oyster; but I'll take
25 my oath on it, till he have made an oyster of me he
shall never make me such a fool. One woman is fair,
yet I am well; another is wise, yet I am well; another
virtuous, yet I am well. But till all graces be in one
woman, one woman shall not come in my grace.
30 Rich she shall be, that's certain; wise, or I'll none;
virtuous, or I'll never cheapen° her; fair, or I'll never
look on her; mild, or come not near me; noble, or
not I for an angel;° of good discourse,° an excellent
musician, and her hair shall be of what color it
35 please God. Ha, the Prince and Monsieur Love!
[*Retiring*] I will hide me in the arbor.

Enter Prince [*Don Pedro*], *Leonato, Claudio,*
[*to the sound of*] *music.*

Don Pedro. Come, shall we hear this music?

Claudio. Yea, my good lord. How still the evening is,
As hushed on purpose to grace harmony!

40 *Don Pedro.* See you where Benedick hath hid himself?

---

15 **tabor and the pipe** music of an unmartial sort   17 **carving the fashion** considering the design   20 **orthography** i.e., into a pedant (?)
31 **cheapen** bargain for   32–33 **noble ... angel** (puns: both words are
Elizabethan coins)   33 **discourse** conversation

Claudio. O, very well, my lord. The music ended,
We'll fit the kid fox with a pennyworth.°

Enter Balthasar with music.

Don Pedro. Come, Balthasar, we'll hear that song
again.

Balthasar. O, good my lord, tax not so bad a voice
To slander music any more than once.   45

Don Pedro. It is the witness still of excellency
To put a strange face on his own perfection.
I pray thee sing, and let me woo no more.

Balthasar. Because you talk of wooing, I will sing,
Since many a wooer doth commence his suit   50
To her he thinks not worthy, yet he woos,
Yet will he swear he loves.

Don Pedro.   Nay, pray thee come;
Or if thou wilt hold longer argument,
Do it in notes.

Balthasar.   Note this before my notes:
There's not a note of mine that's worth the noting.   55

Don Pedro. Why, these are very crotchets° that he
speaks!
Note notes, forsooth, and nothing!°   [*Music.*]

Benedick. [*Aside*] Now divine air! Now is his soul
ravished! Is it not strange that sheep's guts should
hale souls out of men's bodies? Well, a horn for my   60
money, when all's done.   [*Balthasar sings.*]

The Song

Sigh no more, ladies, sigh no more,
   Men were deceivers ever,

---

42 **We'll ... pennyworth** i.e., we'll give Benedick a little something
(perhaps **kid fox** means "young fox," perhaps "known fox")   56 **crotchets**
(1) whims (2) musical notes   57 **nothing** (pronounced "noting," hence
a pun)

One foot in sea, and one on shore,
65   To one thing constant never.
          Then sigh not so,
            But let them go,
        And be you blithe and bonny,
      Converting all your sounds of woe
70   Into hey nonny, nonny.

      Sing no more ditties, sing no moe,
        Of dumps° so dull and heavy;
      The fraud of men was ever so,
          Since summer first was leavy.
75   Then sigh not so, &c.

Don Pedro. By my troth, a good song.

Balthasar. And an ill singer, my lord.

Don Pedro. Ha, no, no, faith! Thou sing'st well enough
      for a shift.°

80 *Benedick.* [*Aside*] And he had been a dog that should
      have howled thus, they would have hanged him; and
      I pray God his bad voice bode no mischief. I had as
      live° have heard the night raven, come what plague
      could have come after it.

85 *Don Pedro.* Yea, marry. Dost thou hear, Balthasar? I
      pray thee get us some excellent music; for tomorrow
      night we would have it at the Lady Hero's chamber
      window.

Balthasar. The best I can, my lord.

90 *Don Pedro.* Do so. Farewell.
                    Exit Balthasar [*with Musicians*].

Come hither, Leonato. What was it you told me of
today? That your niece Beatrice was in love with
Signior Benedick?

Claudio. O, ay! [*In a low voice to Don Pedro*] Stalk on,

---

72 **dumps** sad songs   79 **shift** makeshift   83 **live** lief

stalk on; the fowl sits. [*In full voice*] I did never   *95*
think that lady would have loved any man.

Leonato. No, nor I neither; but most wonderful that she
should so dote on Signior Benedick, whom she
hath in all outward behaviors seemed ever to abhor.

Benedick. [*Aside*] Is't possible? Sits the wind in that   *100*
corner?

Leonato. By my troth, my lord, I cannot tell what to
think of it, but that she loves him with an enraged affection, it is past the infinite of thought.

Don Pedro. May be she doth but counterfeit.   *105*

Claudio. Faith, like enough.

Leonato. O God, counterfeit? There was never counterfeit of passion came so near the life of passion as she
discovers° it.

Don Pedro. Why, what effects of passion shows she?   *110*

Claudio. [*In a low voice*] Bait the hook well! This fish
will bite.

Leonato. What effects, my lord? She will sit you, you
heard my daughter tell you how.

Claudio. She did indeed.   *115*

Don Pedro. How, how, I pray you? You amaze me!
I would have thought her spirit had been invincible
against all assaults of affection.

Leonato. I would have sworn it had, my lord—especially against Benedick.   *120*

Benedick. [*Aside*] I should think this a gull° but that
the white-bearded fellow speaks it. Knavery cannot,
sure, hide himself in such reverence.

Claudio. [*In a low voice*] He hath ta'en th' infection;
hold° it up.   *125*

---

109 **discovers** reveals, betrays   121 **gull** trick   125 **hold** keep

Don Pedro. Hath she made her affection known to
  Benedick?

Leonato. No, and swears she never will. That's her
  torment.

130 *Claudio.* 'Tis true indeed. So your daughter says. "Shall
  I," says she, "that have so oft encount'red him with
  scorn, write to him that I love him?"

Leonato. This says she now when she is beginning to
  write to him; for she'll be up twenty times a night,
135 and there will she sit in her smock till she have writ
  a sheet of paper. My daughter tells us all.

Claudio. Now you talk of a sheet of paper, I remember
  a pretty jest your daughter told us of.

Leonato. O, when she had writ it, and was reading it
140 over, she found "Benedick" and "Beatrice" between
  the sheet?

Claudio. That.

Leonato. O, she tore the letter into a thousand halfpence,° railed at herself that she should be so im-
145 modest to write to one that she knew would flout her.
  "I measure him," says she, "by my own spirit; for I
  should flout him if he writ to me. Yea, though I love
  him, I should."

Claudio. Then down upon her knees she falls, weeps,
150 sobs, beats her heart, tears her hair, prays, curses—
  "O sweet Benedick! God give me patience!"

Leonato. She doth indeed; my daughter says so; and
  the ecstasy° hath so much overborne her that my
  daughter is sometime afeard she will do a des-
155 perate outrage to herself. It is very true.

Don Pedro. It were good that Benedick knew of it by
  some other, if she will not discover it.

143–44 **halfpence** i.e., small pieces   153 **ecstasy** madness

Claudio. To what end? He would make but a sport of it and torment the poor lady worse.

Don Pedro. And he should, it were an alms° to hang   *160*
him! She's an excellent sweet lady, and, out of all suspicion, she is virtuous.

Claudio. And she is exceeding wise.

Don Pedro. In everything but in loving Benedick.

Leonato. O, my lord, wisdom and blood° combating   *165*
in so tender a body, we have ten proofs to one that blood hath the victory. I am sorry for her, as I have just cause, being her uncle and her guardian.

Don Pedro. I would she had bestowed this dotage on me; I would have daffed all other respects° and   *170*
made her half myself. I pray you tell Benedick of it and hear what'a will say.

Leonato. Were it good, think you?

Claudio. Hero thinks surely she will die; for she says she will die if he love her not, and she will die ere   *175*
she make her love known, and she will die, if he woo her, rather than she will bate° one breath of her accustomed crossness.

Don Pedro. She doth well. If she should make tender° of her love, 'tis very possible he'll scorn it; for the   *180*
man, as you know all, hath a contemptible° spirit.

Claudio. He is a very proper° man.

Don Pedro. He hath indeed a good outward happiness.

Claudio. Before God, and in my mind, very wise.

Don Pedro. He doth indeed show some sparks that are   *185*
like wit.°

Claudio. And I take him to be valiant.

---

160 **an alms** a charity   165 **blood** passion   170 **daffed all other respects** put aside all other considerations (i.e., of disparity in rank) 177 **bate** abate, give up   179 **tender** offer   181 **contemptible** disdainful   182 **proper** handsome   186 **wit** intelligence

Don Pedro. As Hector, I assure you. And in the man-
aging of quarrels you may say he is wise, for either
190 he avoids them with great discretion, or undertakes
them with a most Christianlike fear.

Leonato. If he do fear God, 'a must necessarily keep
peace. If he break the peace, he ought to enter into
a quarrel with fear and trembling.

195 *Don Pedro.* And so will he do; for the man doth fear
God, howsoever it seems not in him by some large
jests° he will make. Well, I am sorry for your niece.
Shall we go seek Benedick and tell him of her love?

Claudio. Never tell him, my lord; let her wear it out
200 with good counsel.

Leonato. Nay, that's impossible; she may wear her
heart out first.

Don Pedro. Well, we will hear further of it by your
daughter. Let it cool the while. I love Benedick well,
205 and I could wish he would modestly examine himself to see how much he is unworthy so good a lady.

Leonato. My lord, will you walk? Dinner is ready.
                    [*They walk away.*]

Claudio. If he do not dote on her upon this, I will never
trust my expectation.

210 *Don Pedro.* Let there be the same net spread for her,
and that must your daughter and her gentlewomen
carry.° The sport will be, when they hold one an
opinion of another's dotage, and no such matter.
That's the scene that I would see, which will be
215 merely a dumb show.° Let us send her to call him
in to dinner.
          [*Exeunt Don Pedro, Claudio, and Leonato.*]

Benedick. [*Advancing*] This can be no trick; the conference was sadly° borne. They have the truth of

this from Hero. They seem to pity the lady; it seems
her affections have their full bent.° Love me? Why,   220
it must be requited. I hear how I am censured. They
say I will bear myself proudly if I perceive the love
come from her. They say too that she will rather die
than give any sign of affection. I did never think to
marry; I must not seem proud. Happy are they that   225
hear their detractions and can put them to mending.
They say the lady is fair—'tis a truth, I can bear
them witness; and virtuous—'tis so, I cannot reprove
it; and wise, but for loving me; by my troth, it is
no addition to her wit, nor no great argument of her   230
folly; for I will be horribly in love with her. I may
chance have some odd quirks and remnants of wit
broken on me because I have railed so long against
marriage; but doth not the appetite alter? A man
loves the meat in his youth that he cannot endure   235
in his age. Shall quips and sentences° and these
paper bullets of the brain awe a man from the
career° of his humor? No, the world must be peo-
pled. When I said I would die a bachelor, I did not
think I should live till I were married. Here comes   240
Beatrice. By this day, she's a fair lady. I do spy
some marks of love in her.

Enter Beatrice.

Beatrice. Against my will I am sent to bid you come
   in to dinner.

Benedick. Fair Beatrice, I thank you for your pains.   245

Beatrice. I took no more pains for those thanks than
   you take pains to thank me. If it had been painful,
   I would not have come.

Benedick. You take pleasure then in the message?

Beatrice. Yea, just so much as you may take upon a   250

---

220 **affections have their full bent** emotions are tightly stretched (like a
bent bow)   236 **sentences** maxims   238 **career** course

knife's point, and choke a daw withal.° You have no
stomach,° signior? Fare you well.   *Exit.*

Benedick. Ha! "Against my will I am sent to bid you
come in to dinner." There's a double meaning in
255 that. "I took no more pains for those thanks than
you took pains to thank me." That's as much as to
say, "Any pains that I take for you is as easy as
thanks." If I do not take pity of her, I am a villain;
if I do not love her, I am a Jew. I will go get her
260 picture.   *Exit.*

[ACT 3

Scene 1. *Leonato's garden.*]

*Enter Hero and two Gentlewomen, Margaret
and Ursula.*

Hero. Good Margaret, run thee to the parlor.
  There shalt thou find my cousin Beatrice
  Proposing with° the Prince and Claudio.
  Whisper her ear and tell her, I and Ursley
  Walk in the orchard, and our whole discourse   5
  Is all of her. Say that thou overheard'st us;
  And bid her steal into the pleachèd bower,
  Where honeysuckles, ripened by the sun,
  Forbid the sun to enter—like favorites,
  Made proud by princes, that advance their pride   10
  Against that power that bred it.° There will she hide
    her
  To listen our propose. This is thy office;°
  Bear thee well in it and leave us alone.

Margaret. I'll make her come, I warrant you, presently.
                                      [Exit.]

Hero. Now, Ursula, when Beatrice doth come,   15
  As we do trace° this alley up and down,

___

3.1.3 **Proposing with** talking to   10–11 **Made proud ... bred it** (an
Elizabethan audience of c.1600 would be reminded of the Earl of
Essex)   12 **office** duty   16 **trace** walk

Our talk must only be of Benedick.
When I do name him, let it be thy part
To praise him more than ever man did merit.
20 My talk to thee must be how Benedick
Is sick in love with Beatrice. Of this matter
Is little Cupid's crafty° arrow made,
That only° wounds by hearsay.

Enter Beatrice.

                              Now begin;
For look where Beatrice like a lapwing runs
25 Close by the ground, to hear our conference.

Ursula. The pleasant'st angling is to see the fish
Cut with her golden oars the silver stream
And greedily devour the treacherous bait;
So angle we for Beatrice, who even now
30 Is couchèd in the woodbine coverture.°
Fear you not my part of the dialogue.

Hero. Then go we near her, that her ear lose nothing
Of the false sweet bait that we lay for it.
                    [*They approach the bower.*]
No, truly, Ursula, she is too disdainful.
35 I know her spirits are as coy° and wild
As haggards° of the rock.

Ursula.   But are you sure
That Benedick loves Beatrice so entirely?

Hero. So says the Prince, and my new-trothèd lord.

Ursula. And did they bid you tell her of it, madam?

40 *Hero.* They did entreat me to acquaint her of it;
But I persuaded them, if they loved Benedick,
To wish him wrestle with affection
And never to let Beatrice know of it.

Ursula. Why did you so? Doth not the gentleman

---

22 **crafty** skillfully wrought   23 **only** solely   30 **woodbine coverture**
honeysuckle thicket   35 **coy** disdainful   36 **haggards** wild and in-
tractable hawks

Deserve as full as fortunate a bed   45
  As ever Beatrice shall couch upon?

Hero. O god of love! I know he doth deserve
  As much as may be yielded to a man;
  But Nature never framed a woman's heart
  Of prouder stuff than that of Beatrice.   50
  Disdain and Scorn ride sparkling in her eyes,
  Misprizing° what they look on; and her wit
  Values itself so highly that to her
  All matter else seems weak. She cannot love,
  Nor take no shape nor project° of affection,   55
  She is so self-endeared.

Ursula.   Sure I think so;
  And therefore certainly it were not good
  She knew his love, lest she'll make sport at it.

Hero. Why, you speak truth. I never yet saw man,
  How wise, how noble, young, how rarely featured,   60
  But she would spell him backward. If fair-faced,
  She would swear the gentleman should be her sister;
  If black,° why, Nature, drawing of an antic,°
  Made a foul blot; if tall, a lance ill-headed;
  If low, an agate very vilely cut;°   65
  If speaking, why, a vane blown with all winds;
  If silent, why, a block movèd with none.
  So turns she every man the wrong side out
  And never gives to truth and virtue that
  Which simpleness and merit purchaseth.   70

Ursula. Sure, sure, such carping is not commendable.

Hero. No, not to be so odd, and from all fashions,°
  As Beatrice is, cannot be commendable.
  But who dare tell her so? If I should speak,
  She would mock me into air; O, she would laugh me   75
  Out of myself, press me to death with wit!
  Therefore let Benedick, like covered fire,

---

52 **Misprizing** despising   55 **project** notion   63 **black** dark-complex-
ioned   63 **antic** grotesque figure   65 **agate very vilely cut** poorly done
miniature   72 **from all fashions** contrary

Consume away in sighs, waste inwardly.
It were a better death than die with mocks,
80 Which is as bad as die with tickling.

Ursula. Yet tell her of it. Hear what she will say.

Hero. No; rather I will go to Benedick
And counsel him to fight against his passion.
And truly, I'll devise some honest° slanders
85 To stain my cousin with. One doth not know
How much an ill word may empoison liking.

Ursula. O, do not do your cousin such a wrong!
She cannot be so much without true judgment
(Having so swift and excellent a wit
90 As she is prized to have) as to refuse
So rare a gentleman as Signior Benedick.

Hero. He is the only man of Italy,
Always excepted my dear Claudio.

Ursula. I pray you be not angry with me, madam,
95 Speaking my fancy. Signior Benedick,
For shape, for bearing, argument, and valor,
Goès foremost in report through Italy.

Hero. Indeed he hath an excellent good name.

Ursula. His excellence did earn it ere he had it.
100 When are you married, madam?

Hero. Why, everyday tomorrow!° Come, go in.
I'll show thee some attires, and have thy counsel
Which is the best to furnish° me tomorrow.
                              [*They walk away.*]

Ursula. She's limed,° I warrant you! We have caught
her, madam.

105 *Hero.* If it prove so, then loving goes by haps;°
Some Cupid kills with arrows, some with traps.
                              [*Exeunt Hero and Ursula.*]

---

84 **honest** appropriate   101 **everyday tomorrow** i.e., tomorrow I shall
be married forever   103 **furnish** dress   104 **limed** caught (as a bird is
caught in birdlime, a sticky substance smeared on branches)   105 **haps**
chance

Beatrice. [*Coming forward*] What fire is in mine ears?
    Can this be true?
    Stand I condemned for pride and scorn so much?
Contempt, farewell! And maiden pride, adieu!
    No glory lives behind the back of such.   *110*
And, Benedick, love on; I will requite thee,
    Taming my wild heart to thy loving hand.
If thou dost love, my kindness shall incite thee
    To bind our loves up in a holy band;
For others say thou dost deserve, and I   *115*
Believe it better than reportingly.°   *Exit.*

[Scene 2. *Leonato's house.*]

Enter Prince [*Don Pedro*]*, Claudio, Benedick,
    and Leonato.*

Don Pedro. I do but stay till your marriage be con-
    summate, and then go I toward Aragon.

Claudio. I'll bring you thither, my lord, if you'll vouch-
    safe° me.

Don Pedro. Nay, that would be as great a soil in the   *5*
    new gloss of your marriage as to show a child his
    new coat and forbid him to wear it. I will only be
    bold with Benedick for his company; for, from the
    crown of his head to the sole of his foot, he is all
    mirth. He hath twice or thrice cut Cupid's bow-   *10*
    string,° and the little hangman dare not shoot at him.
    He hath a heart as sound as a bell; and his tongue
    is the clapper, for what his heart thinks, his tongue
    speaks.

Benedick. Gallants, I am not as I have been.   *15*

116 **reportingly** i.e., mere hearsay   3.2.3–4 **vouchsafe** permit   10–11 **cut
Cupid's bowstring** i.e., avoided falling in love

Leonato. So say I. Methinks you are sadder.°

Claudio. I hope he be in love.

Don Pedro. Hang him truant?° There's no true drop of
blood in him to be truly touched with love. If he be
20   sad, he wants money.

Benedick. I have the toothache.

Don Pedro. Draw it.°

Benedick. Hang it!

Claudio. You must hang it first and draw it afterwards.

25 *Don Pedro.* What? Sigh for the toothache?

Leonato. Where is but a humor or a worm.°

Benedick. Well, everyone cannot master a grief but
he that has it.°

Claudio. Yet say I he is in love.

30 *Don Pedro.* There is no appearance of fancy° in him,
unless it be a fancy that he hath to strange disguises;
as to be a Dutchman today, a Frenchman tomorrow; or in the shape of two countries at once, as a
German from the waist downward, all slops,° and
35   a Spaniard from the hip upward, no doublet.° Unless he have a fancy to this foolery, as it appears he
hath, he is no fool for fancy, as you would have
it appear he is.

Claudio. If he be not in love with some woman, there
40   is no believing old signs; 'a brushes his hat o'
mornings. What should that bode?

---

16 **sadder** graver   18 **truant** i.e., as unfaithful to his antiromantic stance
22 **Draw it** extract it (but **draw** also means eviscerate; traitors were
hanged, drawn, and quartered. **Draw it** thus leads to the exclamation
Hang it)   26 **a humor or a worm** (supposed causes of tooth decay, *humor* = secretion)   27–28 **Well ... has it** i.e., a man has to have a grief
first before he can master it (Benedick does not admit that he has a grief;
but some editors emend **cannot** to "can")   30 **fancy** love   34 **slops**
loose breeches   35 **doublet** close-fitting jacket

Don Pedro. Hath any man seen him at the barber's?

Claudio. No, but the barber's man hath been seen with him, and the old ornament of his cheek hath already stuffed tennis balls.° 45

Leonato. Indeed he looks younger than he did, by the loss of a beard.

Don Pedro. Nay, 'a rubs himself with civet.° Can you smell him out by that?

Claudio. That's as much as to say, the sweet youth's in love. 50

Don Pedro. The greatest note of it is his melancholy.

Claudio. And when was he wont to wash his face?

Don Pedro. Yea, or to paint himself?° For the which I hear what they say of him. 55

Claudio. Nay, but his jesting spirit, which is now crept into a lutestring, and now governed by stops.°

Don Pedro. Indeed that tells a heavy tale for him. Conclude, conclude, he is in love.

Claudio. Nay, but I know who loves him. 60

Don Pedro. That would I know too. I warrant, one that knows him not.

Claudio. Yes, and his ill conditions;° and in despite of all,° dies° for him.

Don Pedro. She shall be buried with her face upwards.° 65

Benedick. Yet is this no charm for the toothache. Old

44–45 **the old ornament . . . tennis balls** (cf. Beatrice's remark, 2.1.29–30 "I could not endure a husband with a beard on his face") 48 **civet** perfume 54 **to paint himself** to use cosmetics 57 **stops** frets (on the lute) 63 **conditions** qualities 63–64 **in despite of all** notwithstanding 64 **dies** (1) pines away (2) is willing to "die" in the act of sex 65–66 **She shall . . . upwards** (continues sexual innuendo)

signior, walk aside with me; I have studied eight or
nine wise words to speak to you, which these hobby-
70 horses° must not hear.

> [*Exeunt Benedick and Leonato.*]

Don Pedro. For my life, to break with him about Beatrice!

Claudio. 'Tis even so. Hero and Margaret have by
this played their parts with Beatrice, and then the
75 two bears will not bite one another when they meet.

Enter John the Bastard.

Don John. My lord and brother, God save you.

Don Pedro. Good den,° brother.

Don John. If your leisure served, I would speak with
you.

80 *Don Pedro.* In private?

Don John. If it please you. Yet Count Claudio may
hear, for what I would speak of concerns him.

Don Pedro. What's the matter?

Don John. [*To Claudio*] Means your lordship to be
85 married tomorrow?

Don Pedro. You know he does.

Don John. I know not that, when he knows what I
know.

Claudio. If there be any impediment, I pray you dis-
90 cover it.

Don John. You may think I love you not; let that appear hereafter, and aim better at me° by that° I
now will manifest. For my brother (I think he holds
you well, and in dearness of heart) hath holp to

69–70 **hobbyhorses** jokers (originally an imitation horse fastened around
the waist of a morris dancer)   77 **Good den** good evening   92 **aim better at me** judge better of me   92 **that** that which

effect your ensuing marriage—surely suit ill spent   *95*
and labor ill bestowed!

Don Pedro. Why, what's the matter?

Don John. I came hither to tell you, and, circumstances short'ned (for she has been too long a-talk-
ing of), the lady is disloyal.   *100*

Claudio. Who? Hero?

Don John. Even she—Leonato's Hero, your Hero,
every man's Hero.

Claudio. Disloyal?

Don John. The word is too good to paint out her wick-   *105*
edness. I could say she were worse. Think you of
a worse title, and I will fit her to it. Wonder not
till further warrant. Go but with me tonight, you
shall see her chamber window ent'red, even the
night before her wedding day. If you love her then,   *110*
tomorrow wed her. But it would better fit your
honor to change your mind.

Claudio. May this be so?

Don Pedro. I will not think it.

Don John. If you dare not trust that you see, confess   *115*
not that you know. If you will follow me, I will
show you enough; and when you have seen more
and heard more, proceed accordingly.

Claudio. If I see anything tonight why I should not
marry her tomorrow, in the congregation where I   *120*
should wed, there will I shame her.

Don Pedro. And, as I wooed for thee to obtain her, I
will join with thee to disgrace her.

Don John. I will disparage her no farther till you are
my witnesses. Bear it coldly° but till midnight, and   *125*
let the issue show itself.

125 **coldly** calmly

Don Pedro. O day untowardly turned!

Claudio. O mischief strangely thwarting!

Don John. O plague right well prevented! So will you
130   say when you have seen the sequel.   [*Exeunt.*]

[Scene 3. A street.]

*Enter Dogberry and his compartner [Verges,]
with the Watch.*

Dogberry. Are you good men and true?

Verges. Yea, or else it were pity but they should suffer
salvation,° body and soul.

Dogberry. Nay, that were a punishment too good for
5   them if they should have any allegiance in them,
being chosen for the Prince's watch.

Verges. Well, give them their charge,° neighbor Dogberry.

Dogberry. First, who think you the most desartless
10   man to be constable?

First Watch. Hugh Oatcake, sir, or George Seacole, for
they can write and read.

Dogberry. Come hither, neighbor Seacole. God hath
blessed you with a good name. To be a well-favored°
15   man is the gift of fortune, but to write and read
comes by nature.

Second Watch. Both which, Master Constable—

Dogberry. You have; I knew it would be your answer.
Well, for your favor, sir, why, give God thanks and

3.3.3 **salvation** damnation (the beginning of the malapropisms basic to
the comedy of Dogberry and Verges)   7 **charge** instructions   14 **well-
favored** handsome

make no boast of it; and for your writing and read- 20
ing, let that appear when there is no need of such
vanity. You are thought here to be the most sense-
less and fit man for the constable of the watch.
Therefore bear you the lanthorn. This is your
charge: you shall comprehend all vagrom° men; 25
you are to bid any man stand,° in the Prince's
name.

Second Watch. How if 'a will not stand?

Dogberry. Why then, take no note of him, but let him
go, and presently call the rest of the watch together 30
and thank God you are rid of a knave.

Verges. If he will not stand when he is bidden, he is
none of the Prince's subjects.

Dogberry. True, and they are to meddle with none but
the Prince's subjects. You shall also make no noise 35
in the streets; for, for the watch to babble and to
talk is most tolerable, and not to be endured.

Watch.° We will rather sleep than talk; we know what
belongs to a watch.

Dogberry. Why, you speak like an ancient and most 40
quiet watchman, for I cannot see how sleeping
should offend. Only, have a care that your bills°
be not stol'n. Well, you are to call at all the ale-
houses and bid those that are drunk get them to
bed. 45

Watch. How if they will not?

Dogberry. Why then, let them alone till they are sober.
If they make you not then the better answer, you
may say they are not the men you took them for.

Watch. Well, sir. 50

---

25 **comprehend all vagrom** i.e., apprehend all vagrant 26 **stand** halt,
stop 38 **Watch** (neither the Quarto nor the Folio differentiates again
between First Watch and Second Watch until the end of this scene)
42 **bills** constables' pikes

Dogberry. If you meet a thief, you may suspect him, by virtue of your office, to be no true man; and for such kind of men, the less you meddle or make with them, why, the more is for your honesty.

55 *Watch.* If we know him to be a thief, shall we not lay hands on him?

Dogberry. Truly, by your office you may; but I think they that touch pitch will be defiled. The most peaceable way for you, if you do take a thief, is to 60 let him show himself what he is, and steal out of your company.

Verges. You have been always called a merciful man, partner.

Dogberry. Truly, I would not hang a dog by my will, 65 much more a man who hath any honesty in him.

Verges. If you hear a child cry in the night, you must call to the nurse and bid her still it.

Watch. How if the nurse be asleep and will not hear us?

70 *Dogberry.* Why then, depart in peace and let the child wake her with crying; for the ewe that will not hear her lamb when it baes will never answer a calf when he bleats.

Verges. 'Tis very true.

75 *Dogberry.* This is the end of the charge: you, constable, are to present the Prince's own person. If you meet the Prince in the night, you may stay him.

Verges. Nay, by'r lady, that I think 'a cannot.

Dogberry. Five shillings to one on't, with any man 80 that knows the statutes, he may stay him! Marry, not without the Prince be willing; for indeed the watch ought to offend no man, and it is an offense to stay a man against his will.

Verges. By'r lady, I think it be so.

Dogberry. Ha, ah, ha! Well, masters, good night. And 85
there be any matter of weight chances, call up me.
Keep your fellows' counsels and your own, and good
night. Come, neighbor.

Watch. Well, masters, we hear our charge. Let us go
sit here upon the church bench till two, and then 90
all to bed.

Dogberry. One word more, honest neighbors. I pray
you watch about Signior Leonato's door; for the
wedding being there tomorrow, there is a great coil°
tonight. Adieu. Be vigitant, I beseech you. 95
                 Exeunt [Dogberry and Verges].

          Enter Borachio and Conrade.

Borachio. What, Conrade!

Watch. [*Aside*] Peace! Stir not!

Borachio. Conrade, I say!

Conrade. Here, man. I am at thy elbow.

Borachio. Mass,° and my elbow itched; I thought there 100
would a scab° follow.

Conrade. I will owe thee an answer for that; and now
forward with thy tale.

Borachio. Stand thee close then under this penthouse,°
for it drizzles rain, and I will, like a true drunkard,° 105
utter all to thee.

Watch. [*Aside*] Some treason, masters; yet stand close.

Borachio. Therefore know I have earned of Don John
a thousand ducats.

Conrade. Is it possible that any villainy should be so 110
dear?

---

94 **coil** to-do, turmoil   100 **Mass** (an interjection, from "by the Mass")
101 **scab** (1) crust over a wound (2) contemptible person   104 **penthouse** shed, lean-to   105 **drunkard** (his name is based on the Spanish
borracho, "drunkard")

Borachio. Thou shouldst rather ask if it were possible any villainy should be so rich; for when rich
villains have need of poor ones, poor ones may
115   make what price they will.

Conrade. I wonder at it.

Borachio. That shows thou art unconfirmed.° Thou
knowest that the fashion of a doublet, or a hat, or
a cloak, is nothing to a man.°

120 *Conrade.* Yes, it is apparel.

Borachio. I mean the fashion.

Conrade. Yes, the fashion is the fashion.

Borachio. Tush! I may as well say the fool's the fool.
But seest thou not what a deformed thief this fash-
125   ion is?

Watch. [*Aside*] I know that Deformed; 'a has been a
vile thief this seven year; 'a goes up and down like
a gentleman. I remember his name.

Borachio. Didst thou not hear somebody?

130 *Conrade.* No; 'twas the vane on the house.

Borachio. Seest thou not, I say, what a deformed thief
this fashion is? How giddily 'a turns about all the
hotbloods between fourteen and five-and-thirty?
Sometimes fashioning them like Pharaoh's soldiers
135   in the reechy° painting, sometime like god Bel's
priests° in the old church window, sometime like
the shaven Hercules in the smirched worm-eaten
tapestry, where his codpiece° seems as massy as his
club?

140 *Conrade.* All this I see; and I see that the fashion
wears out more apparel than the man. But art not
thou thyself giddy with the fashion too, that thou

---

117 **unconfirmed** innocent   119 **is nothing to a man** i.e., fails to reveal
his actual character   135 **reechy** grimy, filthy   135–36 **god Bel's priests**
(from the Apocrypha)   138 **codpiece** (decorative pouch at the fly of a sixteenth-century man's breeches)

hast shifted out of thy tale into telling me of the fashion?

Borachio. Not so neither. But know that I have tonight 145
wooed Margaret, the Lady Hero's gentlewoman, by
the name of Hero. She leans me out at her mistress'
chamber window, bids me a thousand times good
night. I tell this tale vilely—I should first tell thee
how the Prince, Claudio, and my master, planted 150
and placed and possessed° by my master Don John,
saw afar off in the orchard this amiable encounter.

Conrade. And thought they Margaret was Hero?

Borachio. Two of them did, the Prince and Claudio;
but the devil my master knew she was Margaret; 155
and partly by his oaths, which first possessed them,
partly by the dark night, which did deceive them,
but chiefly by my villainy, which did confirm any
slander that Don John had made, away went Claudio enraged; swore he would meet her, as he was 160
appointed, next morning at the temple, and there,
before the whole congregation, shame her with
what he saw o'ernight and send her home again
without a husband.

First Watch. We charge you in the Prince's name 165
stand!

Second Watch. Call up the right Master Constable.
We have here recovered the most dangerous piece
of lechery that ever was known in the commonwealth. 170

First Watch. And one Deformed is one of them; I
know him; 'a wears a lock.°

Conrade. Masters, masters—

Second Watch. You'll be made bring Deformed forth,
I warrant you. 175

---

151 **possessed** informed, deluded   172 **lock** lovelock, curl of hair hanging by the ear

Conrade. Masters, never speak; we charge you let us obey you to go with us.°

Borachio. We are like to prove a goodly commodity, being taken up of these men's bills.°

180 *Conrade.* A commodity in question,° I warrant you. Come, we'll obey you.   *Exeunt.*

[Scene 4. *Leonato's house.*]

Enter Hero, and Margaret, and Ursula.

Hero. Good Ursula, wake my cousin Beatrice and desire her to rise.

Ursula. I will, lady.

Hero. And bid her come hither.

5 *Ursula.* Well.   [*Exit.*]

Margaret. Troth, I think your other rabato° were better.

Hero. No, pray thee, good Meg, I'll wear this.

Margaret. By my troth, 's not so good, and I warrant
10 your cousin will say so.

Hero. My cousin's a fool, and thou art another. I'll wear none but this.

Margaret. I like the new tire° within° excellently, if the hair were a thought browner; and your gown's

176–77 **Masters . . . with us** (Conrade is mocking the language of the Second Watch; he means, "Say no more, we will go along with you")   178–79 **We are . . . bills** (Borachio continues the mockery with a series of puns: **commodity** [1] merchandise [2] profit; **taken up** [1] arrested [2] bought on credit; **bills** [1] pikes [2] bonds or sureties) 180 **in question** (1) subject to judicial examination (2) of doubtful value   3.4.6 **rabato** ruff   13 **tire** headdress   13 **within** in the next room

a most rare fashion, i' faith. I saw the Duchess of   15
Milan's gown that they praise so.

Hero. O, that exceeds, they say.

Margaret. By my troth, 's but a nightgown° in respect
of yours—cloth o' gold and cuts,° and laced with
silver, set with pearls, down sleeves, side-sleeves,°   20
and skirts, round underborne with a bluish tinsel.
But for a fine, quaint,° graceful, and excellent fashion, yours is worth ten on't.

Hero. God give me joy to wear it, for my heart is exceeding heavy.   25

Margaret. 'Twill be heavier soon by the weight of a
man.

Hero. Fie upon thee! Art not ashamed?

Margaret. Of what, lady? Of speaking honorably? Is
not marriage honorable in a beggar? Is not your   30
lord honorable without marriage? I think you would
have me say, "saving your reverence, a husband."
And bad thinking do not wrest true speaking, I'll
offend nobody. Is there any harm in "the heavier
for a husband"? None, I think, and it be the right   35
husband and the right wife; otherwise 'tis light,°
and not heavy. Ask my Lady Beatrice else. Here
she comes.

Enter Beatrice.

Hero. Good morrow, coz.

Beatrice. Good morrow, sweet Hero.   40

Hero. Why, how now? Do you speak in the sick tune?

Beatrice. I am out of all other tune, methinks.

---

18 **nightgown** dressing gown   19 **cuts** slashes to show rich fabric underneath   20 **down sleeves, side-sleeves** long sleeves covering the arms,
open sleeves hanging from the shoulder   22 **quaint** pretty, dainty
36 **light** (pun on "wanton")

Margaret. Clap's into° "Light o' love." That goes
without a burden.° Do you sing it, and I'll dance it.

45 *Beatrice.* Ye light o' love with your heels!° Then, if
your husband have stables enough, you'll see he
shall lack no barns.°

Margaret. O illegitimate construction! I scorn that with
my heels.

50 *Beatrice.* 'Tis almost five o'clock, cousin; 'tis time you
were ready. By my troth, I am exceeding ill.
Heigh-ho!

Margaret. For a hawk, a horse, or a husband?

Beatrice. For the letter that begins them all, *H.*°

55 *Margaret.* Well, and you be not turned Turk,° there's
no more sailing by the star.

Beatrice. What means the fool, trow?°

Margaret. Nothing I; but God send everyone their
heart's desire!

60 *Hero.* These gloves the Count sent me, they are an
excellent perfume.

Beatrice. I am stuffed,° cousin; I cannot smell.

Margaret. A maid, and stuffed!° There's goodly catch-
ing of cold.

65 *Beatrice.* O, God help me! God help me! How long
have you professed apprehension?°

Margaret. Ever since you left it. Doth not my wit become me rarely?

Beatrice. It is not seen enough. You should wear it in
70 your cap. By my troth, I am sick.

Margaret. Get you some of this distilled *Carduus*

---

43 **Clap's into** let us sing   44 **burden** bass part (with pun on "the heavier
for a husband")   45 **Ye ... your heels** (sexual innuendo)   47 **barns**
(pun on "bairns," children)   54 **H** ("ache" was pronounced "aitch")
55 **turned Turk** completely changed   57 **trow** I wonder   62 **I am stuffed**
I have a head cold   63 **stuffed** filled (as with a child)   66 **apprehension**
wit

Benedictus° and lay it to your heart. It is the only
thing for a qualm.°

Hero. There thou prick'st her with a thistle.

Beatrice. Benedictus? Why *Benedictus*? You have   75
some moral° in this *Benedictus*.

Margaret. Moral? No, by my troth, I have no moral
meaning. I meant plain holy thistle. You may think
perchance that I think you are in love. Nay, by'r
lady, I am not such a fool to think what I list;° nor   80
I list not to think what I can; nor indeed I cannot
think, if I would think my heart out of thinking,
that you are in love, or that you will be in love, or
that you can be in love. Yet Benedick was such
another, and now is he become a man. He swore   85
he would never marry; and yet now in despite of
his heart he eats his meat without grudging.° And
how you may be converted I know not; but methinks you look with your eyes as other women do.

Beatrice. What pace is this that thy tongue keeps?   90

Margaret. Not a false gallop.

Enter Ursula.

Ursula. Madam, withdraw. The Prince, the Count,
Signior Benedick, Don John, and all the gallants of
the town are come to fetch you to church.

Hero. Help to dress me, good coz, good Meg, good   95
Ursula.   [*Exeunt.*]

[Scene 5. *Another room in Leonato's house.*]

Enter Leonato and the Constable [*Dogberry*], and the Headborough [*Verges*].

71–72 **Carduus Benedictus** blessed thistle, a medicinal herb   73 **qualm**
sensation of sickness   76 **moral** special meaning   80 **list** please   87 **he
eats his meat without grudging** he finds that he can still eat

Leonato. What would you with me, honest neighbor?

Dogberry. Marry, sir, I would have some confidence with you that decerns you nearly.

Leonato. Brief, I pray you, for you see it is a busy
5   time with me.

Dogberry. Marry, this it is, sir.

Verges. Yes, in truth it is, sir.

Leonato. What is it, my good friends?

Dogberry. Goodman Verges, sir, speaks a little off the
10   matter—an old man, sir, and his wits are not so
       blunt as, God help, I would desire they were; but, in
       faith, honest as the skin between his brows.

Verges. Yes, I thank God I am as honest as any man liv-
       ing that is an old man and no honester than I.

15 *Dogberry.* Comparisons are odorous; Palabras,°
       neighbor Verges.

Leonato. Neighbors, you are tedious.

Dogberry. It pleases your worship to say so, but we
       are the poor Duke's officers; but truly, for mine
20   own part, if I were as tedious as a king, I could find
       in my heart to bestow it all of your worship.

Leonato. All thy tediousness on me, ah?

Dogberry. Yea, and 'twere a thousand pound more
       than 'tis; for I hear as good exclamation on your
25   worship as of any man in the city, and though I be
       but a poor man, I am glad to hear it.

Verges. And so am I.

Leonato. I would fain know what you have to say.

Verges. Marry, sir, our watch tonight, excepting your
30   worship's presence, ha' ta'en a couple of as arrant
       knaves as any in Messina.

3.5.15 **Palabras** (for Spanish *pocas palabras*, few words)

Dogberry. A good old man, sir; he will be talking. As
they say, "When the age is in, the wit is out." God
help us! It is a world to see! Well said, i' faith,
neighbor Verges. Well, God's a good man. And   35
two men ride of a horse, one must ride behind. An
honest soul, i' faith, sir, by my troth he is, as ever
broke bread; but God is to be worshiped; all men
are not alike, alas, good neighbor!

Leonato. Indeed, neighbor, he comes too short of you.   40

Dogberry. Gifts that God gives.

Leonato. I must leave you.

Dogberry. One word, sir. Our watch, sir, have indeed
comprehended two aspicious persons, and we would
have them this morning examined before your wor-   45
ship.

Leonato. Take their examination yourself and bring
it me; I am now in great haste, as it may appear
unto you.

Dogberry. It shall be suffigance.   50

Leonato. Drink some wine ere you go. Fare you well.

[*Enter a Messenger.*]

Messenger. My lord, they stay for you to give your
daughter to her husband.

Leonato. I'll wait upon them. I am ready.

> *Exit* [*Leonato,
> with Messenger*].

Dogberry. Go, good partner, go get you to Francis   55
Seacole; bid him bring his pen and inkhorn to the
jail. We are now to examination these men.

Verges. And we must do it wisely.

Dogberry. We will spare for no wit, I warrant you;
here's that shall drive some of them to a non-come.°   60
Only get the learned writer to set down our excom-
munication, and meet me at the jail.   [*Exeunt.*]

60 **non-come** non compos mentis

[ACT 4

Scene 1. *A church.*]

Enter Prince [Don Pedro], [Don John the] Bastard, Leonato, Friar [Francis], Claudio, Benedick, Hero, and Beatrice [and Attendants].

Leonato. Come, Friar Francis, be brief. Only to the plain form of marriage, and you shall recount their particular° duties afterwards.

Friar. You come hither, my lord, to marry this lady?

5 *Claudio.* No.

Leonato. To be married to her; Friar, you come to marry her.

Friar. Lady, you come hither to be married to this count?

10 *Hero.* I do.

Friar. If either of you know any inward impediment why you should not be conjoined, I charge you on your souls to utter it.

Claudio. Know you any, Hero?

15 *Hero.* None, my lord.

4.1.3 **particular** personal

Friar. Know you any, Count?

Leonato. I dare make his answer, none.

Claudio. O, what men dare do! What men may do!
  What men daily do, not knowing what they do!

Benedick. How now? Interjections? Why then, some   20
  be of° laughing, as, ah, ha, he!°

Claudio. Stand thee by,° friar. Father, by your leave,
  Will you with free and unconstrainèd soul
  Give me this maid your daughter?

Leonato. As freely, son, as God did give her me.   25

Claudio. And what have I to give you back whose
    worth
  May counterpoise this rich and precious gift?

Don Pedro. Nothing, unless you render her again.

Claudio. Sweet Prince, you learn me noble thankful-
    ness.
  There, Leonato, take her back again.   30
  Give not this rotten orange to your friend.
  She's but the sign and semblance of her honor.
  Behold how like a maid she blushes here!
  O, what authority and show of truth
  Can cunning sin cover itself withal!   35
  Comes not that blood, as modest evidence,
  To witness simple virtue? Would you not swear,
  All you that see her, that she were a maid,
  By these exterior shows? But she is none.
  She knows the heat of a luxurious° bed;   40
  Her blush is guiltiness, not modesty.

Leonato. What do you mean, my lord?

Claudio.   Not to be married,
  Not to knit my soul to an approvèd° wanton.

Leonato. Dear my lord, if you, in your own proof,°

20–21 **some be of** some are concerned with   21 **ah, ha, he!** (examples of
interjections)   22 **Stand thee by** stand   aside   40 **luxurious** lustful
43 **approvèd** tested   44 **proof** experience

45 Have vanquished the resistance of her youth
And made defeat of her virginity—

Claudio. I know what you would say: if I have known°
her,
You will say she did embrace me as a husband,
And so extenuate the 'forehand sin.
50 No, Leonato,
I never tempted her with word too large,
But, as a brother to his sister, showed
Bashful sincerity and comely love.

Hero. And seemed I ever otherwise to you?

55 *Claudio.* Out on thee, seeming! I will write against it.
You seem to me as Dian in her orb,
As chaste as is the bud ere it be blown;°
But you are more intemperate in your blood°
Than Venus, or those pamp'red animals
60 That rage in savage sensuality.

Hero. Is my lord well that he doth speak so wide?°

Leonato. Sweet Prince, why speak not you?

Don Pedro.   What should I speak?
I stand dishonored that have gone about
To link my dear friend to a common stale.°

65 *Leonato.* Are these things spoken, or do I but dream?

Don John. Sir, they are spoken, and these things are
true.

Benedick. This looks not like a nuptial.

Hero.   "True," O God!

Claudio. Leonato, stand I here?
Is this the Prince? Is this the Prince's brother?
70 Is this face Hero's? Are our eyes our own?

Leonato. All this is so. But what of this, my lord?

---

47 **known** had intercourse with   57 **blown** blossomed   58 **blood** sexual
desire   61 **so wide** so far from the truth   64 **stale** prostitute

Claudio. Let me but move one question to your daugh-
  ter;
 And by that fatherly and kindly° power
 That you have in her, bid her answer truly.

Leonato. I charge thee do so, as thou art my child. *75*

Hero. O, God defend me! How am I beset!
 What kind of catechizing call you this?

Claudio. To make you answer truly to your name.

Hero. Is it not Hero? Who can blot that name
 With any just reproach?

Claudio.   Marry, that can Hero! *80*
 Hero itself can blot out Hero's virtue.
 What man was he talked with you yesternight,
 Out at your window betwixt twelve and one?
 Now, if you are a maid, answer to this.

Hero. I talked with no man at that hour, my lord. *85*

Don Pedro. Why, then are you no maiden. Leonato,
 I am sorry you must hear. Upon mine honor
 Myself, my brother, and this grievèd Count
 Did see her, hear her, at that hour last night
 Talk with a ruffian at her chamber window *90*
 Who hath indeed, most like a liberal° villain,
 Confessed the vile encounters they have had
 A thousand times in secret.

Don John. Fie, fie! They are not to be named, my
  lord—
 Not to be spoke of; *95*
 There is not chastity enough in language
 Without offense to utter them. Thus, pretty lady,
 I am sorry for thy much misgovernment.

Claudio. O Hero! What a Hero hadst thou been
 If half thy outward graces had been placed *100*
 About thy thoughts and counsels of thy heart!
 But fare thee well, most foul, most fair, farewell;

73 kindly natural **91 liberal** licentious

Thou pure impiety and impious purity,
For thee I'll lock up all the gates of love,
105 And on my eyelids shall conjecture° hang,
To turn all beauty into thoughts of harm,
And never shall it more be gracious.

Leonato. Hath no man's dagger here a point for me?
                                                    [*Hero swoons.*]

Beatrice. Why, how now, cousin? Wherefore sink you
down?

Don John. Come, let us go. These things, come thus to
110   light,
Smother her spirits up.
                [*Exeunt Don Pedro, Don John, and Claudio.*]

Benedick. How doth the lady?

Beatrice.   Dead, I think. Help, uncle!
Hero! Why, Hero! Uncle! Signior Benedick! Friar!

Leonato. O Fate, take not away thy heavy hand!
115   Death is the fairest cover for her shame
That may be wished for.

Beatrice.   How now, cousin Hero?

Friar. Have comfort, lady.

Leonato. Dost thou look up?

Friar.   Yea, wherefore should she not?

Leonato. Wherefore? Why, doth not every earthly thing
120   Cry shame upon her? Could she here deny
The story that is printed in her blood?°
Do not live, Hero; do not ope thine eyes;
For, did I think thou wouldst not quickly die,
Thought I thy spirits were stronger than thy shames,
125   Myself would on the rearward of reproaches
Strike at thy life. Grieved I, I had but one?
Chid I for that at frugal nature's frame?°

---

105 **conjecture** suspicion   121 **printed in her blood** written in her blushes
127 **frame** plan

O, one too much by thee! Why had I one?
Why ever wast thou lovely in my eyes?
Why had I not with charitable hand   *130*
Took up a beggar's issue at my gates,
Who smirchèd thus and mired with infamy,
I might have said, "No part of it is mine;
This shame derives itself from unknown loins"?
But mine, and mine I loved, and mine I praised,   *135*
And mine that I was proud on, mine so much
That I myself was to myself not mine,
Valuing of her—why she, O, she is fall'n
Into a pit of ink, that the wide sea
Hath drops too few to wash her clean again,   *140*
And salt too little which may season give°
To her foul tainted flesh!

Benedick.   Sir, sir, be patient.
For my part, I am so attired in wonder,
I know not what to say.

Beatrice. O, on my soul, my cousin is belied!   *145*

Benedick. Lady, were you her bedfellow last night?

Beatrice. No, truly, not; although, until last night,
I have this twelvemonth been her bedfellow.

Leonato. Confirmed, confirmed! O, that is stronger made
Which was before barred up with ribs of iron!   *150*
Would the two princes lie, and Claudio lie,
Who loved her so that, speaking of her foulness,
Washed it with tears? Hence from her! Let her die.

Friar. Hear me a little;
For I have only been silent so long,   *155*
And given way unto this course of fortune,
By noting of the lady. I have marked
A thousand blushing apparitions
To start into her face, a thousand innocent shames
In angel whiteness beat away those blushes,   *160*
And in her eye there hath appeared a fire

---

141 **season give** act as a preservative

       To burn the errors that these princes hold
       Against her maiden truth. Call me a fool;
       Trust not my reading nor my observations,
165   Which with experimental seal° doth warrant
   • The tenor° of my book; trust not my age,
       My reverence, calling, nor divinity,
       If this sweet lady lie not guiltless here
       Under some biting error.

Leonato.   Friar, it cannot be.
170   Thou seest that all the grace that she hath left
       Is that she will not add to her damnation
       A sin of perjury; she not denies it.
       Why seek'st thou then to cover with excuse
       That which appears in proper nakedness?

175 *Friar.* Lady, what man is he you are accused of?

Hero. They know that do accuse me; I know none.
       If I know more of any man alive
       Than that which maiden modesty doth warrant,
       Let all my sins lack mercy! O my father,
180   Prove you that any man with me conversed
       At hours unmeet, or that I yesternight
       Maintained the change° of words with any creature,
       Refuse me, hate me, torture me to death!

Friar. There is some strange misprision° in the princes.

185 *Benedick.* Two of them have the very bent° of honor;
       And if their wisdoms be misled in this,
       The practice° of it lives in John the bastard,
       Whose spirits toil in frame of villainies.

Leonato. I know not. If they speak but truth of her,
190   These hands shall tear her. If they wrong her honor,
       The proudest of them shall well hear of it.
       Time hath not yet so dried this blood of mine,
       Nor age so eat up my invention,°

---

165 **experimental seal** seal of experience 166 **tenor** purport 182 **maintained the change** held exchange 184 **misprision** mistaking 185 **bent** shape (or perhaps "inclination") 187 **practice** scheming 193 **invention** inventiveness

Nor fortune made such havoc of my means,
Nor my bad life reft me so much of friends,   *195*
But they shall find awaked in such a kind
Both strength of limb and policy of mind,
Ability in means, and choice of friends,
To quit° me of them throughly.

Friar.   Pause awhile
And let my counsel sway you in this case.   *200*
Your daughter here the princes left for dead.
Let her awhile be secretly kept in,
And publish it that she is dead indeed;
Maintain a mourning ostentation,°
And on your family's old monument   *205*
Hang mournful epitaphs, and do all rites
That appertain unto a burial.

Leonato. What shall become of this? What will this do?

Friar. Marry, this well carried shall on her behalf
Change slander to remorse; that is some good.   *210*
But not for that dream I on this strange course,
But on this travail look for greater birth.
She dying, as it must be so maintained,
Upon the instant that she was accused,
Shall be lamented, pitied, and excused   *215*
Of every hearer. For it so falls out
That what we have we prize not to the worth
Whiles we enjoy it; but being lacked and lost,
Why, then we rack° the value, then we find
The virtue that possession would not show us   *220*
Whiles it was ours. So will it fare with Claudio.
When he shall hear she died upon his words,
Th' idea of her life shall sweetly creep
Into his study of imagination,°
And every lovely organ° of her life   *225*
Shall come appareled in more precious habit,°
More moving, delicate, and full of life,

---

199 **quit** revenge   204 **Maintain a mourning ostentation** perform the outward show of mourning   219 **rack** stretch   224 **study of imagination** medi-
tation, musing   225 **organ** physical feature   226 **habit** dress

    Into the eye and prospect of his soul
    Than when she lived indeed. Then shall he mourn,
230   If ever love had interest in his liver,°
    And wish he had not so accusèd her,
    No, though he thought his accusation true.
    Let this be so, and doubt not but success°
    Will fashion the event° in better shape
235   Than I can lay it down in likelihood.
    But if all aim, but this, be leveled false,°
    The supposition of the lady's death
    Will quench the wonder of her infamy;
    And if it sort° not well, you may conceal her,
240   As best befits her wounded reputation,
    In some reclusive and religious life,
    Out of all eyes, tongues, minds, and injuries.

Benedick. Signior Leonato, let the friar advise you;
    And though you know my inwardness° and love
245   Is very much unto the Prince and Claudio,
    Yet, by mine honor, I will deal in this
    As secretly and justly as your soul
    Should with your body.

Leonato.   Being that I flow in grief,
    The smallest twine may lead me.

250 *Friar.* 'Tis well consented. Presently away;
      For to strange sores strangely they strain the cure.
    Come, lady, die to live. This wedding day
      Perhaps is but prolonged. Have patience and
      endure.
               Exit [with all but Beatrice and Benedick].

Benedick. Lady Beatrice, have you wept all this while?

255 *Beatrice.* Yea, and I will weep a while longer.

Benedick. I will not desire that.

---

230 **liver** (supposed seat of love) 233 **success** what follows 234 **event**
outcome 236 **But if . . . false** but if all conjecture, except this (i.e., the
mere supposition of Hero's death), be aimed (*leveled*) falsely 239 **sort**
turn out 244 **inwardness** most intimate feelings

Beatrice. You have no reason. I do it freely.

Benedick. Surely I do believe your fair cousin is
   wronged.

Beatrice. Ah, how much might the man deserve of me   *260*
   that would right her!

Benedick. Is there any way to show such friendship?

Beatrice. A very even° way, but no such friend.

Benedick. May a man do it?

Beatrice. It is a man's office, but not yours.   *265*

Benedick. I do love nothing in the world so well as you.
   Is not that strange?

Beatrice. As strange as the thing I know not. It were as
   possible for me to say I loved nothing so well as you.
   But believe me not; and yet I lie not. I confess noth-   *270*
   ing, nor I deny nothing. I am sorry for my cousin.

Benedick. By my sword, Beatrice, thou lovest me.

Beatrice. Do not swear and eat it.

Benedick. I will swear by it that you love me, and I
   will make him eat it that says I love not you.   *275*

Beatrice. Will you not eat your word?

Benedick. With no sauce that can be devised to it. I
   protest° I love thee.

Beatrice. Why then, God forgive me!

Benedick. What offense, sweet Beatrice?   *280*

Beatrice. You have stayed me in a happy hour.° I was
   about to protest I loved you.

Benedick. And do it with all thy heart.

Beatrice. I love you with so much of my heart that none
   is left to protest.   *285*

---

263 **even** direct   278 **protest** avow   281 **in a happy hour** just in time

Benedick. Come, bid me do anything for thee.

Beatrice. Kill Claudio.

Benedick. Ha! Not for the wide world!

Beatrice. You kill me to deny it. Farewell.

290 *Benedick.* Tarry, sweet Beatrice.   [*He holds her.*]

Beatrice. I am gone, though I am here; there is no love
in you. Nay, I pray you let me go!

Benedick. Beatrice—

Beatrice. In faith, I will go!

295 *Benedick.* We'll be friends first.   [*He lets her go.*]

Beatrice. You dare easier be friends with me than fight
with mine enemy.

Benedick. Is Claudio thine enemy?

Beatrice. Is 'a not approved in the height a villain, that
300 hath slandered, scorned, dishonored my kinswoman?
O that I were a man! What, bear her in hand° until
they come to take hands; and then, with public
accusation, uncovered slander, unmitigated rancor—
O God, that I were a man! I would eat his heart in
305 the market place!

Benedick. Hear me, Beatrice—

Beatrice. Talk with a man out at a window! A proper
saying!

Benedick. Nay, but Beatrice—

310 *Beatrice.* Sweet Hero, she is wronged, she is sland'red,
she is undone.

Benedick. Beat—

Beatrice. Princes and counties! Surely, a princely testi-
mony, a goodly count, Count Comfect;° a sweet gal-
315 lant surely! O that I were a man for his sake! Or that

301 **bear her in hand** fool her   314 **Comfect** sugar candy

I had any friend would be a man for my sake! But
manhood is melted into cursies,° valor into compliment, and men are only turned into tongue, and trim
ones too. He is now as valiant as Hercules that only
tells a lie, and swears it. I cannot be a man with　320
wishing; therefore I will die a woman with grieving.

Benedick. Tarry, good Beatrice. By this hand, I love
thee.

Beatrice. Use it for my love some other way than
swearing by it.　325

Benedick. Think you in your soul the Count Claudio
hath wronged Hero?

Beatrice. Yea, as sure as I have a thought or a soul.

Benedick. Enough, I am engaged. I will challenge him.
I will kiss your hand, and so I leave you. By this　330
hand, Claudio shall render me a dear account. As
you hear of me, so think of me. Go comfort your
cousin. I must say she is dead. And so farewell.

　　　　　　　　　　　　　　　　　[Exeunt.]

[Scene 2. *A prison.*]

*Enter the Constables [Dogberry and Verges] and
　the Town Clerk [Sexton] in gowns, Borachio,
　[Conrade, and Watch].*

Dogberry. Is our whole dissembly appeared?

Verges. O, a stool and a cushion for the sexton.

Sexton. Which be the malefactors?

Dogberry. Marry, that am I and my partner.

317 **cursies** curtsies

5 *Verges.* Nay, that's certain. We have the exhibition to
   examine.

   Sexton. But which are the offenders that are to be examined? Let them come before Master Constable.

   Dogberry. Yea, marry, let them come before me. What
10 is your name, friend?

   Borachio. Borachio.

   Dogberry. Pray write down Borachio. Yours, sirrah?°

   Conrade. I am a gentleman, sir, and my name is Conrade.

15 *Dogberry.* Write down Master Gentleman Conrade.
   Masters, do you serve God?

   Both. Yea, sir, we hope.

   Dogberry. Write down that they hope they serve God;
   and write God first, for God defend but God should
20 go before such villains! Masters, it is proved already
   that you are little better than false knaves, and it will
   go near to be thought so shortly. How answer you for
   yourselves?

   Conrade. Marry, sir, we say we are none.

25 *Dogberry.* A marvelous witty fellow, I assure you; but I
   will go about with him.° Come you hither, sirrah; a
   word in your ear. Sir, I say to you, it is thought you
   are false knaves.

   Borachio. Sir, I say to you we are none.°

30 *Dogberry.* Well, stand aside. 'Fore God, they are both
   in a tale.° Have you writ down that they are none?

   Sexton. Master Constable, you go not the way to examine. You must call forth the watch that are their
   accusers.

4.2.12 **sirrah** (term of address used to an inferior)   26 **go about with
him** get the better of him   29 **none** (apparently pronounced the same as
"known," and so taken by Dogberry in his next speech)   30–31 **they are
both in a tale** their stories agree

Dogberry. Yea, marry, that's the eftest° way. Let the   35
watch come forth. Masters, I charge you in the
Prince's name, accuse these men.

First Watch. This man said, sir, that Don John the
Prince's brother was a villain.

Dogberry. Write down Prince John a villain. Why, this   40
is flat perjury, to call a prince's brother villain.

Borachio. Master Constable!

Dogberry. Pray thee, fellow, peace. I do not like thy
look, I promise thee.

Sexton. What heard you him say else?   45

Second Watch. Marry, that he had received a thousand
ducats of Don John for accusing the Lady Hero
wrongfully.

Dogberry. Flat burglary as ever was committed.

Verges. Yea, by mass, that it is.   50

Sexton. What else, fellow?

First Watch. And that Count Claudio did mean, upon
his words, to disgrace Hero before the whole assembly, and not marry her.

Dogberry. O villain! Thou wilt be condemned into   55
everlasting redemption for this.

Sexton. What else?

Watch. That is all.

Sexton. And this is more, masters, than you can deny.   60
Prince John is this morning secretly stol'n away.
Hero was in this manner accused, in this very manner refused, and upon the grief of this suddenly died.
Master Constable, let these men be bound and
brought to Leonato's. I will go before and show him
their examination.   [*Exit.*]   65

35 **eftest** quickest

Dogberry. [*To the Watch*] Come, let them be opinioned.°

Verges. Let them be in the hands of Coxcomb.°

Dogberry. God's my life, where's the sexton? Let him
70   write down the Prince's officer Coxcomb. Come,
bind them. Thou naughty° varlet!

Conrade. Away! You are an ass, you are an ass.

Dogberry. Dost thou not suspect my place? Dost thou
not suspect my years? O that he were here to write
75   me down an ass! But, masters, remember that I am
an ass. Though it be not written down, yet forget
not that I am an ass. No, thou villain, thou art full
of piety, as shall be proved upon thee by good witness. I am a wise fellow; and which is more, an offi-
80   cer; and which is more, a householder; and which is
more, as pretty a piece of flesh as any is in Messina,
and one that knows the law, go to! And a rich fellow
enough, go to! And a fellow that hath had losses; and
one that hath two gowns and everything handsome
85   about him. Bring him away. O that I had been writ
down an ass!   *Exit* [*with the others*].

66–67 **opinioned** (he means "pinioned")   68 **Coxcomb** (apparently
Verges thinks this is an elegant name for one of the Watch; editors commonly emend "of Coxcomb" to "off, coxcomb," and give to Conrade)
71 **naughty** wicked

[ACT 5

Scene 1. *Before Leonato's house.*]

Enter Leonato and his brother [Antonio].

Antonio. If you go on thus, you will kill yourself,
   And 'tis not wisdom thus to second° grief
   Against yourself.

Leonato.   I pray thee cease thy counsel,
   Which falls into mine ears as profitless
   As water in a sieve. Give not me counsel,   5
   Nor let no comforter delight mine ear
   But such a one whose wrongs do suit with° mine.
   Bring me a father that so loved his child,
   Whose joy of her is overwhelmed like mine,
   And bid him speak of patience.   10
   Measure his woe the length and breadth of mine,
   And let it answer every strain° for strain,
   As thus for thus, and such a grief for such,
   In every lineament, branch, shape, and form.
   If such a one will smile and stroke his beard,   15
   And sorrow wag,° cry "hem" when he should groan;
   Patch grief with proverbs, make misfortune drunk
   With candle-wasters;° bring him yet° to me,

5.1.2 **second** assist   7 **suit with** accord with   12 **strain** quality, trait
16 **wag** wave away   18 **candle-wasters** revelers (?) philosophers (?)
18 **yet** then

And I of him will gather patience.
20 But there is no such man. For, brother, men
Can counsel and speak comfort to that grief
Which they themselves not feel; but, tasting it,
Their counsel turns to passion, which before
Would give preceptial medicine° to rage,
25 Fetter strong madness in a silken thread,
Charm ache with air and agony with words.
No, no! 'Tis all men's office to speak patience
To those that wring under the load of sorrow,
But no man's virtue nor sufficiency
30 To be so moral° when he shall endure
The like himself. Therefore give me no counsel;
My griefs cry louder than advertisement.°

Antonio. Therein do men from children nothing differ.

Leonato. I pray thee peace. I will be flesh and blood;
35 For there was never yet philosopher
That could endure the toothache patiently,
However they have writ the style of gods
And made a push at chance and sufferance.°

Antonio. Yet bend not all the harm upon yourself.
40 Make those that do offend you suffer too.

Leonato. There thou speak'st reason. Nay, I will do so.
My soul doth tell me Hero is belied;
And that shall Claudio know; so shall the Prince,
And all of them that thus dishonor her.

Enter Prince [Don Pedro] and Claudio.

45 *Antonio.* Here comes the Prince and Claudio hastily.

Don Pedro. Good den, good den.

Claudio.   Good day to both of you.

Leonato. Hear you, my lords—

Don Pedro.   We have some haste, Leonato.

---

24 **preceptial medicine** medicine of precepts (cf. line 17: "Patch grief with proverbs")   30 **moral** moralizing   32 **advertisement** counsel   38 **made . . . sufferance** defied mischance and suffering

Leonato. Some haste, my lord! Well, fare you well,
   my lord.
   Are you so hasty now? Well, all is one.

Don Pedro. Nay, do not quarrel with us, good old man.   *50*

Antonio. If he could right himself with quarreling,
   Some of us would lie low.

Claudio.   Who wrongs him?

Leonato. Marry, thou dost wrong me, thou dissembler,
      thou!
   Nay, never lay thy hand upon thy sword;
   I fear thee not.

Claudio.   Marry, beshrew° my hand   *55*
   If it should give your age such cause of fear.
   In faith, my hand meant nothing to my sword.

Leonato. Tush, tush, man! Never fleer° and jest at me.
   I speak not like a dotard nor a fool,
   As under privilege of age to brag   *60*
   What I have done being young, or what would do,
   Were I not old. Know, Claudio, to thy head,°
   Thou hast so wronged mine innocent child and me
   That I am forced to lay my reverence by
   And, with gray hairs and bruise of many days,   *65*
   Do challenge thee to trial of a man.°
   I say thou hast belied mine innocent child.
   Thy slander hath gone through and through her
      heart,
   And she lies buried with her ancestors;
   O, in a tomb where never scandal slept,   *70*
   Save this of hers, framed° by thy villainy!

Claudio. My villainy?

Leonato.   Thine, Claudio; thine I say.

Don Pedro. You say not right, old man.

Leonato.   My lord, my lord,

---

55 **beshrew** curse (but not a strong word)   58 **fleer** sneer   62 **head**
face   66 **trial of a man** manly test, i.e., a duel   71 **framed** made

I'll prove it on his body if he dare,
75   Despite his nice fence° and his active practice,
His May of youth and bloom of lustihood.

Claudio. Away! I will not have to do with you.

Leonato. Canst thou so daff° me? Thou hast killed my
child.
If thou kill'st me, boy, thou shalt kill a man.

80 *Antonio.* He shall kill two of us, and men indeed.
But that's no matter; let him kill one first.
Win me and wear me! Let him answer me.
Come, follow me, boy; come, sir boy; come, follow
me.
Sir boy, I'll whip you from your foining° fence!
85   Nay, as I am a gentleman, I will.

Leonato. Brother—

Antonio. Content yourself. God knows I loved my
niece;
And she is dead, slandered to death by villains,
That dare as well answer a man indeed
90   As I dare take a serpent by the tongue.
Boys, apes, braggarts, Jacks,° milksops!

Leonato.   Brother Anthony—

Antonio. Hold you content. What, man! I know them,
yea,
And what they weigh, even to the utmost scruple;°
Scambling,° outfacing, fashionmonging° boys,
95   That lie and cog° and flout, deprave and slander,
Go anticly,° and show outward hideousness,
And speak off half a dozen dang'rous words,
How they might hurt their enemies, if they durst;
And this is all.

Leonato. But, brother Anthony—

---

75 **nice fence** elegant fencing 78 **daff** put off 84 **foining** thrusting
91 **Jacks** (a contemptuous term of no precise meaning) 93 **scruple**
smallest unit 94 **Scambling** brawling 94 **fashionmonging** fashion
following 95 **cog** cheat 96 **anticly** grotesquely dressed

Antonio.   Come, 'tis no matter. *100*
   Do not you meddle; let me deal in this.

Don Pedro. Gentlemen both, we will not wake your
   patience.°
   My heart is sorry for your daughter's death.
   But, on my honor, she was charged with nothing
   But what was true, and very full of proof.   *105*

Leonato. My lord, my lord!

Don Pedro. I will not hear you.

Leonato. No? Come, brother, away! I will be heard!

Antonio. And shall, or some of us will smart for it.
                Exeunt ambo° [Leonato and Antonio].

                Enter Benedick.

Don Pedro. See, see! Here comes the man we went to
   seek.   *110*

Claudio. Now, signior, what news?

Benedick. Good day, my lord.

Don Pedro. Welcome, signior. You are almost come
   to part almost a fray.

Claudio. We had liked to have had our two noses *115*
   snapped off with two old men without teeth.

Don Pedro. Leonato and his brother. What think'st
   thou? Had we fought, I doubt° we should have been
   too young for them.

Benedick. In a false quarrel there is no true valor. I *120*
   came to seek you both.

Claudio. We have been up and down to seek thee; for
   we are high-proof° melancholy, and would fain
   have it beaten away. Wilt thou use thy wit?

---

102 **wake your patience** arouse your indulgence (heavily ironic)   109 s.d
ambo both (Latin)   118 **doubt** suspect   123 **high-proof** in the highest
degree

125 *Benedick.* It is in my scabbard. Shall I draw it?

Don Pedro. Dost thou wear thy wit by thy side?

Claudio. Never any did so, though very many have
been beside their wit. I will bid thee draw, as we do
the minstrels: draw° to pleasure us.

130 *Don Pedro.* As I am an honest man, he looks pale.
Art thou sick, or angry?

Claudio. What, courage, man! What though care killed
a cat, thou hast mettle enough in thee to kill care.

Benedick. Sir, I shall meet your wit in the career° and
135 you charge° it against me. I pray you choose another subject.

Claudio. Nay then, give him another staff. This last
was broke cross.°

Don Pedro. By this light, he changes more and more.
140 I think he be angry indeed.

Claudio. If he be, he knows how to turn his girdle.°

Benedick. Shall I speak a word in your ear?

Claudio. God bless me from a challenge!

Benedick. [*Aside to Claudio*] You are a villain; I jest
145 not; I will make it good how you dare, with what
you dare, and when you dare. Do me right, or I will
protest° your cowardice. You have killed a sweet
lady, and her death shall fall heavy on you. Let me
hear from you.

150 *Claudio.* Well, I will meet you, so I may have good
cheer.

Don Pedro. What, a feast, a feast?

Claudio. I' faith, I thank him; he hath bid me to a

---

129 **draw** i.e., draw not a sword but a fiddle bow   134 **in the career**
headlong   135 **charge** i.e., as in tilting with staves or lances   138 **broke
cross** ineptly broken (by crossing the opponent's shield instead of striking
it headlong)   141 **turn his girdle** challenge me (by reaching for his dagger?)   147 **protest** proclaim

calf's head and a capon; the which if I do not
carve most curiously,° say my knife's naught. Shall   *155*
I not find a woodcock° too?

Benedick. Sir, your wit ambles well; it goes easily.

Don Pedro. I'll tell thee how Beatrice praised thy wit
the other day. I said thou hadst a fine wit. "True,"
said she, "a fine little one." "No," said I, "a great   *160*
wit." "Right," says she, "a great gross one." "Nay,"
said I, "a good wit." "Just," said she, "it hurts nobody." "Nay," said I, "the gentleman is wise."
"Certain," said she, "a wise gentleman." "Nay,"
said I, "he hath the tongues."° "That I believe,"   *165*
said she, "for he swore a thing to me on Monday
night which he forswore on Tuesday morning;
there's a double tongue; there's two tongues." Thus
did she an hour together transshape° thy particular virtues. Yet at last she concluded with a sigh,   *170*
thou wast the prop'rest° man in Italy.

Claudio. For the which she wept heartily and said she
cared not.

Don Pedro. Yea, that she did; but yet, for all that, and
if she did not hate him deadly, she would love him   *175*
dearly. The old man's daughter told us all.

Claudio. All, all! And moreover, God saw him when
he was hid in the garden.

Don Pedro. But when shall we set the savage bull's
horns on the sensible Benedick's head?   *180*

Claudio. Yea, and text underneath, "Here dwells
Benedick, the married man"?

Benedick. Fare you well, boy; you know my mind. I
will leave you now to your gossiplike humor; you
break jests as braggards do their blades, which God   *185*

---

155 **curiously** skillfully   156 **woodcock** stupid bird (Claudio reduces
the duel to a carving up of symbols of stupidity—a calf's head, a capon,
and a woodcock)   165 **hath the tongues** knows foreign languages
169 **transshape** distort   171 **prop'rest** most handsome

be thanked hurt not. [*To Don Pedro*] My lord, for
your many courtesies I thank you. I must discon-
tinue your company. Your brother the bastard is
fled from Messina. You have among you killed a
190 sweet and innocent lady. For my Lord Lackbeard
there, he and I shall meet; and till then peace be
with him.   [*Exit.*]

Don Pedro. He is in earnest.

Claudio. In most profound earnest; and, I'll warrant
195 you, for the love of Beatrice.

Don Pedro. And hath challenged thee?

Claudio. Most sincerely.

Don Pedro. What a pretty thing man is when he goes
in his doublet and hose and leaves off his wit!

Enter Constables [*Dogberry, Verges, and the
Watch, with*] *Conrade and Borachio.*

200 *Claudio.* He is then a giant to an ape; but then is an
ape a doctor to such a man.°

Don Pedro. But, soft you, let me be! Pluck up, my
heart, and be sad. Did he not say my brother was
fled?

205 *Dogberry.* Come you, sir. If justice cannot tame you,
she shall ne'er weigh more reasons in her balance.
Nay, and you be a cursing hypocrite once, you must
be looked to.

Don Pedro. How now? Two of my brother's men
210 bound? Borachio one.

Claudio. Hearken after° their offense, my lord.

Don Pedro. Officers, what offense have these men
done?

200–01 **He is then . . . a man** i.e., an ape would consider him important,
but an ape is actually a scholar (**doctor**) compared to such a fool
211 **Hearken after** inquire into

Dogberry. Marry, sir, they have committed false report; moreover, they have spoken untruths; sec-   *215*
ondarily, they are slanders; sixth and lastly, they
have belied a lady; thirdly, they have verified unjust
things; and to conclude, they are lying knaves.

Don Pedro. First, I ask thee what they have done;
thirdly, I ask thee what's their offense; sixth and   *220*
lastly, why they are committed; and to conclude,
what you lay to their charge.

Claudio. Rightly reasoned, and in his own division;
and, by my troth, there's one meaning well suited.°

Don Pedro. Who have you offended, masters, that you   *225*
are thus bound° to your answer? This learned constable is too cunning° to be understood. What's
your offense?

Borachio. Sweet Prince, let me go no farther to mine
answer. Do you hear me, and let this count kill me.   *230*
I have deceived even your very eyes. What your
wisdoms could not discover, these shallow fools
have brought to light, who in the night overheard
me confessing to this man, how Don John your
brother incensed me to slander the Lady Hero;   *235*
how you were brought into the orchard and saw
me court Margaret in Hero's garments; how you
disgraced her when you should marry her. My
villainy they have upon record, which I had rather
seal with my death than repeat over to my shame.   *240*
The lady is dead upon mine and my master's false
accusation; and briefly, I desire nothing but the
reward of a villain.

Don Pedro. Runs not this speech like iron through
your blood?   *245*

Claudio. I have drunk poison whiles he uttered it.

Don Pedro. But did my brother set thee on to this?

---

224 **well suited** well dressed out   226 **bound** arraigned   227 **cunning**
intelligent

Borachio. Yea, and paid me richly for the practice
of it.

250 *Don Pedro.* He is composed and framed of treachery,
And fled he is upon this villainy.

Claudio. Sweet Hero, now thy image doth appear
In the rare semblance that I loved it first.

Dogberry. Come, bring away the plaintiffs. By this
255 time our sexton hath reformed Signior Leonato of
the matter. And, masters, do not forget to specify,
when time and place shall serve, that I am an ass.

Verges. Here, here comes Master Signior Leonato,
and the sexton too.

*Enter Leonato, his brother [Antonio], and the
Sexton.*

260 *Leonato.* Which is the villain? Let me see his eyes,
That, when I note another man like him,
I may avoid him. Which of these is he?

Borachio. If you would know your wronger, look on
me.

Leonato. Art thou the slave that with thy breath hast
killed
Mine innocent child?

265 *Borachio.*   Yea, even I alone.

Leonato. No, not so, villain! Thou beliest thyself.
Here stand a pair of honorable men;
A third is fled, that had a hand in it.
I thank you, princes, for my daughter's death.
270 Record it with your high and worthy deeds.
'Twas bravely done, if you bethink you of it.

Claudio. I know not how to pray your patience;°
Yet I must speak. Choose your revenge yourself;
Impose me to what penance your invention°

272 **pray your patience** ask your forgiveness   274 **invention** imagination

Can lay upon my sin. Yet sinned I not   275
But in mistaking.

Don Pedro.   By my soul, nor I;
And yet, to satisfy this good old man,
I would bend under any heavy weight
That he'll enjoin me to.

Leonato. I cannot bid you bid my daughter live;   280
That were impossible; but I pray you both,
Possess° the people in Messina here
How innocent she died; and if your love
Can labor aught in sad invention,
Hang her an epitaph upon her tomb,   285
And sing it to her bones, sing it tonight.
Tomorrow morning come you to my house;
And since you could not be my son-in-law,
Be yet my nephew. My brother hath a daughter,
Almost the copy of my child that's dead,   290
And she alone is heir to both of us.
Give her the right° you should have giv'n her
      cousin,
And so dies my revenge.

Claudio.   O noble sir!
Your overkindness doth wring tears from me.
I do embrace your offer; and dispose   295
For henceforth of poor Claudio.

Leonato. Tomorrow then I will expect your coming;
Tonight I take my leave. This naughty man
Shall face to face be brought to Margaret,
Who I believe was packed° in all this wrong,   300
Hired to it by your brother.

Borachio.   No, by my soul, she was not;
Nor knew not what she did when she spoke to me;
But always hath been just and virtuous
In anything that I do know by her.

---

282 **Possess** inform   292 **right** (Hero had a right to claim Claudio as her husband; probably there is also a pun on "rite")   300 **packed** combined, i.e., an
accomplice

305 *Dogberry.* Moreover, sir, which indeed is not under
white and black,° this plaintiff here, the offender,
did call me ass. I beseech you let it be rememb'red
in his punishment. And also the watch heard them
talk of one Deformed; they say he wears a key° in
310 his ear, and a lock hanging by it, and borrows
money in God's name, the which he hath used so
long and never paid that now men grow hard-
hearted and will lend nothing for God's sake. Pray
you examine him upon that point.

315 *Leonato.* I thank thee for thy care and honest pains.

Dogberry. Your worship speaks like a most thankful
and reverent youth, and I praise God for you.

Leonato. There's for thy pains.   [*Gives money.*]

Dogberry. God save the foundation!°

320 *Leonato.* Go, I discharge° thee of thy prisoner, and I
thank thee.

Dogberry. I leave an arrant knave with your worship,
which I beseech your worship to correct yourself,
for the example of others. God keep your worship!
325 I wish your worship well. God restore you to health!
I humbly give you leave to depart; and if a merry
meeting may be wished, God prohibit it! Come,
neighbor.   [*Exeunt Dogberry and Verges.*]

Leonato. Until tomorrow morning, lords, farewell.

Antonio. Farewell, my lords. We look for you tomor-
330 row.

Don Pedro. We will not fail.

Claudio.   Tonight I'll mourn with Hero.
              [*Exeunt Don Pedro and Claudio.*]

305–06 **not under white and black** not in the official record   309 **key**
ring (but perhaps Dogberry merely assumes that if a man wears a lock in
his hair he must wear a key too)   319 **the foundation** (as if Leonato
were a charitable institution)   320 **discharge** relieve

Leonato. [*To the Watch*] Bring you these fellows on.
   We'll talk with Margaret,
How her acquaintance grew with this lewd° fellow.
                        Exeunt [*separately*].

[Scene 2. *Leonato's garden.*]

Enter Benedick and Margaret [*meeting*].

Benedick. Pray thee, sweet Mistress Margaret, deserve
   well at my hands by helping me to the speech of
   Beatrice.

Margaret. Will you then write me a sonnet in praise
   of my beauty?   *5*

Benedick. In so high a style,° Margaret, that no man
   living shall come over it; for in most comely truth
   thou deservest it.

Margaret. To have no man come over me!° Why, shall
   I always keep belowstairs?°   *10*

Benedick. Thy wit is as quick as the greyhound's
   mouth; it catches.

Margaret. And yours as blunt as the fencer's foils,
   which hit but hurt not.

Benedick. A most manly wit, Margaret; it will not hurt   *15*
   a woman. And so, I pray thee call Beatrice. I give
   thee the bucklers.°

Margaret. Give us the swords; we have bucklers of
   our own.

Benedick. If you use them, Margaret, you must put   *20*

---

333 **lewd** low   5.2.6 **style** (pun on "stile," a set of steps for passing over
a fence)   9 **come over me** (the beginning of an interchange of sexual innuendoes)   10 **keep belowstairs** dwell in the servants' quarters
16–17 **I give thee the bucklers** I yield

in the pikes° with a vice;° and they are dangerous
weapons for maids.

Margaret. Well, I will call Beatrice to you, who I think
hath legs.   *Exit Margaret.*

25 *Benedick.* And therefore will come.
      [*Sings*]   The god of love,
                        That sits above
                  And knows me, and knows me,
                        How pitiful I deserve—
30   I mean in singing; but in loving, Leander the good
      swimmer, Troilus° the first employer of panders,
      and a whole book full of these quondam carpet-
      mongers,° whose names yet run smoothly in the
      even road of a blank verse—why, they were never
35   so truly turned over and over as my poor self in love.
      Marry, I cannot show it in rhyme. I have tried.
      I can find out no rhyme to "lady" but "baby," an
      innocent rhyme; for "scorn," "horn," a hard rhyme;
      for "school," "fool," a babbling rhyme. Very omi-
40   nous endings. No, I was not born under a rhyming
      planet, nor I cannot woo in festival terms.

                        Enter Beatrice.

      Sweet Beatrice, wouldst thou come when I called
      thee?

Beatrice. Yea, signior, and depart when you bid me.

45 *Benedick.* O, stay but till then!

Beatrice. "Then" is spoken. Fare you well now. And
      yet, ere I go, let me go with that I came, which is,
      with knowing what hath passed between you and
      Claudio.

50 *Benedick.* Only foul words; and thereupon I will kiss
      thee.

---

21 **pikes** spikes in the center of bucklers   21 **vice** screw   30–31 **Leander . . . Troilus** (legendary lovers; Leander nightly swam the Hellespont
to visit Hero, Troilus was aided in his love for Cressida by Pan-
darus)   32–33 **quondam carpetmongers** ancient boudoir knights

Beatrice. Foul words is but foul wind, and foul wind is but foul breath, and foul breath is noisome. Therefore I will depart unkissed.

Benedick. Thou hast frighted the word out of his right 55
sense, so forcible is thy wit. But I must tell thee plainly, Claudio undergoes my challenge; and either I must shortly hear from him or I will subscribe him° a coward. And I pray thee now tell me, for which of my bad parts didst thou first fall in love 60
with me?

Beatrice. For them all together, which maintained so politic a state° of evil that they will not admit any good part to intermingle with them. But for which of my good parts did you first suffer love for me? 65

Benedick. Suffer love! A good epithet. I do suffer love indeed, for I love thee against my will.

Beatrice. In spite of your heart, I think. Alas, poor heart! If you spite it for my sake, I will spite it for yours, for I will never love that which my friend 70
hates.

Benedick. Thou and I are too wise to woo peaceably.

Beatrice. It appears not in this confession. There's not one wise man among twenty that will praise himself.

Benedick. An old, an old instance,° Beatrice, that 75
lived in the time of good neighbors. If a man do not erect in this age his own tomb ere he dies, he shall live no longer in monument than the bell rings and the widow weeps.

Beatrice. And how long is that, think you? 80

Benedick. Question: why, an hour in clamor and a quarter in rheum;° therefore is it most expedient for the wise, if Don Worm, his conscience, find no impediment to the contrary, to be the trumpet of

---

58–59 **subscribe him** write him down   63 **politic a state** well-ordered a community   75 **instance** example   82 **rheum** tears

85   his own virtues, as I am to myself. So much for
praising myself, who, I myself will bear witness, is
praiseworthy. And now tell me, how doth your
cousin?

Beatrice. Very ill.

90 *Benedick.* And how do you?

Beatrice. Very ill too.

Benedick. Serve God, love me, and mend. There will
I leave you too, for here comes one in haste.

Enter Ursula.

Ursula. Madam, you must come to your uncle. Yon-
95   der's old coil° at home. It is proved my Lady Hero
hath been falsely accused, the Prince and Claudio
mightily abused, and Don John is the author of all,
who is fled and gone. Will you come presently?

Beatrice. Will you go hear this news, signior?

100 *Benedick.* I will live in thy heart, die in thy lap, and
be buried in thy eyes; and moreover, I will go with
thee to thy uncle's.   *Exit [with Beatrice and Ursula].*

[Scene 3. *A church.*]

*Enter Claudio, Prince [Don Pedro, Lord,] and
three or four with tapers [followed by Musicians].*

Claudio. Is this the monument of Leonato?

Lord. It is, my lord.

[*Claudio reads from a scroll.*]

---

95 **old coil** plenty of confusion

Epitaph.

Done to death by slanderous tongues
   Was the Hero that here lies;
Death, in guerdon° of her wrongs,   5
   Gives her fame which never dies.
So the life that died with shame
 .Lives in death with glorious fame.
              [*Hangs up the scroll.*]
Hang thou there upon the tomb,
Praising her when I am dumb.   10

Claudio. Now, music, sound, and sing your solemn
   hymn.

Song.

Pardon, goddess of the night,°
Those that slew thy virgin knight;
For the which, with songs of woe,
Round about her tomb they go.   15
Midnight, assist our moan;
Help us to sigh and groan,
   Heavily, heavily.
Graves, yawn and yield your dead,
Till death be utterèd,   20
   Heavily, heavily.

Claudio. Now unto thy bones good night!
   Yearly will I do this rite.

Don Pedro. Good morrow, masters; put your torches
   out.
   The wolves have preyed, and look, the gentle
   day,   25
Before the wheels of Phoebus,° round about
   Dapples the drowsy east with spots of gray.
Thanks to you all, and leave us. Fare you well.

Claudio. Good morrow, masters; each his several way.

5.3.5 **guerdon** reward   12 **goddess of the night** Diana, goddess of the moon
and of chastity   26 **wheels of Phoebus** wheels of the sun god's chariot

Don Pedro. Come, let us hence and put on other
30   weeds,°
       And then to Leonato's we will go.

Claudio. And Hymen° now with luckier issue speeds°
       Than this for whom we rend'red up this woe.

                                             Exeunt.

[Scene 4. *Leonato's house.*]

*Enter Leonato, Benedick, [Beatrice,] Margaret,
Ursula, Old Man [Antonio], Friar [Francis],
Hero.*

Friar. Did I not tell you she was innocent?

Leonato. So are the Prince and Claudio, who accused
       her
       Upon the error that you heard debated.
       But Margaret was in some fault for this,
5   Although against her will, as it appears
       In the true course of all the question.°

Antonio. Well, I am glad that all things sorts° so well.

Benedick. And so am I, being else by faith enforced
       To call young Claudio to a reckoning for it.

10 **Leonato.** Well, daughter, and you gentlewomen all,
       Withdraw into a chamber by yourselves,
       And when I send for you, come hither masked.
       The Prince and Claudio promised by this hour
       To visit me. You know your office, brother;
15   You must be father to your brother's daughter,
       And give her to young Claudio.   *Exeunt Ladies.*

Antonio. Which I will do with confirmed° counte-
       nance.

---

30 **weeds** apparel   32 **Hymen** god of marriage   32 **speeds** succeeds
5.4.6 **question** investigation   7 **sorts** turn out   17 **confirmed** steady

Benedick. Friar, I must entreat your pains, I think.

Friar. To do what, signior?

Benedick. To bind me, or undo me—one of them.   20
  Signior Leonato, truth it is, good signior,
  Your niece regards me with an eye of favor.

Leonato. That eye my daughter lent her; 'tis most true.

Benedick. And I do with an eye of love requite her.

Leonato. The sight whereof I think you had from me,   25
  From Claudio, and the Prince. But what's your will?

Benedick. Your answer, sir, is enigmatical.
  But, for my will, my will is, your good will
  May stand with ours, this day to be conjoined
  In the state of honorable marriage;   30
  In which, good friar, I shall desire your help.

Leonato. My heart is with your liking.

Friar.   And my help.
  Here comes the Prince and Claudio.

    Enter Prince [Don Pedro] and Claudio and two
        or three other.

Don Pedro. Good morrow to this fair assembly.

Leonato. Good morrow, Prince; good morrow, Clau-
  dio.   35
  We here attend you. Are you yet determined
  Today to marry with my brother's daughter?

Claudio. I'll hold my mind, were she an Ethiope.

Leonato. Call her forth, brother. Here's the friar
  ready.   [*Exit Antonio.*]

Don Pedro. Good morrow, Benedick. Why, what's the
  matter   40
  That you have such a February face,
  So full of frost, of storm, and cloudiness?

Claudio. I think he thinks upon the savage bull.°
    Tush, fear not, man! We'll tip thy horns with gold,°
45 And all Europa° shall rejoice at thee,
    As once Europa did at lusty Jove
    When he would play the noble beast in love.

Benedick. Bull Jove, sir, had an amiable low,
    And some such strange bull leaped your father's
      cow
50 And got a calf in that same noble feat
    Much like to you, for you have just his bleat.°

    Enter [Leonato's] brother [Antonio], Hero,
  Beatrice, Margaret, Ursula, [the ladies wearing
            masks].

Claudio. For this I owe you.° Here comes other
    reck'nings.
    Which is the lady I must seize upon?

Antonio. This same is she, and I do give you her.

Claudio. Why then, she's mine. Sweet, let me see your
55   face.

Leonato. No, that you shall not till you take her hand
    Before this friar and swear to marry her.

Claudio. Give me your hand; before this holy friar
    I am your husband if you like of me.

60 *Hero.* And when I lived I was your other wife; *[un-
    masking]*
    And when you loved you were my other husband.

Claudio. Another Hero!

Hero.   Nothing certainer.
    One Hero died defiled; but I do live,
    And surely as I live, I am a maid.

---

43 savage bull (refers to 1.1.252)   **44 tip thy horns with gold** i.e., make
your cuckolding something to be proud of   **45 Europa** Europe (though
in the next line the word designates the girl that Jupiter wooed in the guise
of a bull)   **52 I owe you** i.e., I will pay you back (for calling me a calf
and a bastard)

Don Pedro. The former Hero! Hero that is dead! 65

Leonato. She died, my lord, but whiles° her slander
lived.

Friar. All this amazement can I qualify,°
When, after that the holy rites are ended,
I'll tell you largely° of fair Hero's death.
Meantime let wonder seem familiar, 70
And to the chapel let us presently.

Benedick. Soft and fair, friar. Which is Beatrice?

Beatrice. [*Unmasking*] I answer to that name. What is
your will?

Benedick. Do not you love me?

Beatrice.　　　　　Why, no; no more than reason.

Benedick. Why, then your uncle, and the Prince, and
Claudio 75
Have been deceived—they swore you did.

Beatrice. Do not you love me?

Benedick.　　　　　Troth, no; no more than reason.

Beatrice. Why, then my cousin, Margaret, and Ursula
Are much deceived; for they did swear you did.

Benedick. They swore that you were almost sick for
me. 80

Beatrice. They swore that you were well-nigh dead for
me.

Benedick. 'Tis no such matter. Then you do not love
me?

Beatrice. No, truly, but in friendly recompense.

Leonato. Come, cousin, I am sure you love the gentleman.

Claudio. And I'll be sworn upon't that he loves her; 85
For here's a paper written in his hand,

---

66 **but whiles** only while   67 **qualify** abate   69 **largely** in detail

A halting° sonnet of his own pure brain,
Fashioned to Beatrice.

Hero.   And here's another,
Writ in my cousin's hand, stol'n from her pocket,
90 Containing her affection unto Benedick.

Benedick. A miracle! Here's our own hands against our
hearts. Come, I will have thee; but, by this light, I
take thee for pity.

Beatrice. I would not deny you; but, by this good day,
95 I yield upon great persuasion, and partly to save
your life, for I was told you were in a consumption.

Benedick.° Peace! I will stop your mouth. [*Kisses her.*]

Don Pedro. How dost thou, Benedick, the married
man?

100 *Benedick.* I'll tell thee what, Prince: a college of wit-
crackers cannot flout me out of my humor. Dost
thou think I care for a satire or an epigram? No. If
a man will be beaten with brains, 'a shall wear nothing handsome about him. In brief, since I do pur-
105 pose to marry, I will think nothing to any purpose
that the world can say against it; and therefore never
flout at me for what I have said against it; for man
is a giddy thing, and this is my conclusion. For thy
part, Claudio, I did think to have beaten thee; but in
110 that thou art like to be my kinsman, live unbruised,
and love my cousin.

Claudio. I had well hoped thou wouldst have denied
Beatrice, that I might have cudgeled thee out of thy
single life, to make thee a double-dealer,° which out
115 of question thou wilt be if my cousin do not look
exceeding narrowly to thee.

Benedick. Come, come, we are friends. Let's have a

---

87 **halting** limping   97 **Benedick** (both Quarto and Folio assign this line
to Leonato; possibly the original reading is correct, and Leonato forces
Benedick to kiss Beatrice)   114 **double-dealer** (1) married man (2) unfaithful husband

dance ere we are married, that we may lighten our
own hearts and our wives' heels.

Leonato. We'll have dancing afterward.   *120*

Benedick. First, of my word; therefore play, music.
Prince, thou art sad; get thee a wife, get thee a wife!
There is no staff more reverend than one tipped with
horn.°
                    Enter Messenger.

Messenger. My lord, your brother John is ta'en in
     flight,   *125*
And brought with armèd men back to Messina.

Benedick. Think not on him till tomorrow. I'll devise
thee brave punishments for him. Strike up, pipers!
                    Dance. [*Exeunt.*]

                    FINIS.

123–24 **with horn** (final reference to the horns of a cuckold)

Textual Note

The present text of *Much Ado About Nothing* is based upon the Quarto edition of the play, published in 1600. The Folio text of 1623 is a slightly edited version of this Quarto.

The first stage direction in the Quarto (repeated in the Folio) includes what is sometimes called a phantom character, a character who never speaks and who is never addressed. After "Leonato Governor of Messina" the stage direction adds "Innogen his wife" (see page lxxiii). Presumably Shakespeare thought he would create this character, but then found, as he wrote the scene, that he had no need for her. In all probability we have evidence here that the printer's copy was Shakespeare's manuscript, rather than a theatrical promptbook. Other bits of evidence tend to confirm this view that we are close to the author's table. In 1.2, Antonio is designated "Old" in the Quarto, meaning old man. In 2.1, Antonio's speeches are assigned to "Brother." In 4.2, "Kemp" and "Cowley," the actors intended for the roles, are assigned the speeches for Dogberry and Verges. At the beginning of 5.3, a stage direction calls for "three or four with tapers."

The present edition regularizes all speech prefixes. All act and scene divisions are bracketed, since (like indications of locale) these are not in the Quarto. Spelling and punctuation have been modernized, and obvious typographical errors have been corrected. The positions of a few stage directions have been slightly altered; necessary directions that are not given in the Quarto are added in brackets. Other substantial departures from the Quarto are listed below, the adopted reading first, in italics, and then the Quarto's reading in roman type. If the adopted reading comes from the Folio, the fact is indicated by [F] following it.

1.1. s.d. [Q has "Innogen his wife," i.e., Leonato's wife, before "Hero"; she does not appear in the play]   1*Don Pedro* Don Peter   9–10 *Don Pedro* Don Peter   195 *Enter Don Pedro* Enter don Pedro, Iohn the bastard

2.1. s.d. *Hero* his wife, Hero *niece* neece, and a kinsman 84 s.d. *Don John* or dumb Iohn   208 s.d. [Q adds "Iohn and Borachio, and Conrade"]

2.3.138 *us of* [F] of vs

3.2.52 *Don Pedro* [F] Bene

4.2 s.d. [Q places "Borachio" immediately after "Constables"]

5.3.10 *dumb* [F] dead   22 *Claudio* Lo[rd]

5.4.54 *Antonio* Leo   97 *Benedick* Leon

A Note on the Sources of
Much Ado About Nothing

Much Ado About Nothing combines two plots, the Hero-Claudio tragicomic one and the Beatrice-Benedick comic one. Shakespeare himself seems to have hit on the idea of joining the two, though if he knew of an earlier work in which they had already been combined, he surely would not have scrupled to follow suit.

The gist of the Hero-Claudio plot—a girl is said to be false and her fiancé is so deceived that he denounces her, though later they are reconciled—is ancient. It is also the basis of a series of stories popular in the sixteenth century. It can scarcely be doubted that Shakespeare knew it in the versions of Ariosto (*Orlando Furioso* was translated by Sir John Harington and plundered by Edmund Spenser) and Bandello (the *Novelle* were translated into French by Belleforest). Quite possibly Shakespeare was acquainted with a number of other versions. Shakespeare's own addition of Dogberry and Verges, for which at best he had only bare hints, gives this Hero-Claudio plot most of its vitality.

The comic intrigue of Beatrice and Benedick is scarcely a plot, and it would be foolish to attempt to isolate a source for it. Sixteenth-century literature offers numerous ladies and gentlemen who wittily scorn each other. In the English drama before Shakespeare, John Lyly had made something of a specialty of such combats. There are, moreover, nondramatic works (Lyly is again reluctant) that may also have given Shakespeare hints. Possibly a paragraph in Castiglione's *Il Cortegiano* (translated by Sir Thomas Hoby) sparked his imagination:

> I have also seen a most fervent love spring in the heart of a woman toward one that seemed at first not to bear him the least

affection in the world, only for that they heard say that the opinion of many was that they loved together.

It should be remembered, too, that Beatrice and Benedick are not Shakespeare's first witty, bickering lovers. In *Love's Labor's Lost*, Biron ("not a word with him but a jest") and Rosaline ("A wightly wanton") anticipate Beatrice and Benedick.

Passages from several books that probably influenced *Much Ado* are given in the second volume of Geoffrey Bullough's *Narrative and Dramatic Sources of Shakespeare*, but when one has read *Much Ado* each source seems like Charles Lamb's poor relation: "the most irrelevant thing in nature—a piece of impertinent correspondency."

Commentaries

CHARLES GILDON

The Argument of *Much Ado About Nothing*

The scene lies at Messina in Sicily and in and near the house of Leonato. Don Pedro of Aragon with his favorite Claudio, and Benedick a gay young cavalier of Padua, and Don John the bastard brother of Don Pedro, come to Leonato's, the Governor of Messina. Claudio is in love with Hero, Leonato's daughter, whom Don Pedro obtains for him, and while they wait the wedding day, they consult how to make Benedick and Beatrice, the niece of Leonato, in love with each other, both being gay and easy and averse to love and like great talkers, railing always at each other. However, by letting them overhear their discourse they persuade them that they are in love with each other. In the meantime Don John, the very soul of envy and mischief, contrives how to break the match betwixt Claudio and Hero, and to this purpose, by his engines, Conrade and Borachio, they make Claudio and the Prince believe that Hero is a wanton and put a plausible cheat on them to confirm the suspicion by having Borachio talk to Hero's maid, Margaret, at the chamber window at midnight, as if she were Hero. Convinced by this fallacy, Claudio and Don Pedro disgrace her in the church where he went to marry her, rejecting her, and accusing her of wantonness with another. Hero swoons away, and the priest interposing and, joining in the attestation she makes of her virtue, she is privately conveyed away and reported dead. The rogue Borachio being taken by the watch, as he

From *The Works of Mr. William Shakespear*, 1710.

was telling the adventure to his comrade, discovers the villainy and clears Hero; but Don John is fled. Her innocence being known, her father is satisfied with Claudio, that he hang verses on her tomb that night and marry a niece of his the next morning without seeing her face, which he agrees to and performs, and then it is discovered that it is Hero whom he married and so the play ends with an account of Don John's being taken.

This fable is as full of absurdities as the writing is full of beauties: the first I leave to the reader to find out by the rules I have laid down; the second I shall endeavor to show and point out some few of the many that are contained in the play. Shakespear indeed had the misfortune which other of our poets have since had of laying his scene in a warm climate where the manners of the people are very different from ours, and yet he has made them talk and act generally like men of a colder country; *Marriage à la Mode* has the same fault.

This play we must call a comedy, though some of the incidents and discourses too are more in a tragic strain; and that of the accusation of Hero is too shocking for either tragedy or comedy; nor could it have come off in nature, if we regard the country, without the death of more than Hero. The imposition on the Prince and Claudio seems very lame, and Claudio's conduct to the woman he loved highly contrary to the very nature of love, to expose her in so barbarous a manner and with so little concern and struggle, and on such weak grounds without a farther examination into the matter, yet the passions this produces in the old father make a wonderful amends for the fault. Besides which there is such a pleasing variety of characters in the play, and those perfectly maintained, as well as distinguished, that you lose the absurdities of the conduct in the excellence of the manners, sentiments, diction, and topics. Benedick and Beatrice are two sprightly, witty, talkative characters, and, though of the same nature, yet perfectly distinguished, and you have no need to read the names to know who speaks. As they differ from each other, though so near akin, so do they from that of Lucio in *Measure for Measure*, who is likewise a very talkative person; but there is a gross abusiveness, calumny, lying, and lewdness in Lucio, which Benedick is free from. One is a rake's mirth and tattle; the other that of a gentleman and a man of spirit and wit.

The stratagem of the Prince on Benedick and Beatrice is managed with that nicety and address that we are very well pleased with the success and think it very reasonable and just.

The character of Don John the Bastard is admirably distinguished, his manners are well marked, and everywhere convenient or agreeable. Being a sour, melancholy, saturnine, envious, selfish, malicious temper—manners necessary to produce these villainous events they did—these were productive of the catastrophe, for he was not a person brought in to fill up the number only, because without him the fable could not have gone on.

To quote all the comic excellencies of this play would be to transcribe three parts of it. For all that passes betwixt Benedick and Beatrice is admirable. His discourse against love and marriage in the later end of the second act is very pleasant and witty, and that which Beatrice says of wooing, wedding, and repenting. And the aversion that the poet gives Benedick and Beatrice for each other in their discourse heightens the jest of making them in love with one another. Nay, the variety and natural distinction of the vulgar humors of this play are remarkable.

The scenes of this play are something obscure, for you can scarce tell where the place is in the two first acts, though the scenes in them seem pretty entire and unbroken. But those are things we ought not to look much for in Shakespear. But whilst he is out in the dramatic imitation of the fable, he always draws men and women so perfectly that when we read, we can scarce persuade ourselves but that the discourse is real and no fiction.

LEWIS CARROLL

A Letter to Ellen Terry

Now I'm going to put before you a "Hero-ic" puzzle of mine, but please remember I do not ask for your solution of it, as you will persist in believing, if I ask your help in a Shakespeare difficulty, that I am only jesting! However, if you won't attack it yourself, perhaps you would ask Mr. Irving someday how *he* explains it?

My difficulty is this: Why in the world did not Hero (or at any rate Beatrice on her behalf) prove an "alibi" in answer to the charge? It seems certain that she did *not* sleep in her room that night; for how could Margaret venture to open the window and talk from it, with her mistress asleep in the room? It would be sure to wake her. Besides Borachio says, after promising that Margaret shall speak with him out of Hero's chamber window, "I will so fashion the matter that Hero shall be absent." (*How* he could possibly manage any such thing is another difficulty, but I pass over that.) Well then, granting that Hero slept in some other room that night, why didn't she say so? When Claudio asks her: "What man was he talked with you yesternight out at your window betwixt twelve and one?" why doesn't she reply: "I talked with no man at that hour, my lord. Nor was I in my chamber yesternight, but in another, far from it, remote." And this she could, of course, prove by the evidence of the housemaids, who must have known that she had occupied another room that night.

But even if Hero might be supposed to be so distracted as not to remember where she had slept the night before, or

From *The Story of My Life* by Ellen Terry. 2nd ed. (London: Hutchinson and Company, n.d.).

even whether she had slept *anywhere*, surely *Beatrice* has her wits about her! And when an arrangement was made, by which she was to lose, for one night, her twelve-months' bedfellow, is it conceivable that she didn't know *where* Hero passed the night? Why didn't *she* reply:

> But good my lord sweet Hero slept not there:
> She had another chamber for the nonce.
> 'Twas sure some counterfeit that did present
> Her person at the window, aped her voice,
> Her mien, her manners, and hath thus deceived
> My good Lord Pedro and this company?

With all these excellent materials for proving an "alibi" it is incomprehensible that no one should think of it. If only there had been a barrister present, to cross-examine Beatrice! "Now, ma'am, attend to me, please, and speak up so that the jury can hear you. Where did you sleep last night? Where did Hero sleep? Will you swear that she slept in her own room? Will you swear that you do not know where she slept?" I feel inclined to quote old Mr. Weller and to say to Beatrice at the end of the play (only I'm afraid it isn't etiquette to speak across the footlights):

"Oh, Samivel, Samivel, vy vornt there a halibi?"

GEORGE BERNARD SHAW

Shakespear's Merry Gentlemen

MUCH ADO ABOUT NOTHING. St. James's Theatre, 16
February 1898.   [26 *February* 1898]

   Much Ado is perhaps the most dangerous actor-manager
trap in the whole Shakespearean repertory. It is not a safe
play like *The Merchant of Venice* or *As You Like It*, nor a
serious play like *Hamlet*. Its success depends on the way it
is handled in performance; and that, again, depends on
the actor-manager being enough of a critic to discriminate
ruthlessly between the pretension of the author and his
achievement.
   The main pretension in *Much Ado* is that Benedick and
Beatrice are exquisitely witty and amusing persons. They
are, of course, nothing of the sort. Benedick's pleasantries
might pass at a singsong in a public-house parlor; but a
gentleman rash enough to venture on them in even the very
mildest £52-a-year suburban imitation of polite society today would assuredly never be invited again. From his first
joke, "Were you in doubt, sir, that you asked her?" to his
last, "There is no staff more reverend than one tipped with
horn," he is not a wit, but a blackguard. He is not Shakespear's only failure in that genre. It took the Bard a long
time to grow out of the provincial conceit that made him
so fond of exhibiting his accomplishments as a master of
gallant badinage. The very thought of Biron, Mercutio,
Gratiano, and Benedick must, I hope, have covered him
with shame in his later years. Even Hamlet's airy compli-
ments to Ophelia before the court would make a cabman
blush. But at least Shakespear did not value himself on

From *Our Theatres in the Nineties* by George Bernard Shaw. 3 vols. (London: Constable & Co., Ltd., 1932). Reprinted by permission of the Public
Trustee and the Society of Authors.

Hamlet's indecent jests as he evidently did on those of the four merry gentlemen of the earlier plays. When he at last got conviction of sin, and saw this sort of levity in its proper light, he made masterly amends by presenting the blackguard *as* a blackguard in the person of Lucio in *Measure for Measure*. Lucio, as a character study, is worth forty Benedicks and Birons. His obscenity is not only inoffensive, but irresistibly entertaining, because it is drawn with perfect skill, offered at its true value, and given its proper interest, without any complicity of the author in its lewdness. Lucio is much more of a gentleman than Benedick, because he keeps his coarse sallies for coarse people. Meeting one woman, he says humbly, "Gentle and fair: your brother kindly greets you. Not to be weary with you, he's in prison." Meeting another, he hails her sparkingly with "How now? which of your hips has the more profound sciatica?" The woman is a lay sister, the other a prostitute. Benedick or Mercutio would have cracked their low jokes on the lay sister, and been held up as gentlemen of rare wit and excellent discourse for it. Whenever they approach a woman or an old man, you shiver with apprehension as to what brutality they will come out with.

Precisely the same thing, in the tenderer degree of her sex, is true of Beatrice. In her character of professed wit she has only one subject, and that is the subject which a really witty woman never jests about, because it is too serious a matter to a woman to be made light of without indelicacy. Beatrice jests about it for the sake of the indelicacy. There is only one thing worse than the Elizabethan "merry gentleman," and that is the Elizabethan "merry lady."

Why is it then that we still want to see Benedick and Beatrice, and that our most eminent actors and actresses still want to play them? Before I answer that very simple question let me ask another. Why is it that Da Ponte's "dramma giocosa," entitled *Don Giovanni,* a loathsome story of a coarse, witless, worthless libertine, who kills an old man in a duel and is finally dragged down through a trapdoor to hell by his twaddling ghost, is still, after more than a century, as "immortal" as *Much Ado*? Simply because Mozart clothed it with wonderful music, which turned the worthless words and thoughts of Da Ponte into a magical human drama of

moods and transitions of feeling. That is what happened in a
smaller way with *Much Ado*. Shakespear shews himself in it
a commonplace librettist working on a stolen plot, but a
great musician. No matter how poor, coarse, cheap, and obvious the thought may be, the mood is charming, and the
music of the words expresses the mood. Paraphrase the encounters of Benedick and Beatrice in the style of a blue-
book, carefully preserving every idea they present, and it
will become apparent to the most infatuated Shakespearean
that they contain at best nothing out of the common in
thought or wit, and at worst a good deal of vulgar naughti-
ness. Paraphrase Goethe, Wagner, or Ibsen in the same way,
and you will find original observation, subtle thought, wide
comprehension, far-reaching intuition, and serious psychological study in them. Give Shakespear a fairer chance in
the comparison by paraphrasing even his best and maturest
work, and you will still get nothing more than the platitudes
of proverbial philosophy, with a very occasional curiosity in
the shape of a rudiment of some modern idea, not followed
up. Not until the Shakespearean music is added by replacing
the paraphrase with the original lines does the enchantment
begin. Then you are in another world at once. When a
flower girl tells a coster to hold his jaw, for nobody is listening to him, and he retorts, "Oh, you're there, are you, you
beauty?" they reproduce the wit of Beatrice and Benedick
exactly. But put it this way: "I wonder that you will still be
talking, Signior Benedick: nobody marks you." "What! my
dear Lady Disdain, are you yet living?" You are miles away
from costerland at once. When I tell you that Benedick and
the coster are equally poor in thought, Beatrice and the
flower girl equally vulgar in repartee, you reply that I might
as well tell you that a nightingale's love is no higher than a
cat's. Which is exactly what I do tell you, though the
nightingale is the better musician. You will admit, perhaps,
that the love of the worst human singer in the world is accompanied by a higher degree of intellectual consciousness
than that of the most ravishingly melodious nightingale.
Well, in just the same way, there are plenty of quite second-
rate writers who are abler thinkers and wits than William,
though they are unable to weave his magic into the expression of their thoughts.

It is not easy to knock this into the public head, because comparatively few of Shakespear's admirers are at all conscious that they are listening to music as they hear his phrases turn and his lines fall so fascinatingly and memorably; whilst we all, no matter how stupid we are, can understand his jokes and platitudes, and are flattered when we are told of the subtlety of the wit we have relished, and the profundity of the thought we have fathomed. Englishmen are specially susceptible to this sort of flattery, because intellectual subtlety is not their strong point. In dealing with them you must make them believe that you are appealing to their brains when you are really appealing to their senses and feelings. With Frenchmen the case is reversed: you must make them believe that you are appealing to their senses and feelings when you are really appealing to their brains. The Englishman, slave to every sentimental ideal and dupe of every sensuous art, will have it that his great national poet is a thinker. The Frenchman, enslaved and duped only by systems and calculations, insists on his hero being a sentimentalist and artist. That is why Shakespear is esteemed a mastermind in England and wondered at as a clumsy barbarian in France.

However indiscriminate the public may be in its Shakespear worship, the actor and actress who are to make a success of *Much Ado* must know better. Let them once make the popular mistake of supposing that what they have to do is to bring out the wit of Benedick and Beatrice, and they are lost. Their business in the "merry" passages is to cover poverty of thought and coarseness of innuendo by making the most of the grace and dignity of the diction. The sincere, genuinely dramatic passages will then take care of themselves. Alas! Mr. Alexander and Miss Julia Neilson have made the plunge without waiting for my advice. Miss Neilson, throwing away all her grace and all her music, strives to play the merry lady by dint of conscientious gamboling. Instead of uttering her speeches as exquisitely as possible, she rattles through them, laying an impossible load of archness on every insignificant conjunction, and clipping all the important words until there is no measure or melody left in them. Not even the wedding scene can stop her: after an indignant attitude or two she redoubles her former skittishness. I can only implore her to give up all her deep-laid Beatricisms, to discard the movements of Miss Ellen Terry, the voice of Mrs. Patrick Campbell, and the gaiety of Miss Kitty Loftus, and try the effect of Julia Neilson in all her grave grace taken quite seriously. Mr. Alexander makes the same mistake, though, being more judicious than Miss Neilson, he does not carry it out so disastrously. His merry gentleman is patently a dutiful assumption from beginning to end. He smiles, rackets, and bounds up and down stairs like a quiet man who has just been rated by his wife for habitual dullness before company. It is all hopeless: the charm of Benedick cannot be realized by the spryness of the actor's legs, the flashing of his teeth, or the rattle of his laugh: nothing but the music of the words—above all, not their meaning—can save the part. I wish I could persuade Mr. Alexander that if he were to play the part exactly as he played Guy Domville, it would at once become ten times more fascinating. He should at least take the revelation of Beatrice's supposed love for him with perfect seriousness. The more remorsefully sympathetic Benedick is when she comes to bid him to dinner after he has been gulled into believing she loves him, the more exquisitely ridiculous the scene becomes. It is the audience's turn to laugh then, not Benedick's.

Of all Sir Henry Irving's manifold treasons against Shakespear, the most audacious was his virtually cutting Dogberry out of *Much Ado*. Mr. Alexander does not go so far; but he omits the fifth scene of the third act, upon which the whole effect of the later scenes depends, since it is from it that the audience really gets Dogberry's measure. Dogberry is a capital study of parochial character. Sincerely played, he always comes out as a very real and highly entertaining person. At the St. James's, I grieve to say, he does not carry a moment's conviction: he is a mere mouthpiece for malapropisms, all of which he shouts at the gallery with intense consciousness of their absurdity, and with open anxiety lest they should pass unnoticed. Surely it is clear, if anything histrionic is clear, that Dogberry's first qualification must be a complete unconsciousness of himself as he appears to others.

Verges, even more dependent than Dogberry on that cut-out

scene with Lenato, is almost annihilated by its excision; and it was hardly worth wasting Mr. Esmond on the remainder.

When I have said that neither Benedick nor Beatrice have seen sufficiently through the weakness of Shakespear's merriments to concentrate themselves on the purely artistic qualities of their parts, and that Dogberry is nothing but an excuse for a few laughs, I have made a somewhat heavy deduction from my praises of the revival. But these matters are hardly beyond remedy; and the rest is excellent. Miss Fay Davis's perfect originality contrasts strongly with Miss Neilson's incorrigible imitativeness. Her physical grace is very remarkable; and she creates her part between its few lines, as Hero must if she is to fill up her due place in the drama. Mr. Fred Terry is a most engaging Don Pedro; and Mr. H. B. Irving is a striking Don John, though he is becoming too accomplished an actor to make shift with that single smile which is as well known at the St. James's by this time as the one wig of Mr. Pinero's hero was at "The Wells." Mr. Vernon and Mr. Beveridge are, of course, easily within their powers as Leonato and Antonio; and all the rest come off with credit—even Mr. Loraine, who has not a trace of Claudio in him. The dresses are superb, and the scenery very handsome, though Italy contains so many palaces and chapels that are better than handsome that I liked the opening scenes best. If Mr. Alexander will only make up his mind that the piece is irresistible as poetry, and hopeless as epigrammatic comedy, he need not fear for its success. But if he and Miss Neilson persist in depending on its attempts at wit and gallantry, then it remains to be seen whether the public's sense of duty or its boredom will get the upper hand.

I had intended to deal here with the O.U.D.S. and its performance of *Romeo and Juliet*; but *Much Ado* has carried me too far; so I must postpone Oxford until next week.

DONALD A. STAUFFER

From Shakespeare's World of Images

The spirit of the farces, *The Taming of the Shrew* and *The Merry Wives of Windsor*, most nearly parallels the approach to romantic love in *Much Ado About Nothing*. Like them, this play is written with more than a dash of prosaic common sense. Portia's real home had been in the gardens and galleries of Belmont, from which she sallies forth into the world of action like a feminine and effective Don Quixote. But in *Much Ado About Nothing* Shakespeare's sympathy from the beginning lies with the hardheaded and sharp-tongued Benedick and Beatrice. The play constitutes his severest criticism to date of the weaknesses lying in romantic love. He takes as his main plot a highly fanciful story—what could be more romantic than a crucial scene in which a lady swoons into supposed death upon hearing her honor falsely traduced by her lover at the altar? Yet the lady Hero, shadowy and almost silent, is strangely ineffective, the villain is little more than a conventional malcontent, and Shakespeare is satisfied to develop in a few fine touches the weak impulses of his smart young gentleman Claudio.[1]

So full of tricks is fancy, that Claudio in his melodramatic scene of accusation, rails against the "cunning sin" and "savage sensuality" of his Hero, who is as modest, chaste, and sincere in reality as he accuses her of being only in "exterior

From *Shakespeare's World of Images* by Donald A. Stauffer (New York: W. W. Norton and Company, Inc., 1949; London: Oxford University Press, 1952). Copyright, 1949, by W. W. Norton and Company, Inc., and reprinted by their permission.

[1] His misliking is as sudden as his liking, and at the first zephyr of suspicion he is quick to note that "beauty is a witch /Against whose charms faith melteth into blood" (2.1.177–78). Benedick sees him as a "poor hurt fowl" that will "now . . . creep into sedges" (2.1.200–01).

shows." He willfully makes over the world to his own mistaken misogyny:

> On my eyelids shall conjecture hang,
> To turn all beauty into thoughts of harm,
> And never shall it more be gracious.   (4.1.105–7)

Before he is forgiven and restored to his happiness, the Friar insists that the crime must be purged and punished in the place where it was committed—Claudio's own mind. Slander must change to remorse.

> Th' idea of her life shall sweetly creep
> Into his study of imagination, . . .
> Into the eye and prospect of his soul . . .
>   Then shall he mourn . . .
> And wish he had not so accusèd her.   (223–31)

The reconciliation scene is as melodramatic as the denunciation. It too plays with the paradoxes of true love that transcends, or runs counter to, this world of shadows. The resurrected Hero presents the truth as a conceit:

> And when I lived I was your other wife;
> And when you loved you were my other husband.   (5.4.60–61)

Leonato enforces love's transcendence: "She died, my lord, but whiles her slander liv'd." And the Friar reaffirms the joy and the remorse before the miraculous grace of love that will not die: "Meantime let wonder seem familiar."

The trouble is that in the main plot wonder does not seem familiar enough. The operatic situations and the ill-developed or poorly motivated characters are not convincing. Shakespeare rescues them through his favorites, Benedick and Beatrice. The denunciation scene turns from verse to prose, from melodrama to drama, when the stage is left to the two lovers and Benedick asks the question that shows again Shakespeare's dramatic use of silence: "Lady Beatrice, have you wept all this while?" (4.1.254) She does not weep much longer, nor does she allow Benedick to fall into conventional vows of love. When he protests: "Bid me do anything for thee," she answers in two words: "Kill Claudio." (287)[2] As she thinks of Claudio, her bitter eloquence pronounces a moral judgment not only on his blindness but on the unnecessary cruelty of his procedure:

> O that I were a man! What, bear her in hand until they come to take hands; and then with public accusation, uncovered slander, unmitigated rancor—O God, that I were a man! I would eat his heart in the market place! (301-5)

Mere words are useless. When Benedick swears "By this hand, I love thee," Beatrice retorts: "Use it for my love some other way than swearing by it" (322–25). And Benedick replies with equal economy: "Enough, I am engag'd, I will challenge him." Actions will speak, and "As you hear of me, so think of me." Benedick has had to choose between loyalty to Claudio and love for Beatrice. The greater love eclipses the smaller, and Benedick acts contrary to the presented evidence, on the strength of his trust in Beatrice's loyal love. Faith begets faith. He has asked but one question: "Think you *in your soul* the Count Claudio hath wronged Hero?" She answers: "Yea, as sure as I have a thought or a soul" (326–28). And the debate in his mind has been decided in favor of Beatrice.

This is serious matter for comedy. But Shakespeare had long felt restive at the thought of mere manners passing for sound coin. In the court of love, there had been too much courtliness and courtesy, not enough love. This is evident in Berowne's renunciation of "taffeta phrases, silken terms precise," as well as in the portrayal of the villain Tybalt in *Romeo and Juliet* as one of "these antic, lisping, affecting fantasticoes–these new tuners of accent!" Portia herself waxes sarcastic against the tribe of immature swaggerers and the "thousand raw tricks of these bragging Jacks." And

---

[2]Another book on Shakespeare waiting to be written is *Shakespeare's Short Speeches*. Cf. Shylock's "I am content," and the many other examples, increasing as he learns his art, in which a short speech of not more than four words, usually monosyllables, marks a turn in the action or the highest dramatic point of a scene or of a whole play.

Beatrice showers vitriol on such courageous captains of compliment:

> But manhood is melted into cursies, valor into compliment, and men are only turned into tongue, and trim ones too. He is now as valiant as Hercules that only tells a lie, and swears it.
>
> (4.1.316–20)

Old Antonio, uncle to Beatrice and Hero, grieving at the younger generation, carries on the tongue-lashing of these "Boys, apes, braggarts, Jacks, milksops!" "I know them," he says:

> I know them, yea,
> And what they weigh, even to the utmost scruple;
> Scambling, outfacing, fashionmonging boys,
> That lie and cog and flout, deprave and slander,
> Go anticly, and show outward hideousness,
> And speak off half a dozen dang'rous words,
> How they might hurt their enemies, if they durst;
> And this is all.
>
> (5.1.92–99)

Why has Shakespeare taken such an antipathy to the vain young slanderers, the hotheaded lying Jacks of which Tybalt, and Claudio in *Much Ado*, show possible varieties? In part because he loathed particularly those evil elements that base their hostile actions on unfounded suspicion or on nothing whatever. Jealousy and slander he viewed with special aversion, for how can chastity and integrity oppose them? They mock our eyes with air. Of the two, slander may be the more sordid, since jealousy at least springs from misguided passion, whereas slander is purely malicious, destructive, and irresponsible. Who steals my purse steals trash; and outlaws are not such bad fellows, as *The Two Gentlemen of Verona* and *As You Like It* testify. But the slanderers, almost alone among Shakespeare's sinners, are nearly unforgivable; and Shakespeare, like Spenser, treats with revulsion the Blatant Beast whose myriad tongues wound for sheer spite. In the plays with political implications, of course, slander becomes even more criminal than in the dramas of personal fortune.

Partly Shakespeare is bitter against the young swaggering slanderers out of his usual contempt for pretension in any form. And partly he seems to have developed, with considerable deliberation, a distrust for the cocksureness of callow youth. He works himself into a rather curious position: The smooth, privileged young men are too young to know what they are talking about; on the other hand, old age with its wise saws is impotent in convincing anybody. There seems little left for Shakespeare to acknowledge as a principle for conduct except Poor Richard's adage, "Experience keeps a dear school, but fools will learn in no other." Men's passions make all of them fools, incapable of accepting any sage advice or profiting from any hard-won experience except their own. Let us take a formally developed illustration. When old Leonato is grieving for his daughter Hero's shame, his yet older brother Antonio admonishes him:

> If you go on thus, you will kill yourself,
> And 'tis not wisdom thus to second grief
> Against yourself.
>
> (5.1.1–3)

Leonato answers in a thirty-line speech, "I pray thee cease thy counsel," the gist of which is that no one can console him except a comforter "whose wrongs do suit with mine," that no man can patch his grief with a few proverbs, that only those who do not feel grief mouth comfortable counsel, that aches cannot be charmed with air, nor agony with words. He ends with certainty:

> No, no! 'Tis all men's office to speak patience
> To those that wring under the load of sorrow,
> But no man's virtue nor sufficiency
> To be so moral when he shall endure
> The like himself. Therefore give me no counsel;
> My griefs cry louder than advertisement.
>
> (27–32)

And old brother Antonio answers with too much truth: "Therein do men from children nothing differ." Knowledge of this lamentable fact in human behavior is not the monopoly of the old men. Benedick has said earlier in the play: "Well, everyone cannot master a grief but he that has it" (3.2.27–28). And Romeo had answered the Friar's soothing wisdom in some irritation: "Thou canst not speak of that thou dost not feel" (3.3.64).[3]

To sum it up, Shakespeare is no believer in the schoolroom. Copybook maxims, admirable as they may be, are ineffective. The only school is experience, and axioms are proved upon the pulses. Believing this, Shakespeare finds the drama a most excellent moral instrument, since in the drama characters reach conclusions by putting their various conflicting beliefs into action. Their passions and philosophies are forced to work out practicable solutions, in conflict with a larger world and with unsympathetic alien forces or personalities. The audience may profit vicariously from the display of life in action. This belief, so slowly affirmed, accounts for the greater soundness and sanity of Shakespeare's handling of love in the Golden Comedies. Romantic love, in the characters that interest him in *Much Ado About Nothing*, is not to be a doctrine promulgated to puppet lovers and forced upon them. Benedick and Beatrice will fight it to the last gasp. They take their stand against sentimentality, and carry on the war between the sexes with gusto.

The main interest of the play, then, starts in the world of common sense. Raillery and wit will protect light hearts. "There is measure in everything," (2.1.70) says Beatrice, and lest that remark on moderation sound immoderately serious, she makes it into a pun and dances out her conviction. The lovers are too clear-eyed not to be self-critical. When Beatrice overhears her disdain, scornful wit, and self-endearment exaggerated, she abandons them. "Contempt, farewell! and maiden pride, adieu!" (3.1.109). And when Benedick also overhears a conversation on his character—that he will scorn Beatrice's love, since he "hath a contemptible spirit"—he decides to forsake "quips and sentences

---

[3]Shakespeare does not forget the ineffectiveness of sage advice. Compare Brabantio's bitter reply to the Duke of Venice (*Othello*, 1.3. 199–219) or Hamlet's attitude toward the sage counsel of Claudius (1.2.87–120). See also Polonius and Laertes, the Duke of Vienna and Claudio, and the more knowing course of action Ulysses adopts toward both Achilles and Troilus.

and these paper bullets of the brain" (2.3.236–37) because, he says, "I must not seem proud. Happy are they that hear their detractions and can put them to mending" (225–26). Part of this, of course, is not the result of the lovers' good resolutions, but of their instinctive attraction toward each other. "Good Lord, for alliance!" cries Beatrice, as she watches Claudio and Hero making love, and there is a touch of envy and self-pity in her jest: "Thus goes everyone to the world but I. . . . I may sit in a corner and cry 'Heigh-ho for a husband!' " (2.1.314–16).

"Alliance," then, catches these two independent spirits, who have too much good sense to resist nature. Leonato in his passion of grief had asserted:

> I will be flesh and blood;
> For there was never yet philosopher
> That could endure the toothache patiently.
>
> (5.1.34–36)

Now Benedick feels the pangs of love, and when his friends twit him on his sadness, he replies: "I have the toothache." (3.2.21) They ascribe it to love and suggest a remedy, but Benedick already knows well that "Yet is this no charm for the toothache." (66)

To himself, he will not deny the effects and the power of love. Yet he will try to keep it in proportion through humor:

> Leander the good swimmer, Troilus the first employer of panders, and a whole book full of these quondam carpet-mongers, whose names yet run smoothly in the even road of a blank verse—why, they were never so truly turned over and over as my poor self in love.
>
> (5.2.30–36)

He has too much respect for his genuine feelings to transform them into fashionable conventions; he "cannot woo in festival terms," and when he looks for rhymes for "lady," "scorn," and "school," he can only come out with "baby," "horn," and "fool." Sentiment—even when it is experienced directly—is to be kept in its place by antisentiment.

His sincerity is best shown in that excellently conceived

dramatic scene of his challenge to Claudio. Here we have dramatic reversal of moods, for the perpetual giber Benedick is now in deadly earnest—"You have among you killed a sweet and innocent lady" (5.1.189–90)—and his friends Pedro and Claudio are uneasily jesting against his estrangement and their own bad consciences. In critical moments Benedick controls both his emotion and his wit; their interaction protects him at once against the affectations of intellect and the extreme sallies of passion.

The integrity and sincerity of his love, based so broadly, make him in the end impervious to mockery, and it is "Benedick, the married man" who, after kissing Beatrice heartily, replies in all surety: "I'll tell thee what, Prince: a college of wit-crackers cannot flout me out of my humor," (5.2.100–11) who demands music and dancing, and who advises Pedro: "Prince, thou art sad. Get thee a wife!" (123). In the wedding of Benedick and Beatrice, humor has been married to love on both sides of the family. Since humor presupposes a greater consciousness of the world and of one's self, the wedding promises more stability and happiness than in any of Shakespeare's previous imaginings. "Man is a giddy thing," says Benedick, "and this is my conclusion" (107–8). Man is less giddy, surer in his moral sense, in direct proportion to his awareness of his own giddiness.

W. H. AUDEN

From The Dyer's Hand

The called-for songs in *Much Ado About Nothing*, *As You Like It*, and *Twelfth Night* illustrate Shakespeare's skill in making what might have been beautiful irrelevancies contribute to the dramatic structure.

> *Much Ado About Nothing*
> Act 2. Scene 3.
> *Song.* Sigh no more, ladies.
> *Audience. Don Pedro, Claudio, and Benedick (in hiding).*

In the two preceding scenes we have learned of two plots, Don Pedro's plot to make Benedick fall in love with Beatrice, and Don John's plot to make Claudio believe that Hero, his wife-to-be, is unchaste. Since this is a comedy, we, the audience, know that all will come right in the end, that Beatrice and Benedick, Claudio and Hero will get happily married.

The two plots of which we have just learned, therefore, arouse two different kinds of suspense. If the plot against Benedick succeeds, we are one step nearer the goal; if the plot against Claudio succeeds, we are one step back.

At this point, between their planning and their execution, action is suspended, and we and the characters are made to listen to a song.

The scene opens with Benedick laughing at the thought of the lovesick Claudio and congratulating himself on being heart-whole, and he expresses their contrasted states in musical imagery.

From *The Dyer's Hand and Other Essays* by W. H. Auden (New York: Random House, Inc., 1962; London: Faber & Faber, Ltd., 1963). © Copyright, 1957, by W. H. Auden. Reprinted by permission of the publishers.

I have known him when there was no music with him but the
drum and the fife; and now had he rather hear the tabor and the
pipe. . . . Is it not strange that sheep's guts should hale souls out
of men's bodies?—Well, a horn for my money, when all's
done.

We, of course, know that Benedick is not as heart-whole as
he is trying to pretend. Beatrice and Benedick resist each
other because, being both proud and intelligent, they do not
wish to be the helpless slaves of emotion or, worse, to become what they have often observed in others, the victims
of an imaginary passion. Yet whatever he may say against
music, Benedick does not go away, but stays and listens.

Claudio, for his part, wishes to hear music because he is
in a dreamy, lovesick state, and one can guess that his *petit
roman* as he listens will be of himself as the ever-faithful
swain, so that he will not notice that the mood and words of
the song are in complete contrast to his daydream. For the
song is actually about the irresponsibility of men and the
folly of women taking them seriously, and recommends as
an antidote good humor and common sense. If one imagines
these sentiments being the expression of a character, the
only character they suit is Beatrice.

> *Leonato.* . . . She is never sad but when she sleeps, and not ever
> sad then; for I have heard my daughter say she hath often
> dreamt of unhappiness and waked herself with laughing.
> *Don Pedro.* She cannot endure to hear tell of a husband.
> *Leonato.* O, by no means! She mocks all her wooers out of suit.

I do not think it too farfetched to imagine that the song
arouses in Benedick's mind an image of Beatrice, the tenderness of which alarms him. The violence of his comment
when the song is over is suspicious:

> I pray God, his bad voice bode no mischief! I had as lief have
> heard the night-raven, come what plague could have come
> after it.

And, of course, there *is* mischief brewing. Almost immediately he overhears the planned conversation of Claudio and

Don Pedro, and it has its intended effect. The song may not have compelled his capitulation, but it has certainly softened him up.

More mischief comes to Claudio who, two scenes later, shows himself all too willing to believe Don John's slander before he has been shown even false evidence, and declares that, if it should prove true, he will shame Hero in public. Had his love for Hero been all he imagined it to be, he would have laughed in Don John's face and believed Hero's assertion of her innocence, despite apparent evidence to the contrary, as immediately as her cousin does. He falls into the trap set for him because as yet he is less a lover than a man in love with love. Hero is as yet more an image in his own mind than a real person, and such images are susceptible to every suggestion.

For Claudio, the song marks the moment when his pleasant illusions about himself as a lover are at their highest. Before he can really listen to music he must be cured of imaginary listening, and the cure lies through the disharmonious experiences of passion and guilt.

CAROL THOMAS NEELY

Broken Nuptials in *Much Ado About Nothing*

Poised at the center of Shakespeare's thirteen comedies, *Much Ado About Nothing* uniquely blends elements from them all. It is linked with both the romantic comedies and problem comedies by virtue of the interactions of its two couples, its two plots. In the Claudio/Hero plot, the anxieties and risks underlying the conventions of romantic love are expressed and contained by the broken nuptials, Hero's vilification and mock death, and Claudio's penitence and acceptance of a substitute bride, motifs that are developed further in the problem comedies, *All's Well That Ends Well* and *Measure for Measure*, and in the late romances. In the Beatrice/Benedick plot, the mutual mockery, double gulling, and Benedick's acceptance of Beatrice's command to "kill Claudio" function, as do the mockery, trickery, parody, and tamings of the festive comedies, to break down resistance and to release desire and affection. The Beatrice/Benedick plot protects the Hero/Claudio plot by ventilating and displacing it and by transforming its romance elements. In turn, the impasse of the Hero/Claudio plot generates movement in the Beatrice-Benedick plot and, by permitting the witty couple the expression of romantic affection, initiates the transformation of their "merry wars" into a witty truce.[1] Together the two plots maintain an equilibrium between male control and female initiative, between male reform and female submission, which is characteristic of the romantic comedies. In this play, wit clarifies the vulnerability of romantic idealization while romance alters the static, self-defensive gestures of wit.

From *Broken Nuptials in Shakespeare's Plays* (New Haven: Yale University Press, 1985), pp. 38–57, abridged by the author.

The two plots are played out against a backdrop of patri-archal authority; this authority is protected by the extensive bawdy, especially the cuckoldry jokes. This bawdy expresses and mutes sexual anxieties; it turns them into a communal joke and provides comic release and relief in specific ways. It manifests sexuality as the central component of mar-riage and emphasizes male power and female weakness. The bawdy persistently views sex as a male assault on women. Men "board" women (2.1.142), "put in the pikes" (5.2.21), and women cheerfully resign themselves to being "made heavier . . . by the weight of a man," and "stuffed" (3.4.26–27,62–63). The women counterattack by mocking the virility that threatens them: the "blunt foils" (5.2.13), "short horns" (2.1.23), and "fine little" wit (5.1.165) of the men. They do not, however, see their own sexuality as a weapon. They joke about female "lightness" (3.4.36,43,45) to warn each other against it, not to threaten men; even the term itself identifies women with weakness rather than strength.

But women's proverbial "lightness' is also a source of male anxiety. Men, perceiving sexuality as power over women, fear its loss through female betrayal. They de-fend themselves against betrayal in three ways: They deny its possibility through idealization, anticipate it through misogyny, or transform it, through the motif of cuckoldry, into an emblem of male virility. As Coppélia Kahn shows, cuckoldry is associated with virility through the horn, which symbolizes both.[2] The reiterated motif "In time the savage bull doth bear the yoke" (1.1.252) emphasizes the bull's po-tency as well as his submission to dull domestic life and in-evitable cuckoldry. Similarly, to be "horn-mad" (260) is to be both furious with jealousy and sexually voracious; both halves of the pun imply aggressiveness. The defensive func-tion of these jokes is especially apparent in the extended one that precedes the couples' pledge to marry. In Claudio's ac-count, the scorn due the cuckold is ingeniously swallowed up in the acclaim awarded the cuckolder for his "noble feat" by which he attains power over both the woman and the husband:

Tush, fear not, man! We'll tip thy horns with gold,
And all Europa shall rejoice at thee,

> As once Europa did at lusty Jove
> When he would play the noble beast in love.   (5.4.44–47)

All rejoice with the woman. The cuckold is crowned, the cuckolder is noble, and even the illegitimate calf will be proud of, if intimidated by, his father's virility—and may even inherit it (48–51). Cuckoldry has thus been deftly dissociated from female power and infidelity and identified instead with masculinity, virility, and solidarity.

In *Much Ado*, marriage and cuckoldry, both potentially threatening to male bonds and power, become assurances of them. But male authority in the play remains lame and diffused. Leonato is a weak father; Claudio, a passive protagonist; Don John, a conventional villain. Don Pedro is potentially the most powerful man in the play, but he phases himself out of the plots he initiates. Male power in the play is blunted by its ineffectuality and rendered comic by Dogberry's parody of it. In 4.2, Dogberry parodies the inept strategies and good fortune of the other men; his arraignment reenacts as farce Hero's trial in the preceding scene. The arraignment occurs before any examination of the evidence; "malefactors" and "benefactors" are indistinguishable, and judges as well as accused have charges brought against them. Dogberry's self-defense becomes a comic defense of his betters which articulates the men's testy response to insults real or imagined, their reliance on conventions to protect and confirm their self-importance, and the potential for asininity that goes along with their desires for swaggering and safety:

> I am a wise fellow; and which is more, an officer; and which is more, a householder; and which is more, as pretty a piece of flesh as any is in Messina, and one that knows the law, go to! And a rich fellow enough, go to! And a fellow that hath had losses; and one that hath two gowns and everything handsome about him.
>
> (79–85)

Yet in spite of the men's rivalry, ineffectuality, and silliness, they control all of the play's plot-generating deceits and revelations. They fit women with husbands, and their authority and solidarity are confirmed in the play's conclusion.

But first, conflicts disrupt both the male bonds and the two couples. The Claudio/Hero alliance is thinly sketched as a conventional one in which the functions of romantic idealization are made clear. Claudio protects himself from Hero's sexuality by viewing her as a remote, idealized love object who is not to be touched or even talked to: "she is the sweetest lady that ever I looked on" (1.1.181–82).[3] Patriarchal marriage customs conveniently coalesce with romantic rhetoric, enabling him to maintain Hero as an object of social exchange and possession: "Lady, as you are mine, I am yours," he cautiously vows (2.1.304–05). He lets Don Pedro do his wooing for him. He scarcely acknowledges Hero's sexual attractiveness, and his only reference to his own desires seems oddly passive and gynecocentric in a play crammed with aggressively phallic innuendo: "But now I am returned and that war-thoughts / Have left their places vacant, in their rooms / Came thronging soft and delicate desires, / All prompting me how fair young Hero is" (1.1.291–94). Claudio thus alleviates his anxieties about marriage by viewing it both as a romantic ideal and as a conventional social arrangement.

Hero's willingness to be the passive object of her father's negotiations, Don Pedro's decorous wooing, and Claudio's low-keyed proposal provide her with a parallel defense against sexuality. She is as unforthcoming as Claudio at their first exchange, and perhaps she welcomes his silence, for she asks Don Pedro as he begins his wooing to "say nothing" (2.1.87–88). Her own uneasiness about sex is suggested in her unhappiness on her wedding day; the one bawdy innuendo that she contributes to the women's banter, "There, thou prick'st her with a thistle" (3.4.74) is as tentative as Claudio's allusion. Hero is the perfect object of his "delicate" desires: modest, chaste, virtuous, silent.

The witty verbal skirmishes comprising Beatrice's and Benedick's "merry wars" explicitly express the anxieties about loss of power through sexuality, love, and marriage that are suppressed by Claudio's and Hero's silent romanticism. Their verbal wars fill up the silence of the Hero/Claudio plot and reveal the fundamental asymmetry of the battle of the sexes. Benedick expressly equates loving with humiliation and loss of potency; he imagines it as a castrating torture: "Prove that ever I lose more blood with love than I will get again with drinking, pick out mine eyes with a ballad marker's pen and hang me up at the door of a brothel house for the sign of blind Cupid" (1.1.241–45). He likewise fears being separated from his friends by marriage and loss of status with them if he must "sigh away Sundays" or, feminized, "turn spit" like Hercules (1.1.194; 2.1.251).

He defends himself from fears of love, marriage, and female betrayal by distrust of women—"I will do myself the right to trust none" (1.1.235). Distrust, coupled with the claim that all women dote on him, allows him to profess virility without putting it to the proof. Mocking Claudio's romantic idealization, he is similarly protected by misogyny. The parallel function of the two poses is evident in Benedick's admission that if he could find an ideal woman, he would abandon the pose: "But till all graces be in one woman, one woman shall not come into my grace" (2.3.28–29). Benedick's misogyny puts him in a position of unchallengeable power; his wit is consistently belligerent, protective, and self-aggrandizing.

Instead of defensively asserting power, Beatrice's sallies often reveal weakness and ambivalence; her wit, in contrast to Benedick's, is consistently self-deprecating. Her mockery of marriage and men poignantly reveals her desire for both. Her repartee expresses as much anxiety about being unmarried, as it does about being married: "So, by being too curst, God will send you no horns" (2.1.25–26). She does not mock Hero's marriage plans as Benedick does Claudio's but only urges her to marry a man who pleases her. Hero's engagement does not engender smug self-satisfaction in her but a sense of isolation: "Thus goes everyone to the world but I, and I am sunburnt. I may sit in a corner and cry 'Heigh-ho for a husband!' " (314–16). Even her allusion to "living as merry as the day is long" in heaven "where the bachelors sit" shows a desire to continue to share equally in easy male camaraderie rather than a desire to remain single (48–49).

Beatrice's ambivalence about marriage is rooted in her fear of the social and sexual power it grants to men. Her bawdy jests manifest both her desire for Benedick and her fear of the potential control over her which her desire gives him. In the first scene she refers to Benedick as "Signior Mountanto," suggestively initiates dialogue by asking, "Is it possible Disdain should die while she hath such meet food to feed it as Signior Benedick?" (1.1.29,116–17), and from behind the safety of her mask admits to Benedick (of him)—"I would he had boarded me" (2.1.142). But her jesting about the unsuitability of husbands with beards and those without them mocks Benedick's beard and reveals her ambivalent attitude toward virility: "He that hath a beard is more than a youth, and he that hath no beard is less than a man; and he that is more than a youth is not for me; and he that is less than a man, I am not for him" (36–39). Because she is apprehensive about the social and sexual submission demanded of women in marriage and wary of men's volatile mixture of earthly frailty with arrogant authority, Beatrice does not want a husband:

> Not till God make men of some other metal than earth. Would it not grieve a woman to be overmastered with a piece of valiant dust? To make an account of her life to a clod of wayward marl? No, uncle, I'll none. Adam's sons are my brethren, and truly I hold it a sin to match in my kindred. (59–64)

Given the play's dominant metaphor of sex as a male assault, the subordination demanded of Renaissance women in marriage, and the valiant cloddishness of many of the men in the comedies, Beatrice's fear of being "overmastered" seems judicious. But her anxieties, like Benedick's, grow out of pride and fear of risk as well as out of justified wariness.

Beatrice and Benedick, both proud mockers of love, cannot dispel these anxieties or admit to love without intervention. The asymmetrical gullings perpetrated by their friends displace Hero's and Claudio's silent engagement and act out contrasted male and female anxieties there left unspoken. The men gently mock Benedick's witty misogyny while nurturing his ego. Their gentle ribbing of Benedick's "contemptible spirit" is tempered with much praise of his virtues; he is proper, wise, witty, and valiant "As Hector" (2.3.181–88). They alleviate his fears about Beatrice's aggressiveness by a lengthy, exaggerated tale of her desperate passion for him: "then down upon her knees she falls, weeps, sobs, beats her heart, tears her hair, prays, curses— 'O sweet Benedick! God give me patience!' " (149–51). The story dovetails perfectly with his fantasy that all women dote on him (and presumably it gratifies the other men to picture the disdainful Beatrice in this helpless state). The men also reassure Benedick that Beatrice is sweet and "out of all suspicion, she is virtuous" (161–62). The gulling permits Benedick to love with his friends' approval while remaining complacently self-satisfied. Even these protective assurances of his power win from him only a grudgingly impersonal acknowledgment of his feelings: "Love me? Why, it must be requited" (220–21).

The women's gulling of Beatrice is utterly different in strategy and effect. They make only one unembroidered mention of Benedick's love for her, and even that is interrogative— "But are you sure / That Benedick loves Beatrice so entirely?" (3.1.36–37). They praise his virtues, not Beatrice's. Throughout most of the staged scene, they attack at length and with gusto Beatrice's proud wit, deflating rather than bolstering her self-esteem. The men emphasize Beatrice's love whereas the women emphasize her inability to love as a means of exorcising it: "She cannot love, / Nor take no shape nor project of affection, / She is so self-endeared" (54–56). Beatrice, accepting unabashedly the accuracy of these charges—"Contempt, farewell! And maiden pride, adieu!" (109)—is released into an undefensive and personal declaration of love and of passionate submission to Benedick: "Benedick, love on; I will requite thee, / Taming my wild heart to thy loving hand. / If thou dost love, my kindness shall incite thee / To bind our loves up in a holy band" (111–14). She views marriage not as a social inevitability but as a ritual expressing affectionate commitment. Benedick's "love" will be requited with "kindness," not merely with the production of "kind."

The men's anxieties about sexuality and submission then erupt violently in Don John's slander. It is ironically appropriate that, though Hero has never talked to Claudio at all and he had "never tempted her with word too large" (4.1.51), he should immediately accept Don John's report that she "talk[ed] with a man out at a window" (307) as proof of her infidelity. Though he does not "see her chamber window ent'red" (3.2.109), his suppositions about the act transform defensive idealization to vicious degradation, as will occur later with Angelo, Troilus, Hamlet, Othello, Posthumus, and Leontes. Once his suspicions are aroused, Claudio's silent worship explodes into extravagantly lascivious denunciation:

> Out on thee, seeming! I will write against it,
> You seem to me as Dian in her orb,
> As chaste as is the bud ere it be blown;
> But you are more intemperate in your blood
> Than Venus, or those pamp'red animals
> That rage in savage sensuality. (4.1.55–60)

He perverts the ceremony that had seemed to protect him and now seeks his friends' confirmation of Hero's corruption.

When unanchored idealization turns to degradation here, nuptials are shattered more violently and irretrievably than in the other comedies. The possibility of future reconciliation is kept alive, however, by the friar's scheme for Hero's mock death, by Dogberry and his crew's knowledge of the truth about Don John's deceit, and by Beatrice's command to Benedick. The slander of Hero tempers Beatrice's commitment to love. But Claudio's failure of romantic faith in Hero parallels and helps to rectify Benedick's lack of romantic commitment to Beatrice. Both men, along with Hero, must risk a comic death and effect a comic transformation to affirm their love. Although only Dogberry's revelation influences the plot, the three "deaths" function together to engender the play's comic reconciliations and festive release.

Hero's mock death, transforming the strategies of self-concealment through masking, disguise, or withdrawal practiced by women in romantic comedies, anticipates the development of the motif in later plays. The mock death, designed by the woman and her confidante to mend nuptials shattered by men, is both an involuntary, passive escape from degradation and a voluntary constructive means to alter it. Friar Francis, who engineers the death with Leonato's

approval, outlines its constructive purpose and potential
effects. The death—real or imagined—of the slandered
woman satisfies the lover's desire for revenge while
alleviating his fear of infidelity: "Yet she must die, else
she'll betray more men" (*Othello*, 5.2.6). Then relief and
guilt working together will change "slander to remorse"
(4.1.210). Freed from the pain of desiring her and the fear of
losing her, the lover can re-idealize the woman, a process
that is described in detail by the friar, walked through in this
play, and dramatized more completely in *All's Well That
Ends Well*, *Hamlet*, *Othello*, *Antony and Cleopatra*, *Cymbeline*, and *The Winter's Tale*.

> For it so falls out
> That what we have we prize not to the worth
> Whiles we enjoy it; but being lacked and lost,
> Why, then we rack the value, then we find
> The virtue that possession would not show us
> Whiles it was ours. So will it fare with Claudio.
> When he shall hear she died upon his words,
> Th' idea of her life shall sweetly creep
> Into his study of imagination,
> And every lovely organ of her life
> Shall come appareled in more precious habit,
> More moving, delicate, and full of life,
> Into the eye and prospect of his soul
> Than when she lived indeed.   (216–29)

Through the death—pretended or actual—of the corrupted
beloved, the lover can repossess her, purified.

But for women the strategy is bold, painful, and risky.
Whereas, in earlier comedies, female disguise, control, and
wit brought men to their senses, in later ones, more dis-
turbingly, female submission generates male affection.
Hero must put herself in the hands of the friar, practice patience, and accept, if the trick fails, chaste seclusion in a re-
ligious retreat. Women pretend to die of unrequited love as
Beatrice is said to be doing; they "die" sexually, validating
male virility as Helen (*All's Well*) and Mariana (*Measure
for Measure*) do in bed tricks whose deceit makes them a
form of mock death; and they die, or pretend to, as retribu-

tion for their imagined betrayals. Juliet undergoes the death-like swoon induced by the friar's potion and her interment with dead bodies in the Capulet monument, while Hermione must remain in seclusion sixteen years. In the tragedies, Ophelia, Desdemona, and Cleopatra actually die.

The woman's pretended death, even when combined with a vigorous defense of her virtues by her friends,[4] does not by itself ensure penitence. Claudio seems utterly unaffected by the death until Borachio testifies to Hero's innocence; then re-idealization is instantaneous: "Sweet Hero, now thy image doth appear / In the rare semblance that I loved it first" (5.1.252–53). Although the motif appears in all genres, playing dead can perhaps be seen as a female version of the tragic heroes' literal and symbolic journeys.[5] Its effect is not to transform the woman as the tragic hero is transformed, but to achieve the transformation of her image in the eyes of the hero and to alter and complicate the audience's view of her. The motif satisfies the male characters' fantasies of control and the audience's need to sympathize with the slandered women.

But in *Much Ado* the festive conclusion is not only made possible by Hero's mock death, Claudio's enforced penance, and Dogberry's apprehension of the "benefactors" who expose the deceit. Equally important is Benedick's willingness to comply with Beatrice's command to "Kill Claudio" (4.1.287). Extravagant and coercive as her demand may be, Benedick's willingness to comply is a necessary antidote to the play's pervasive misogyny and a necessary rehabilitation of romance from Claudio's corruption of it. Benedick's challenge to Claudio, by affirming his faith in both Hero's and Beatrice's fidelity, repudiates his former mistrust of women and breaks his bonds with the male friends who shared this attitude. Romantic vows have proved empty and must now be validated through deeds. Male aggression is to be used not in war but for love, not against women but on their behalf. Beatrice calls on Benedick to become a hero of romance in order to qualify his wit and verify his commitment to her. Although the duel does not take place, Benedick's acquiescence and delivery of the challenge to Claudio signals his transformation and reconciles him with Beatrice. The dynamics of the Beatrice/Benedick plot invert and counteract the dynamics of the Claudio/Hero plot. Whereas Hero must "die" in response to Claudio's misogynistic fantasies of her corruption, Benedick must agree to kill Claudio in compliance with Beatrice's demand in order to replace witty misogyny with romantic commitment.

At the conclusion, Claudio's and Hero's pat reaffirmation of their wedding vows ignores rather than transforms the conflicts which erupted through the broken nuptials. First Claudio performs a ritualistic but impersonal penance. Then he asserts his faith in women by agreeing to accept a substitute bride. But his willingness to "seize upon" any bride suggests that the possessiveness and conventionality which fuel romance are not exorcised. When she unmasks, Claudio declares, "Another Hero," but there is no sense of rebirth. However, Beatrice and Benedick, displacing the Claudio/Hero plot one final time, create the festive conclusion. Disruptive elements continue to be expressed and exorcised in their bantering movement into marriage. Their refusal to love "more than reason" or other than "for pity" or "in friendly recompense" (5.4.74, 93, 83) acknowledges wittily the fear each still has of submission and the desire each has to subordinate the other. The discovery of their "halting" sonnets signals their mutual release into the extravagance of romance and is followed by a kiss which, manifesting their mutual desire, serves as a truce in their merry wars. This kiss "stop[s]" Beatrice's mouth; affirming mutuality in one way, it ends it in another, for it silences Beatrice for the rest of the play as other strong, articulate women are subdued at the ends of their comedies—Julia, Kate, Titania, Rosalind, Viola.[6] This inequality is confirmed as Benedick presides over the play's conclusion, using his wit to affirm the compatibility of manhood, friendship, and marriage. Beatrice's and Benedick's sparring is transformed by the broken nuptials into romantic attachment, and Hero's mock death and the revelation of her innocence transform Claudio's degradation of her into a ritualistic penance. Throughout the comedies broken nuptials, even when initiated by men, give women the power to resist, control, or alter the movement of courtship. But with the celebration of completed nuptials at the conclusion, male control is reestablished, and the women take their subordinate places in the dance. While rejoicing in the festive conclusion of *Much Ado* we should perhaps remember Beatrice's acute satire on wooing and wedding—and their aftermath:

> wooing, wedding, and repenting is as a Scotch jig, a measure, and a cinquepace. The first suit is hot and hasty like a Scotch jig (and full as fantastical); the wedding, mannerly modest, as a measure, full of state and ancientry; and then comes Repentance and with his bad legs falls into the cinquepace faster and faster till he sink into his grave. (2.1.72–79)

Beatrice's description, which sees marriage as a precarious beginning, not as a happy ending, is anticipated in the irregular nuptials of the earlier comedies and is enacted in the troubling unresolved endings of the problem comedies and the "repenting" which follows in the tragedies. And in *Much Ado About Nothing* there is one final nuptial irregularity: The dancing begins even before the weddings are celebrated.

BIBLIOGRAPHIC NOTE
1. See A. P. Rossiter, *Angel with Horns: Fifteen Lectures on Shakespeare* (New York: Theatre Arts Books, 1974), pp. 72–74; Barbara Everett, *"Much Ado About Nothing," The Critical Quarterly* 3 (1961): 32; and John Traugott, "Creating a Rational Rinaldo: A Study in the Mixture of the Genres of Comedy and Romance in *Much Ado About Nothing*," in *The Forms of Power and the Power of Forms in the Renaissance*, ed. Stephen Greenblatt (Norman, OK: University of Oklahoma Press, 1982), pp. 157–81 for valuable discussions of the relationships between the two plots.
2. Coppélia Kahn, *Man's Estate: Masculine Identity in Shakespeare* (Berkeley: University of California Press, 1981), p. 122.
3. Janice Hays, "Those 'soft and delicate desires': *Much Ado* and the Distrust of Women," in *The Woman's Part: Feminist Criticism of Shakespeare*, ed. Carolyn Swift Lenz,

Gayle Greene, and Carol Thomas Neely (Urbana: University of Illinois Press, 1980), pp. 79–99, discusses in detail Claudio's defenses against sexuality.

4. For example, Beatrice, the Countess in *All's Well,* Paulina in *Winter's Tale.* Marilyn Williamson, "Doubling, Women's Anger, and Genre," *Women's Studies* 9 no. 2 (1982): 107–19, discusses the function of the anger of the slandered women's defenders in *Much Ado, Othello,* and *Winter's Tale.*

5. Maynard Mack, "The Jacobean Shakespeare: Some Observations on the Construction of the Tragedies," in the Signet Classic edition of *Othello* and in Alvin B. Kernan, *Modern Shakespearean Criticism* (New York: Harcourt, Brace and World, 1970), pp. 344–45, discusses the symbolic functions of the tragic heroes' journeys, and Kirby Farrell, *Shakespeare's Creation* (Amherst: University of Massachusetts Press, 1975), Chapter 6, discusses the symbolic functions of heroines' mock deaths.

6. Clara Claiborne Park, "As We Like It: How a Girl Can be Smart and Still Popular," in *The Woman's Part,* ed. Lenz, Greene, and Neely, pp. 100–116, analyzes how the assertiveness of the comic heroines is curtailed.

ROBERT SMALLWOOD

Three Ways to Begin
Much Ado About Nothing

Folio (and Quarto) opening stage directions nearly always begin with the instruction "Enter" followed by a list of characters usually in some discernibly hierarchical order. Strict adherence to what is printed would presumably mean a reasonably brisk parade onto the stage, or perhaps simultaneous manifestation through several doors, followed immediately by the first line of dialogue.... Modern directors have found much to exploit in the alluringly vague area between the house lights going down and the first word of dialogue. Three versions of *Much Ado About Nothing* will provide examples. "Enter Leonato, Governor of Messina, Innogen his wife, Hero his daughter and Beatrice, his niece, with a messenger" says the Folio (and Quarto) direction. All three productions left out Innogen (a "ghost" character who never speaks) and all three created a space between the appearance of the family and the arrival of the messenger, half a minute or so in which interpretative intentions were made clear and the production's manifesto declared.

On the Stratford main stage in 1988, in a modern-dress production by Di Trevis, the stage lights came up on Leonato's family lounging in the sunshine on the terrace of what was clearly their very expensive villa. They looked languid and listless, each isolated from the other, clearly rather irritable; and into this scene of bored wealth came the messenger in battle-dress. The image of a society that was

From Robert Smallwood, "Director's Shakespeare," in *Shakespeare: An Illustrated Stage History*, ed. Jonathan Bate and Russell Jackson (Oxford University Press, 1996), pp. 192–93. Used by permission of Oxford University Press.

rich, decadent, and selfish had been economically created with not a word spoken and was to color our response to the rest of the play. In the preceding year Judi Dench's production for the Renaissance Theatre Company, set in the nineteenth century, had also presented Leonato's family sitting on a sunny terrace, but the relationships we saw were of cooperation and mutuality—Beatrice helping Leonato with a jigsaw puzzle, Margaret and Hero winding wool together— a community at peace with itself, in contented interdependence. One director wished the disintegrating events of the play to be unsurprising, almost what such a society deserved; the other made them seem a shocking intrusion into harmony, eliciting from us a response of pain and pity. In Bill Alexander's production, at Stratford in 1990, in splendid Renaissance costumes, the performance began with the somewhat incongruous spectacle of Beatrice and Leonato enjoying a little bout of rapier-fencing together, with Beatrice, in spite of the encumbrance of long, flowing skirts, winning rather easily. And then the messenger arrived and "the play" began—except that it had really begun for the audience with this image of a woman defeating a man at what, in the period presented, was a man's game. "O God, that I were a man!," Beatrice will say later, and here in this little directorial pre-play we were invited to think about the restrictions and frustrations imposed upon an intelligent woman in the play's patriarchal society. Here were three productions of *Much Ado About Nothing,* then, each postponing the entry of the messenger for a few seconds to create directorial space that would present a strong interpretative angle on the play.

SYLVAN BARNET

Much Ado About Nothing
on Stage and Screen

When *Much Ado* was first published, the text announced that the play had been "sundry times publicly acted," but despite this implication of popularity the play was not reprinted until 1623, when it was included in the volume that collected Shakespeare's dramatic works. The only reference to a specific performance in Shakespeare's day is in the Lord Chamberlain's account of May 20, 1613, which records payment to the company for a performance of *Much Ado* at court as part of the celebration of the marriage of Princess Elizabeth. Despite the lack of references to particular performances, however, there is evidence that the play was popular. In 1640, in a commendatory poem prefacing an edition of Shakespeare's poems, Leonard Digges wrote:

> Let but Beatrice
> And Benedick be seen, lo in a trice
> The Cockpit, galleries, and boxes are all full.

Aside from testifying to the popularity of the play in the early seventeenth century, this statement is interesting because it locates the center of interest in Beatrice and Benedick, a view shared by Charles I, who in his copy of the text retitled it *Benedick and Beatrice*.

Of the original presentation of the play we know little besides what can be gleaned from some stage directions, but one of the few things we know from the Quarto text is that the part of Dogberry was played by the famous clown Will Kempe, since Kempe's name appears as a speech prefix instead of Dogberry. Another interesting bit of information, though it casts a glimmer on Shakespeare's method of

composition rather than on the staging, is conveyed in the
first stage direction of the Quarto of 1600, which includes,
after "Enter Leonato, Governor of Messina" these words:
"Innogen his wife." Innogen is mentioned again in the
Quarto in the first stage direction in 2.1, but no lines are
given to her anywhere in the play, suggesting that although
Shakespeare at first thought of her as a character in the
story, as he worked on the play he decided to omit her but
neglected to go back and correct the stage directions.

After the reference in Leonard Digges's poem, the next
thing we hear about *Much Ado* on the stage is a reference in
1660 assigning the play (along with eight of Shakespeare's
other plays) as the exclusive property of Sir William
Davenant. Davenant combined the Benedick and Beatrice
material of *Much Ado* with a version of *Measure for Measure* in a play he called *The Law Against Lovers*, first performed in 1662. But Shakespeare's original play may also
have been produced in the late seventeenth century and in
the early eighteenth, since a revival of *Much Ado* in 1721
announced that the play was "not acted these twenty years,"
a comment that can allow one to conclude (at least tenta-
tively) that *Much Ado* endured on the stage until about
1690. Between 1721 and 1746 it was given a few times, but
it apparently lived chiefly in Charles Johnson's *Love in a
Forest* (1723), which incorporated some passages into a
version of *As You Like It*, and in a curious work by James
Miller, *The Universal Passion* (1737), which combined
parts of *Much Ado* with Molière's *La Princesse d'Elide*,
along with bits of *Two Gentlemen of Verona* and *Twelfth
Night*.

Shakespeare's play returned to the stage when David
Garrick played Benedick at Drury Lane in 1748. The performance was well received, and Garrick kept it in his repertory until he retired in 1776. From 1788 John Philip Kemble
staged it (he played Benedick), and then, in 1803, his
brother Charles took the part. In 1858 Charles Kean staged
Much Ado—he too played Benedick—in a production that
was famous for its splendid sets. John William Cole, Kean's
biographer, briefly describes the beginning of this revival,
an illusion of the harbor of Messina, which he characterized
as "a pictorial gem":

The gradual illumination of the lighthouse and various mansions, in almost every window, the moon slowly rising and throwing her silver light upon the deep waters of the Mediterranean, were managed with imposing reality. Then followed the masquerade, with its variegated lamps, bridges, gardens, and lake, seen through the arches of the palace.

As this description indicates, the second half of the nineteenth century was an age of spectacle, especially in the form of illusionistic sets; no expense was spared in creating elaborate sets, and Kean's staging of the church scene (4.1) was especially marveled at.

The tradition of Kean was continued by Henry Irving, who staged *Much Ado* in 1882 for a run of a hundred and two consecutive performances. He then took the production to America, and then back to London, where he staged it for thirty-one performances. For Irving *Much Ado* was chiefly two things: a play about Beatrice and Benedick, and a play that allowed the designer to present an elaborate, illusionistic reconstruction of aspects of sixteenth-century Sicily. The Dogberry material was heavily cut, since it hardly seemed to belong in this world. The wedding scene (4.1), for instance, was set in a side chapel of a Sicilian cathedral with three-dimensional columns, sunlight entering through a stained-glass window, and acolytes genuflecting. A contemporary described Irving's set for the church:

> The altar stands at the left-hand side of the stage, and the beautifully ornamented roof is supported by massive pillars. These accessories, the massive pillars, the figured iron gates, the decorated roof, the pictures, the stained glass, the elaborate and costly altar, the carved oak benches, the burning lights, and the perfume of incense, all combine to render this a scene of such richness and grandeur as at first to arrest all thought of the play and to delight only the eye with the beautiful sight.

Given this elaborate setting it is not surprising that Irving cut Leonato's first line in the scene, "Come, Friar Francis, be brief. Only to the plain form of marriage." The sets and the acting were immensely successful, but John Gielgud in 1963 summed up an unintended side effect of Irving's production: "An outstandingly successful production of a classical play can kill that play's popularity for many years afterward. So it happened in England with *Much Ado About Nothing*."

Irving, like the great actors before him, played Benedick; his Beatrice was Ellen Terry, and they, as well as the sets—and perhaps the text of the play—were responsible for the play's enormous success in the last decades of the nineteenth century. It's worth mentioning that Ellen Terry (like Helen Faucit, who had played Beatrice from 1836 to 1879), brought to the role a lighthearted mirth and a delightful raillery that apparently had not been present in the later eighteenth century, when the role was played somewhat more shrewishly. Despite her enormous success in the role, Ellen Terry was not fully satisfied with her performance. In her diary she wrote of a performance in 1891:

> I did some parts better, I think—made Beatrice a nobler woman. Yet I failed to please myself in the Cathedral scene.

Two days later she wrote:

> Played the Church Scene all right at last. More of a *blaze*. The little scene in the garden, too, I did better (in the last act). Beatrice has *confessed* her love, and is now *softer*. Her voice should be beautiful now, breaking out into playful defiance now and again, as of old. The last scene, too, I made much more merry, happy, *soft*.

And the next day she wrote:

> I must make Beatrice more *flashing* at first, and *softer* afterwards. This will be an improvement upon my old reading of the part. She must always be *merry* and by turns scornful, tormenting, vexed, self-communing, absent, melting, teasing, brilliant, indignant, *sad-merry*, thoughtful, withering, gentle, humorous, and gay, Gay, Gay! Protecting (to Hero), motherly, very intellectual—a gallant creature and complete in mind and feature.

But years later, reflecting on her performances, she confessed that she never fulfilled her own ideals:

I have played Beatrice hundreds of times, but not once as I know she ought to be played. I was never swift enough, not nearly swift enough at the Lyceum where I had a too deliberate, though polished and thoughtful Benedick in Henry Irving. But at least I did not make the mistake of being arch and skittish.

Two other points about Irving's *Much Ado* should be mentioned: The first is that in addition to cutting much of the Dogberry scenes, he cut most of the jokes about cuckoldry and most of the references to God, substituting "Heaven" for "God," though not when Beatrice (after Claudio's monstrous behavior at the wedding) explodes, "O God, that I were a man" (4.1.304). Second, he followed Kemble in adding dialogue at the end of 4.1. The original text ends with Benedick speaking these lines to Beatrice:

> Enough, I am engaged. I will challenge him. I will kiss your hand, and so I leave you. By this hand, Claudio shall render me a dear account. As you hear of me, so think of me. Go comfort your cousin. I must say she is dead. And so farewell.

Irving's version, almost identical with Kemble's, runs thus:

> *Benedick.* Enough. I am engaged; I will challenge him.
> *Beatrice.* You will?
> *Benedick.* By those bright eyes, I will. I will kiss your hand, and so leave you. By this hand, Claudio shall render me a dear account.
> *Beatrice.* My dear friend, kiss my hand again.
> *Benedick.* As you hear of me, so think of me. Go, comfort your cousin; I must say, she is dead.
> *Beatrice.* Benedick, kill him, kill him if you can.
> *Benedick.* As sure as he's alive, I will.

It is to Ellen Terry's credit that she protested against this change—but her protests were unavailing.

Elaborate illusionistic sets of the sort used by Kean and Irving continued in favor in the early twentieth century— Beerbohm Tree's production of 1905 was in this tradition— but a counter movement was already afoot in the late

nineteenth century, when scholarly knowledge of the Elizabethan stage began to move from the study to the theater, and
experiments were made in staging Shakespeare in what was
thought to be the Elizabethan manner, i.e. on a relatively bare
stage with only minimal props. In 1912 Granville-Barker took
a middle course between the illusionistic settings of the previous age and the virtually bare stage of its opponents, and produced some of the plays with simple, stylized, elegant decor
that he called "decorative" and that we would call "symbolic."
And then in 1925 Barry Jackson assaulted the late nineteenth-
century approach from a different angle, by staging *Hamlet*
in modern dress. The way was now open for all sorts of settings, with the consequence that we have had productions of
Much Ado in (to name only a few styles) Elizabethan dress, in
seventeenth-century dress (ranging from that of the Cavaliers
to the Three Musketeers), in nineteenth-century dress (early,
middle, and late, including the production by John Houseman
and Jack Landau, set in northern Mexico—now Texas or
southern California—in which the performers wore sombreros
and highly decorated outfits), and in twentieth-century dress
(ranging from the beginning of the century to the present).

Directors occasionally justify the change simply by saying that something fresh is needed, but more often they
claim that the new setting clarifies the play in some way.
Thus, the northern Mexican setting was justified on the
grounds that Messina was a Spanish colony (the Aragonese,
led by King Pedro, had defeated Charles II of Naples and
had transferred the court to Messina), and that, since American audiences have little sense of Messina as a Spanish
colony, Mexico is a fitting substitute. But John Gielgud,
who in 1949 chose the Renaissance ("I had always imagined *Much Ado* with scenery and dresses of the Boccaccio
period"), in 1963, in *Stage Directions*, expressed his dissat-
isfaction with these novelties:

> *Much Ado*, it seems to me, is above all a play of the Renais-
> sance. It may conceivably be played in a decor of an earlier
> period than Shakespeare's. But I have been amazed, in the last
> few years, to find it, both at Stratford-on-Avon, the Old Vic,
> Stratford Ontario, and Stratford Connecticut, decked out in Vic-

torian or Regency scenery and costumes, without much protest from audiences or critics. Surely the period between 1800 and 1900, when women barely showed their ankles and conversation between the sexes was intensely prudish and reserved, is in direct contradiction of Shakespeare's whole intention in the text.

One can imagine what Gielgud, the greatest Benedick of our century and the director of what has been esteemed the greatest production of the play, would have thought of the northern Mexican version, or of A. J. Antoon's version of 1971 (set in a small town in the United States, around 1900), or of John Barton's version of 1976 (set in India).

Antoon's *Much Ado,* produced as part of the Shakespeare Festival in Central Park, New York, began and ended with a brass band, dressed in blue and gold uniforms. The background was an elegant pavilion in a more or less Victorian style, Don Pedro became Captain Pedro, the soldiers seemed to be vestiges of Teddy Roosevelt's Rough Riders, and when dressed more formally they wore striped blazers and carried pocket flasks. The ladies carried parasols and sneaked cigarettes, and much fun was had with police who resembled Keystone Kops. The production was later televised, with the result, it was said, that the number of people who saw this production far exceeded all of the audience put together who saw earlier productions of the play.

Judging from numerous reviews, John Barton's Anglo-Indian production for the Royal Shakespeare Company in 1976, with Judi Dench as Beatrice and Donald Sinden as Benedick, was a much more thoughtful affair. Barton saw the Hero-Claudio plot as largely about pleasure-seeking men with elegant manners and coarse moral values; he found in British India a setting which seemed appropriate to this interpretation. Moreover, he was able to make memorable some scenes which, when merely read in a book, seem a trifle dull. Here is Roger Warren (in *Shakespeare Survey* 30 [1977]) describing the beginning of 5.3, the scene in which Claudio and Don Pedro offer a rather stiff, formal repentance at the supposed tomb of Hero, while a song describes their action, "Round about her tomb they go":

"Round about her tomb they go" indeed: Claudio and Don Pedro marched in a formal circle with military precision, half
drew and then completely drew their sabres by numbers, then
reversed the process to sheathe them again. These mechanical
military honors exactly fitted the mechanical formality of the
text. But then dawn broke, and Don Pedro gave full value to his
warmly flexible lines about the gentle day as the play moved us
into (literally) the light again.

Writing in 1966, a decade before Barton's production,
J. R. Mulryne in *Shakespeare: "Much Ado About Nothing"*
called attention to the ease with which a reader may pass
over the potent drama in this scene, which on the page consists, as Mulryne says, of "the mere reading of one rather
undistinguished verse and the singing of another, followed
by a resolve to repeat the practice yearly." As Mulryne said,
and as Barton went on to demonstrate, if the scene is properly staged

the audience undergoes, in fact, an experience that is deeply im-
pressive at the time and distinctly memorable during the rest of
the play and when it is over. An ill-defined experience certainly,
but one that investigates Claudio's remorseful consciousness,
or specifies his moral reflection on his behavior. But this is precisely what Shakespeare wants at this point. With the play de-
veloping as it has, moral analysis would be out of place; to
interest us now in the idiosyncratic movement of Claudio's
mind would open up perspectives the play has not otherwise ex-
plored. We need only to be assured about the depth of Claudio's
emotional response, not its precise nature: and this the theatrical
experience to which the words-on-the-page appropriately give
rise will do for us.

The analyses by Roger Warren and J. R. Mulryne are not
overly subtle. A performance of the play supports them, and
though inevitably the "merry war" between Beatrice and
Benedick and the malaprops of Dogberry are more easily
appreciated, the Hero-Claudio plot is equally dramatic
if properly staged, or if envisioned in the theater in one's
mind.

Although *Much Ado About Nothing* continues to be regularly produced, no stage productions of the last two decades have established themselves as landmarks, and the image that we are likely to have of the play in performance will probably be shaped chiefly by the BBC television version and a film made by Kenneth Branagh. The television version (1984), virtually uncut—it runs for two and a half hours—was made in a studio, but it is quite handsome. The chief set is a large courtyard planted with fruit trees, and the costumes, seeking to evoke a place (Messina, in northeastern Sicily) that for the Elizabethans was remote, are vaguely seventeenth-century Turkish. Although in the early part of this version Beatrice and Benedick seem sulky rather than witty, it picks up and is a creditable production.

Kenneth Branagh's film (1993) is a considerably abridged version of the play (it runs for a bit less than two hours), but it shows some material not dramatized in the play, notably Hero's alleged infidelity. In the play we are merely told about it, but in the film we see Hero (actually Hero's waiting-woman, Margaret, whom Claudio takes to be Hero), nude, at an upper window, with Borachio. And at the end of the film, we see (as we do not, in Shakespeare's text) Don John brought in under guard. The longest addition is near the beginning, when the camera pans across a Tuscan landscape (Branagh has said that Sicily is not green enough to suit his vision), and cuts back and forth between the tanned playful women in their white billowing dresses and the eager men in their nineteenth-century military uniforms raising a cloud of dust as they ride (they are returning from battle) toward the women. "Some grateful teacher," Branagh said, "with a gasp of relief will be able to say, 'Here are girls with cleavages and boys with tight trousers, class. You will now shut up for an hour and a half and pay attention.' " And the film, with Branagh as Benedick, Emma Thompson as Beatrice, Denzel Washington as Don Pedro, and Keanu Reeves as Don John, does hold our attention, and in its way it disproves John Gielgud's comment, quoted a moment ago, to the effect that the play cannot be coherently set in the nineteenth century. Despite Michael Keaton, of *Batman* fame, who gives a disastrous performance as a demented Dogberry, it's a delightful romp.

Bibliographic Note: For a stage history somewhat longer than the present one, but still fairly short, see A. R. Humphreys's Arden edition of the play. The ways of delivering one episode, the "Kill Claudio" passage (4.2.297*ff*), have been examined at length by J. F. Cox, in *Shakespeare Survey* 32 (1979). Biographies and autobiographies of actors who have performed the roles usually include helpful material; for reviews of productions staged during the second half of the twentieth century, consult *Shakespeare Survey* (an annual) and especially *Shakespeare Quarterly*. For the text of Branagh's screenplay, with some pictures and a short introduction, see Kenneth Branagh, *"Much Ado About Nothing" by William Shakespeare* (1993).

Suggested References

The number of possible references is vast and grows alarmingly. (The *Shakespeare Quarterly* devotes one issue each year to a list of the previous year's work, and *Shakespeare Survey*—an annual publication—includes a substantial review of biographical, critical, and textual studies, as well as a survey of performances.) The vast bibliography is best approached through James Harner, *The World Shakespeare Bibliography on CD-Rom: 1900–Present*. The first release, in 1996, included more than 12,000 annotated items from 1990–93, plus references to several thousand book reviews, productions, films, and audio recordings. The plan is to update the publication annually, moving forward one year and backward three years. Thus, the second issue (1997), with 24,700 entries, and another 35,000 or so references to reviews, newspaper pieces, and so on, covered 1987–94.

Though no works are indispensable, those listed below have been found especially helpful. The arrangement is as follows:

1. Shakespeare's Times
2. Shakespeare's Life
3. Shakespeare's Theater
4. Shakespeare on Stage and Screen
5. Miscellaneous Reference Works
6. Shakespeare's Plays: General Studies
7. The Comedies
8. The Romances
9. The Tragedies
10. The Histories
11. *Much Ado About Nothing*

The titles in the first five sections are accompanied by brief explanatory annotations.

1. Shakespeare's Times

Andrews, John F., ed. *William Shakespeare: His World, His Work, His Influence,* 3 vols. (1985). Sixty articles, dealing not only with such subjects as "The State," "The Church," "Law," "Science, Magic, and Folklore," but also with the plays and poems themselves and Shakespeare's influence (e.g., translations, films, reputation)

Byrne, Muriel St. Clare. *Elizabethan Life in Town and Country* (8th ed., 1970). Chapters on manners, beliefs, education, etc., with illustrations.

Dollimore, John, and Alan Sinfield, eds. *Political Shakespeare: New Essays in Cultural Materialism* (1985). Essays on such topics as the subordination of women and colonialism, presented in connection with some of Shakespeare's plays.

Greenblatt, Stephen. *Representing the English Renaissance* (1988). New Historicist essays, especially on connections between political and aesthetic matters, statecraft and stagecraft.

Joseph, B. L. *Shakespeare's Eden: the Commonwealth of England 1558–1629* (1971). An account of the social, political, economic, and cultural life of England.

Kernan, Alvin. *Shakespeare, the King's Playwright: Theater in the Stuart Court 1603–1613* (1995). The social setting and the politics of the court of James I, in relation to *Hamlet, Measure for Measure, Macbeth, King Lear, Antony and Cleopatra, Coriolanus,* and *The Tempest.*

Montrose, Louis. *The Purpose of Playing: Shakespeare and the Cultural Politics of the Elizabethan Theatre* (1996). A poststructuralist view, discussing the professional theater "within the ideological and material frameworks of Elizabethan culture and society," with an extended analysis of *A Midsummer Night's Dream.*

Mullaney, Steven. *The Place of the Stage: License, Play, and Power in Renaissance England* (1988). New Historicist analysis, arguing that popular drama became a cultural institution "only by . . . taking up a place on the margins of society."

Schoenbaum, S. *Shakespeare: The Globe and the World*

(1979). A readable, abundantly illustrated introductory book on the world of the Elizabethans.

Shakespeare's England, 2 vols. (1916). A large collection of scholarly essays on a wide variety of topics, e.g., astrology, costume, gardening, horsemanship, with special attention to Shakespeare's references to these topics.

2. Shakespeare's Life

Andrews, John F., ed. *William Shakespeare: His World, His Work, His Influence,* 3 vols. (1985). See the description above.

Bentley, Gerald E. *Shakespeare: A Biographical Handbook* (1961). The facts about Shakespeare, with virtually no conjecture intermingled.

Chambers, E. K. *William Shakespeare: A Study of Facts and Problems,* 2 vols. (1930). The fullest collection of data.

Fraser, Russell. *Young Shakespeare* (1988). A highly readable account that simultaneously considers Shakespeare's life and Shakespeare's art.

———. *Shakespeare: The Later Years* (1992).

Schoenbaum, S. *Shakespeare's Lives* (1970). A review of the evidence and an examination of many biographies, including those of Baconians and other heretics.

———. *William Shakespeare: A Compact Documentary Life* (1977). An abbreviated version, in a smaller format, of the next title. The compact version reproduces some fifty documents in reduced form. A readable presentation of all that the documents tell us about Shakespeare.

———. *William Shakespeare: A Documentary Life* (1975). A large-format book setting forth the biography with facsimiles of more than two hundred documents, and with transcriptions and commentaries.

3. Shakespeare's Theater

Astington, John H., ed. *The Development of Shakespeare's Theater* (1992). Eight specialized essays on theatrical companies, playing spaces, and performance.

Beckerman, Bernard. *Shakespeare at the Globe, 1599–1609* (1962). On the playhouse and on Elizabethan dramaturgy, acting, and staging.

Bentley, Gerald E. *The Profession of Dramatist in Shakespeare's Time* (1971). An account of the dramatist's status in the Elizabethan period.

———. *The Profession of Player in Shakespeare's Time, 1590–1642* (1984). An account of the status of members of London companies (sharers, hired men, apprentices, managers) and a discussion of conditions when they toured.

Berry, Herbert. *Shakespeare's Playhouses* (1987). Usefully emphasizes how little we know about the construction of Elizabethan theaters.

Brown, John Russell. *Shakespeare's Plays in Performance* (1966). A speculative and practical analysis relevant to all of the plays, but with emphasis on *The Merchant of Venice, Richard II, Hamlet, Romeo and Juliet,* and *Twelfth Night.*

———. *William Shakespeare: Writing for Performance* (1996). A discussion aimed at helping readers to develop theatrically conscious habits of reading.

Chambers, E. K. *The Elizabethan Stage,* 4 vols. (1945). A major reference work on theaters, theatrical companies, and staging at court.

Cook, Ann Jennalie. *The Privileged Playgoers of Shakespeare's London, 1576–1642* (1981). Sees Shakespeare's audience as wealthier, more middle-class, and more intellectual than Harbage (below) does.

Dessen, Alan C. *Elizabethan Drama and the Viewer's Eye* (1977). On how certain scenes may have looked to spectators in an Elizabethan theater.

Gurr, Andrew. *Playgoing in Shakespeare's London* (1987). Something of a middle ground between Cook (above) and Harbage (below).

———. *The Shakespearean Stage, 1579–1642* (2nd ed., 1980). On the acting companies, the actors, the playhouses, the stages, and the audiences.

Harbage, Alfred. *Shakespeare's Audience* (1941). A study of the size and nature of the theatrical public, emphasizing the representativeness of its working class and middle-class audience.

Hodges, C. Walter. *The Globe Restored* (1968). A conjectural restoration, with lucid drawings.

Hosley, Richard. "The Playhouses," in *The Revels History of Drama in English*, vol. 3, general editors Clifford Leech and T. W. Craik (1975). An essay of a hundred pages on the physical aspects of the playhouses.

Howard, Jane E. "Crossdressing, the Theatre, and Gender Struggle in Early Modern England," *Shakespeare Quarterly* 39 (1988): 418–40. Judicious comments on the effects of boys playing female roles.

Orrell, John. *The Human Stage: English Theatre Design, 1567–1640* (1988). Argues that the public, private, and court playhouses are less indebted to popular structures (e.g., innyards and bear-baiting pits) than to banqueting halls and to Renaissance conceptions of Roman amphitheaters.

Slater, Ann Pasternak. *Shakespeare the Director* (1982). An analysis of theatrical effects (e.g., kissing, kneeling) in stage directions and dialogue.

Styan, J. L. *Shakespeare's Stagecraft* (1967). An introduction to Shakespeare's visual and aural stagecraft, with chapters on such topics as acting conventions, stage groupings, and speech.

Thompson, Peter. *Shakespeare's Professional Career* (1992). An examination of patronage and related theatrical conditions.

———. *Shakespeare's Theatre* (1983). A discussion of how plays were staged in Shakespeare's time.

4. Shakespeare on Stage and Screen

Bate, Jonathan, and Russell Jackson, eds. *Shakespeare: An Illustrated Stage History* (1996). Highly readable essays on stage productions from the Renaissance to the present.

Berry, Ralph. *Changing Styles in Shakespeare* (1981). Discusses productions of six plays (*Coriolanus, Hamlet, Henry V, Measure for Measure, The Tempest,* and *Twelfth Night*) on the English stage, chiefly 1950–1980.

————. *On Directing Shakespeare: Interviews with Contemporary Directors* (1989). An enlarged edition of a book first published in 1977, this version includes the seven interviews from the early 1970s and adds five interviews conducted in 1988.

Brockbank, Philip, ed. *Players of Shakespeare: Essays in Shakespearean Performance* (1985). Comments by twelve actors, reporting their experiences with roles. See also the entry for Russell Jackson (below).

Bulman, J. C., and H. R. Coursen, eds. *Shakespeare on Television* (1988). An anthology of general and theoretical essays, essays on individual productions, and shorter reviews, with a bibliography and a videography listing cassettes that may be rented.

Coursen, H. P. *Watching Shakespeare on Television* (1993). Analyses not only of TV versions but also of films and videotapes of stage presentations that are shown on television.

Davies, Anthony, and Stanley Wells, eds. *Shakespeare and the Moving Image: The Plays on Film and Television* (1994). General essays (e.g., on the comedies) as well as essays devoted entirely to *Hamlet*, *King Lear*, and *Macbeth*.

Dawson, Anthony B. *Watching Shakespeare: A Playgoer's Guide* (1988). About half of the plays are discussed, chiefly in terms of decisions that actors and directors make in putting the works onto the stage.

Dessen, Alan. *Elizabethan Stage Conventions and Modern Interpretations* (1984). On interpreting conventions such as the representation of light and darkness and stage violence (duels, battles).

Donaldson, Peter. *Shakespearean Films/Shakespearean Directors* (1990). Postmodernist analyses, drawing on Freudianism, Feminism, Deconstruction, and Queer Theory.

Jackson, Russell, and Robert Smallwood, eds. *Players of Shakespeare 2: Further Essays in Shakespearean Performance by Players with the Royal Shakespeare Company* (1988). Fourteen actors discuss their roles in productions between 1982 and 1987.

————. *Players of Shakespeare 3: Further Essays in Shake-*

spearean Performance by Players with the Royal Shakespeare Company (1993). Comments by thirteen performers.

Jorgens, Jack. *Shakespeare on Film* (1977). Fairly detailed studies of eighteen films, preceded by an introductory chapter addressing such issues as music, and whether to "open" the play by including scenes of landscape.

Kennedy, Dennis. *Looking at Shakespeare: A Visual History of Twentieth-Century Performance* (1993). Lucid descriptions (with 170 photographs) of European, British, and American performances.

Leiter, Samuel L. *Shakespeare Around the Globe: A Guide to Notable Postwar Revivals* (1986). For each play there are about two pages of introductory comments, then discussions (about five hundred words per production) of ten or so productions, and finally bibliographic references.

McMurty, Jo. *Shakespeare Films in the Classroom* (1994). Useful evaluations of the chief films most likely to be shown in undergraduate courses.

Rothwell, Kenneth, and Annabelle Henkin Melzer. *Shakespeare on Screen: An International Filmography and Videography* (1990). A reference guide to several hundred films and videos produced between 1899 and 1989, including spinoffs such as musicals and dance versions.

Sprague, Arthur Colby. *Shakespeare and the Actors* (1944). Detailed discussions of stage business (gestures, etc.) over the years.

Willis, Susan. *The BBC Shakespeare Plays: Making the Televised Canon* (1991). A history of the series, with interviews and production diaries for some plays.

5. Miscellaneous Reference Works

Abbott, E. A. *A Shakespearean Grammar* (new edition, 1877). An examination of differences between Elizabethan and modern grammar.

Allen, Michael J. B., and Kenneth Muir, eds. *Shakespeare's Plays in Quarto* (1981). One volume containing facsimiles of the plays issued in small format before they were collected in the First Folio of 1623.

Bevington, David. *Shakespeare* (1978). A short guide to hundreds of important writings on the subject.

Blake, Norman. *Shakespeare's Language: An Introduction* (1983). On vocabulary, parts of speech, and word order.

Bullough, Geoffrey. *Narrative and Dramatic Sources of Shakespeare*, 8 vols. (1957–75). A collection of many of the books Shakespeare drew on, with judicious comments.

Campbell, Oscar James, and Edward G. Quinn, eds. *The Reader's Encyclopedia of Shakespeare* (1966). Old, but still the most useful single reference work on Shakespeare.

Cercignani, Fausto. *Shakespeare's Works and Elizabethan Pronunciation* (1981). Considered the best work on the topic, but remains controversial.

Dent, R. W. *Shakespeare's Proverbial Language: An Index* (1981). An index of proverbs, with an introduction concerning a form Shakespeare frequently drew on.

Greg, W. W. *The Shakespeare First Folio* (1955). A detailed yet readable history of the first collection (1623) of Shakespeare's plays.

Harner, James. *The World Shakespeare Bibliography*. See headnote to Suggested References.

Hosley, Richard. *Shakespeare's Holinshed* (1968). Valuable presentation of one of Shakespeare's major sources.

Kökeritz, Helge. *Shakespeare's Names* (1959). A guide to pronouncing some 1,800 names appearing in Shakespeare.

———. *Shakespeare's Pronunciation* (1953). Contains much information about puns and rhymes, but see Cercignani (above).

Muir, Kenneth. *The Sources of Shakespeare's Plays* (1978). An account of Shakespeare's use of his reading. It covers all the plays, in chronological order.

Miriam Joseph, Sister. *Shakespeare's Use of the Arts of Language* (1947). A study of Shakespeare's use of rhetorical devices, reprinted in part as *Rhetoric in Shakespeare's Time* (1962).

The Norton Facsimile: The First Folio of Shakespeare's Plays (1968). A handsome and accurate facsimile of the first collection (1623) of Shakespeare's plays, with a valuable introduction by Charlton Hinman.

Onions, C. T. *A Shakespeare Glossary*, rev. and enlarged by

R. D. Eagleson (1986). Definitions of words (or senses of words) now obsolete.

Partridge, Eric. *Shakespeare's Bawdy*, rev. ed. (1955). Relatively brief dictionary of bawdy words; useful, but see Williams, below.

Shakespeare Quarterly. See headnote to Suggested References.

Shakespeare Survey. See headnote to Suggested References.

Spevack, Marvin. *The Harvard Concordance to Shakespeare* (1973). An index to Shakespeare's words.

Vickers, Brian. *Appropriating Shakespeare: Contemporary Critical Quarrels* (1993). A survey—chiefly hostile—of recent schools of criticism.

Wells, Stanley, ed. *Shakespeare: A Bibliographical Guide* (new edition, 1990). Nineteen chapters (some devoted to single plays, others devoted to groups of related plays) on recent scholarship on the life and all of the works.

Williams, Gordon. *A Dictionary of Sexual Language and Imagery in Shakespearean and Stuart Literature*, 3 vols. (1994). Extended discussions of words and passages; much fuller than Partridge, cited above.

6. Shakespeare's Plays: General Studies

Bamber, Linda. *Comic Women, Tragic Men: A Study of Gender and Genre in Shakespeare* (1982).

Barnet, Sylvan. *A Short Guide to Shakespeare* (1974).

Callaghan, Dympna, Lorraine Helms, and Jyotsna Singh. *The Weyward Sisters: Shakespeare and Feminist Politics* (1994).

Clemen, Wolfgang H. *The Development of Shakespeare's Imagery* (1951).

Cook, Ann Jennalie. *Making a Match: Courtship in Shakespeare and His Society* (1991).

Dollimore, Jonathan, and Alan Sinfield. *Political Shakespeare: New Essays in Cultural Materialism* (1985).

Dusinberre, Juliet. *Shakespeare and the Nature of Women* (1975).

Granville-Barker, Harley. *Prefaces to Shakespeare*, 2 vols. (1946–47; volume 1 contains essays on *Hamlet*, *King*

Lear, Merchant of Venice, Antony and Cleopatra, and *Cymbeline*; volume 2 contains essays on *Othello, Coriolanus, Julius Caesar, Romeo and Juliet, Love's Labor's Lost*).

————. *More Prefaces to Shakespeare* (1974; essays on *Twelfth Night, A Midsummer Night's Dream, The Winter's Tale, Macbeth*).

Harbage, Alfred. *William Shakespeare: A Reader's Guide* (1963).

Howard, Jean E. *Shakespeare's Art of Orchestration: Stage Technique and Audience Response* (1984).

Jones, Emrys. *Scenic Form in Shakespeare* (1971).

Lenz, Carolyn Ruth Swift, Gayle Greene, and Carol Thomas Neely, eds. *The Woman's Part: Feminist Criticism of Shakespeare* (1980).

Novy, Marianne. *Love's Argument: Gender Relations in Shakespeare* (1984).

Rose, Mark. *Shakespearean Design* (1972).

Scragg, Leah. *Discovering Shakespeare's Meaning* (1994).

————. *Shakespeare's "Mouldy Tales": Recurrent Plot Motifs in Shakespearean Drama* (1992).

Traub, Valerie. *Desire and Anxiety: Circulations of Sexuality in Shakespearean Drama* (1992).

Traversi, D. A. *An Approach to Shakespeare,* 2 vols. (3rd rev. ed, 1968–69).

Vickers, Brian. *The Artistry of Shakespeare's Prose* (1968).

Wells, Stanley. *Shakespeare: A Dramatic Life* (1994).

Wright, George T. *Shakespeare's Metrical Art* (1988).

7. The Comedies

Barber, C. L. *Shakespeare's Festive Comedy* (1959; discusses *Love's Labor's Lost, A Midsummer Night's Dream, The Merchant of Venice, As You Like It, Twelfth Night*).

Barton, Anne. *The Names of Comedy* (1990).

Berry, Ralph. *Shakespeare's Comedy: Explorations in Form* (1972).

Bradbury, Malcolm, and David Palmer, eds. *Shakespearean Comedy* (1972).

Bryant, J. A., Jr. *Shakespeare and the Uses of Comedy* (1986).

Carroll, William. *The Metamorphoses of Shakespearean Comedy* (1985).

Champion, Larry S. *The Evolution of Shakespeare's Comedy* (1970).

Evans, Bertrand. *Shakespeare's Comedies* (1960).

Frye, Northrop. *Shakespearean Comedy and Romance* (1965).

Leggatt, Alexander. *Shakespeare's Comedy of Love* (1974).

Miola, Robert S. *Shakespeare and Classical Comedy: The Influence of Plautus and Terence* (1994).

Nevo, Ruth. *Comic Transformations in Shakespeare* (1980).

Ornstein, Robert. *Shakespeare's Comedies: From Roman Farce to Romantic Mystery* (1986).

Richman, David. *Laughter, Pain, and Wonder: Shakespeare's Comedies and the Audience in the Theater* (1990).

Salingar, Leo. *Shakespeare and the Traditions of Comedy* (1974).

Slights, Camille Wells. *Shakespeare's Comic Commonwealths* (1993).

Waller, Gary, ed. *Shakespeare's Comedies* (1991).

Westlund, Joseph. *Shakespeare's Reparative Comedies: A Psychoanalytic View of the Middle Plays* (1984).

Williamson, Marilyn. *The Patriarchy of Shakespeare's Comedies* (1986).

8. The Romances (*Pericles, Cymbeline, The Winter's Tale, The Tempest, The Two Noble Kinsmen*)

Adams, Robert M. *Shakespeare: The Four Romances* (1989).

Felperin, Howard. *Shakespearean Romance* (1972).

Frye, Northrop. *A Natural Perspective: The Development of Shakespearean Comedy and Romance* (1965).

Mowat, Barbara. *The Dramaturgy of Shakespeare's Romances* (1976).

Warren, Roger. *Staging Shakespeare's Late Plays* (1990).

Young, David. *The Heart's Forest: A Study of Shakespeare's Pastoral Plays* (1972).

9. The Tragedies

Bradley, A. C. *Shakespearean Tragedy* (1904).

Brooke, Nicholas. *Shakespeare's Early Tragedies* (1968).

Champion, Larry. *Shakespeare's Tragic Perspective* (1976).

Drakakis, John, ed. *Shakespearean Tragedy* (1992).

Evans, Bertrand. *Shakespeare's Tragic Practice* (1979).

Everett, Barbara. *Young Hamlet: Essays on Shakespeare's Tragedies* (1989).

Foakes, R. A. *Hamlet versus Lear: Cultural Politics and Shakespeare's Art* (1993).

Frye, Northrop. *Fools of Time: Studies in Shakespearean Tragedy* (1967).

Harbage, Alfred, ed. *Shakespeare: The Tragedies* (1964).

Mack, Maynard. *Everybody's Shakespeare: Reflections Chiefly on the Tragedies* (1993).

McAlindon, T. *Shakespeare's Tragic Cosmos* (1991).

Miola, Robert S. *Shakespeare and Classical Tragedy: The Influence of Seneca* (1992).

———. *Shakespeare's Rome* (1983).

Nevo, Ruth. *Tragic Form in Shakespeare* (1972).

Rackin, Phyllis. *Shakespeare's Tragedies* (1978).

Rose, Mark, ed. *Shakespeare's Early Tragedies: A Collection of Critical Essays* (1995).

Rosen, William. *Shakespeare and the Craft of Tragedy* (1960).

Snyder, Susan. *The Comic Matrix of Shakespeare's Tragedies* (1979).

Wofford, Susanne. *Shakespeare's Late Tragedies: A Collection of Critical Essays* (1996).

Young, David. *The Action to the Word: Structure and Style in Shakespearean Tragedy* (1990).

———. *Shakespeare's Middle Tragedies: A Collection of Critical Essays* (1993).

10. The Histories

Blanpied, John W. *Time and the Artist in Shakespeare's English Histories* (1983).

Campbell, Lily B. *Shakespeare's "Histories": Mirrors of Elizabethan Policy* (1947).

Champion, Larry S. *Perspective in Shakespeare's English Histories* (1980).

Hodgdon, Barbara. *The End Crowns All: Closure and Contradiction in Shakespeare's History* (1991).

Holderness, Graham. *Shakespeare Recycled: The Making of Historical Drama* (1992).

————, ed. *Shakespeare's History Plays: "Richard II" to "Henry V"* (1992).

Leggatt, Alexander. *Shakespeare's Political Drama: The History Plays and the Roman Plays* (1988).

Ornstein, Robert. *A Kingdom for a Stage: The Achievement of Shakespeare's History Plays* (1972).

Rackin, Phyllis. *Stages of History: Shakespeare's English Chronicles* (1990).

Saccio, Peter. *Shakespeare's English Kings: History, Chronicle, and Drama* (1977).

Tillyard, E. M. W. *Shakespeare's History Plays* (1944).

Velz, John W., ed. *Shakespeare's English Histories: A Quest for Form and Genre* (1996).

11. *Much Ado About Nothing*

In addition to the references given at the end of *Much Ado About Nothing* on Stage and Screen (p. 152), and those listed in Section 7, The Comedies, the following titles are recommended.

Berger, Harry. "Against the Sink-a-Pace: Sexual and Family Politics in *Much Ado About Nothing*." *Shakespeare Quarterly* 33 (1982): 302–13.

Brown, John Russell, ed. *Shakespeare: "Much Ado About Nothing" and "As You Like It": A Casebook* (1979).

Cook, Carol. "The Sign and Semblance of Her Honor: Reading Gender Difference in *Much Ado About Nothing*. *PMLA* 101 (1986): 186–202.

Davis, Walter R., ed. *Twentieth Century Interpretations of "Much Ado About Nothing"* (1969).

Everett, Barbara. "*Much Ado About Nothing*: the Unsociable

Comedy," in *English Comedy.* Ed. Michael Cordner, Peter Holland, and John Kerrigan (1994), pp. 68–84.

Levin, Richard A. *Love and Society in Shakespearean Comedy* (1985).

Mulryne, J. R. *Shakespeare: "Much Ado About Nothing"* (1965).

Rossiter, A. P. *"Angel with Horns" and Other Shakespeare Lectures.* Ed. Graham Storey (1961).

Stevenson, David L. *The Love-Game Comedy* (1946).